THE SEPHARDIM
IN THE
OTTOMAN EMPIRE

THE
SEPHARDIM
IN THE
OTTOMAN
EMPIRE

by Avigdor Levy

THE DARWIN PRESS, INC.
PRINCETON, NEW JERSEY
In Cooperation with
THE INSTITUTE OF TURKISH STUDIES, INC.
WASHINGTON, D.C.

Library of Congress Cataloging in Publication Data

Levy, Avigdor.
    The Sephardim in the Ottoman Empire / by Avigdor Levy.
        p.   cm.
    Includes bibliographical references and index.
    ISBN 0–87850–088–X (hardbound).—ISBN 0–87850–089–8
    (paperbound)
    1. Sephardim—Turkey—History.   2. Jews—Turkey—History.
    3. Turkey—Ethnic relations.   I. Title.
DS135. T8L47   1992
956'.004924—dc20   92–2992
                                                          CIP

The paper in this book is acid-free neutral pH stock and meets the guidelines for permanence and durability of the Committee on Production Guidelines for Book Longevity of the Council on Library Resources.

Printed in the United States of America.

For Jonathan

Contents

List of Illustrations

(Following page 80)

Acknowledgments. The author is grateful to the following institutions for their permission to reproduce photographs of books or documents in their possession:

American Jewish Historical Society, Waltham, Massachusetts: No. 21.

Başbakanlık Arşivi, Istanbul: Nos. 17, 18, 19, and 20.

Brandeis University Library, Waltham, Massachusetts: Nos. 6, 7, 8, 9, 15, 16, and 22.

Hebrew Union College—Jewish Institute of Religion Library, Cincinnati, Ohio: Nos. 3, 4, and 5.

Nos. 10, 11, 12, and 13 were reproduced from Nicholas de Nicolay, *The Nauigations into Turkie* (London, 1585).

No. 23 was reproduced from C. Oscanyan, *The Sultan and His People* (New York, 1857).

Nos. 1, 2, 14, and 24 were reproduced from Edwin A. Grosvenor, *Constantinople* (2 vols., Boston, 1900).

Nos. 25 through 33 were reproduced from R. Mayer, *The Jews of Turkey* (privately printed, 1913).

1. Plan of Istanbul, 1481.
2. Sultan Süleyman the Magnificent (ruled 1520–66).
3. Introductory page of *Arba'ah Turim*, a widely-accepted code of Jewish law compiled by Jacob ben Asher (ca. 1270–1340), printed in Istanbul, 1493–94. First Hebrew book printed in the Ottoman Empire.
4. First page of *Arba'ah Turim*.
5. Last page of *Arba'ah Turim* with colophon naming the printers, David and Samuel Nahmias, and dating the book 4 Tevet, 5254/13 December, 1493.
6. A page of *Sefer ha-Halakhot*, a comprehensive compendium of the Talmud by Isaac ben Jacob Alfasi (ca. 1013–1103), printed in Istanbul, 1509.
7. Front page (bearing censor's markings) of *Sefer Bereshit Rabbah*, an anthology of biblical exegesis dating from the fifth century, printed in Istanbul, 1512.

List of Tables

Preface

The expulsion of the Jews from Spain (1492) and Portugal (1497) brought the curtain down on the largest, most vigorous, and creative Jewish community in the world at the time, which had thrived on Iberian soil for more than a thousand years. The same events, however, also led to the rise of a wide-flung Sephardic diaspora in the countries of the Mediterranean and the Atlantic seaboard. For wherever the Iberian Jews, the *Sephardim,* went, they carried with them their languages, cultural heritage, traditions, and customs. The largest of the new Sephardic centers were formed in the Ottoman Empire, which emerged as the most secure and desirable haven for the Iberian refugees. Records from the early sixteenth century indicate that, within two to three decades after their expulsion, tens of thousands of Iberian Jews had become established in many Ottoman cities and towns.

In the Ottoman Empire the Sephardim encountered other Jewish groups, not only local residents, but also refugees from other European countries, especially Italy, France, Germany, and Hungary. The contacts and cross-fertilization between these various Jewish groups led to the emergence of a new, uniquely vibrant and multifaceted society, rich in culture and scholarship. Due to their large numbers and high cultural and educational standards, the Sephardim emerged as the dominant group within Ottoman Jewry. Their impact was especially strong and long-lasting in the Jewish communities of the Balkans, western Anatolia, and the urban centers of Palestine. Under Sephardic leadership, the Ottoman Jewish communities became the most important centers of Jewish scholarship and learning in the world, a position they maintained for a long time. Religious and intellectual currents originating within Ottoman Jewry resounded throughout the Jewish diaspora.

Within the Ottoman sociopolitical order, for much of the period, the Jews occupied an important, if not unique, position. In the fifteenth and sixteenth centuries they were instrumental in developing and expanding the Ottoman economy and administration, and they continued to maintain a prominent role in these areas for a long time thereafter. Jews made significant contributions in science, technology, culture, and entertainment. In return, Ottoman Jewry experienced unprecedented levels of individual and religious freedom and long periods of material comfort, security, and prominence.

In spite of this record, the study of Ottoman Jewry has long been relegated to a marginal position within modern Jewish historiography, and basic facets of Ottoman Jewish life remain obscure and uninvestigated. Recent years have witnessed, however, a surge of interest in the subject. This has been due, in large measure, to the expansion of Jewish studies and historical research into areas that had been traditionally neglected or little investigated, such as the study of Sephardic communities and the Jews of the Islamic lands. This surge would not have been possible, however, without a collateral development in Ottoman social and economic history and the greater accessibility that scholars have gained to Ottoman sources and archival materials. Improved understanding of Ottoman social and political institutions has shed new light also on the life of the religious minorities, including the Jews, and the place they occupied in Ottoman society.

The present volume grew out of a larger collaborative work edited by this author and scheduled for publication by The Darwin Press in 1992, under the title *The Jews of the Ottoman Empire*. The present volume was originally written to serve as the introductory essay in the collaborative work and it is reprinted there with some necessary changes. For this reason the references to the contributions in the latter work are included in the body of this text by reference to the contributor (in parentheses), and not in the notes. A list of authors and their contributions is included in this book as an appendix.

The publication of this work would not have been possible without the support and cooperation of two institutions and several individuals. A special debt of gratitude is due to Brandeis University for facilitating my work on this volume in various ways. I am particularly indebted to my colleagues, Charles Cutter, Marvin Fox, Benjamin Ravid, Jehuda Reinharz, and Gregory Shesko, for their steadfast assistance and encouragement. The Institute of Turkish Studies and its Executive Director, Heath W. Lowry, deserve special recognition for consistently supporting this work through its various stages, until its completion. Without their enthusiastic encouragement, this endeavor would never have been launched. Yael Even and Stephanie Fine ably contributed to the preparation of the manuscript. Their commitment and diligence are greatly appreciated.

A Note on Transliteration

Hebrew terms and proper names have been transliterated according to a simplified method intended to approximate their pronunciation in modern Hebrew. The spelling of Turkish terms and proper names follows modern Turkish orthography. Please note, however, that the Turkish *c* is pronounced as the English *j*, *ç* as *ch*, *ş* as *sh*. Thus, *cizye, çelebi, şura* are pronounced *jizye, chelebi, shura*. In general, wherever feasible, familiar anglicized forms have been used.

Abbreviations Used in the Notes

AG   Archives de la Guerre, Paris.

BA   Başbakanlık Arşivi, Istanbul. Archives of the Prime Minister's Office.

EJ   *Encyclopaedia Judaica.* Jerusalem: Keter Publishing House, 1971.

FO   Foreign Office Archives, London.

GMC   *Gayr-ı Müslim Cemaatlere Ait Defterler.* Registers pertaining to non-Muslim communities in BA.

IA   *Islâm Ansiklopedisi* [Encyclopedia of Islam]. Istanbul: Millî Eğitim Basımevi, 1940 to date.

TV   *Takvim-i-Vakayı,* Istanbul. Official Ottoman government newspaper.

I
JEWISH SETTLEMENT IN THE OTTOMAN EMPIRE

Modern Perceptions of the Origins of Ottoman Jewry

During the month of April 1892, the Jews of the Ottoman Empire celebrated what was described as "the fourth centennial of their immigration to Turkey."[1] On the first day of Passover (April 12), a special prayer, in Hebrew, was offered in all the synagogues of the realm for the reigning Sultan Abdülhamid II (Abdul-Hamid II; r. 1876–1909), as well as for Sultan Bayezid II (r. 1481–1512) in whose time the event being commemorated had taken place.[2] On that same day, the Acting Chief Rabbi, Moshe Levy (Ha-Levy), presented the Sultan with a Turkish translation of the prayer, as well as an album, containing a statement of gratitude and homage signed by leaders said to represent all the Jewish communities of the empire. In the preceding weeks, the Ottoman Jewish press published special commemorative editions containing numerous contributions in prose and verse, in Turkish, Hebrew, French, and Judeo-Spanish.[3] The weekly *Le Nouvelliste* (*El Nuvelista*), published in Izmir in both French and Judeo-Spanish,[4] carried a poem entitled "The Outcasts," penned by Lucien Sciuto, a journalist from Salonica.[5] The following excerpts, translated from the original French, convey some of the themes expressed in the Ottoman Jewish press:

> When, in galleons heavy with a sad load,
> The eternally outcast wander from sea to sea,
> Asking for asylum with bitter cries,
> Nations, watching them go by, call out: Keep away! . . .
>
> Tempest! The hurricane blows aloft;
> The navigators, thoughtful, their brows furrowed;
> And the somber vessels sail on aimlessly,
> Searching without finding the route of exile.

1

They go on, steering for empty horizons.
Who will say to them "Hello!" when they already told
    them "Good-bye"?
Unknown on the earth and lost in the waves,
Despairing of all, don't they have any hope except in God? . . .

And, in the galleons lost in the storm,
O miracle! One hears neither lament nor cry,
Israel, prepared to die, has raised his head,
And serene, he awaits the opening of the waves. . . .

But God, who had put them in the most difficult trial,
Said: "Enough, you will live, what is the use of death?
Of your strong faith, I have the greatest proof.
You who would know how to die, no, you will not die . . . ."

"Go on, son of Israel, it is I who support you.
Over there, in the Orient, there lies a triumphant country:
Its sky is merciful, its earth fertile;
He who rules it has my name in his heart . . . ."

There it is! There it is! The Orient has become illuminated!
The haven is there! Stamboul in the distance is all bright red.
Towards the mighty city, Israel proceeds
And his hymns of thanks burst in the sunshine.

And when those whom yesterday all seemed to revile
Arrived in Stamboul, wretched and destitute,
For the first time one could hear the words:
"You who are the outcasts, be welcome."

The tenor of the 1892 celebrations by Ottoman Jewry was distinctly different from the attitudes with which Jews elsewhere have traditionally regarded the events of 1492. In the collective Jewish memory, this date represented, first and foremost, a tragedy of catastrophic proportions: the world's leading Jewish community, efflorescent and long-established, was suddenly uprooted and destroyed.[6] However, the poem cited above, and similar expressions, appear to highlight different themes: true, the Iberian Jews suffered much and were almost lost, but they were saved at the end. The expulsion from Spain, the tribulations along the way, and the eventual resettlement in the Ottoman Empire, were all part of one act of divine Providence. In fact, it was a latter-day Exodus, hence its celebration on Passover, a holiday commemorating the flight of the ancient Israelites from Egyptian bondage to freedom. This theme appears to have been long-held and widespread among Ottoman Jews.[7] Some contemporary Ottoman Jewish expressions dwelt primarily, and even exclusively, on the aspects of redemption and resettlement, rather than that of expulsion. The one sentiment which they all shared was a deep sense of gratitude to the Ottoman state. The special commemorative prayer speaks of "the four hundred years since the Jews had come to find shelter under the wings of the righteous and compassionate king, Sultan Bayezid Han the Second."[8] Western Jewish organizations also contributed to this celebratory mood. The Central Committee of the Alliance Israélite Universelle (henceforth Alliance) in Paris sent a congratulatory message to Abdülhamid II, which read, in part:

> In the spring of the year 1492, the Jews expelled from Spain found shelter in Turkey. While they were oppressed in the rest of the world, they enjoyed in the lands of your glorious ancestors a protection that had never ceased. It permitted them to live in security, to work and to develop . . . .
>
> The Alliance Israélite Universelle joins the Jews of Turkey; and our coreligionists of all countries join us in celebrating the fourth centennial of the settlement of the Jews in Turkey.[9]

The Realities of Jewish Settlement

The main celebrants must have known, however, that the date chosen for commemorating Jewish "settlement" in the Ottoman Empire was more symbolic than real. In the first place, in the fourteenth century, when the Ottoman state was in its early formative stages, Jews were already settled in Anatolia and the Balkans, where they had lived for many centuries. Most of these were Greek-speaking, whose traditions and culture had formed under Byzantine rule. They were known as *Benei Romania*, or *Romaniot* Jews, since Byzantium and other Greek-ruled lands were known by contemporary Jews as *Romania*, that is, the land of the Romans.[10] These Jews followed a ritual known as *Minhag Romania*.[11]

In the course of the fifteenth century, German Jews, known as *Ashkenazim,* had come to the Ottoman Empire. Rosanes places the beginning of Ashkenazi settlement during the reign of Murad II (1421–51).[12] Their numbers grew appreciably around 1470 as a result of persecution and eventual expulsion from the Kingdom of Bavaria[13] (see Chronology). Another small but distinct component in the mosaic of pre-1492 Ottoman Jewry were the Italian Jews, who, with the exception of the Sicilian Jews, followed their own ritual known as *Minhag Italiano,* or *Mahzor Benei Roma.* The Sicilian Jews followed a ritual, which resembled that of the Spanish Jews, the Sephardim.[14] Also during the fifteenth century, as the oppression of Iberian Jews had gained momentum, Sephardim began arriving in the Ottoman Empire. Around 1481, several distinguished Iberian rabbis settled in Istanbul.[15]

In 1492, when King Ferdinand and Queen Isabella expelled the Jews of Spain, only small numbers actually set out for the Ottoman Empire.[16] The hazards and expense of maritime travel and the small size of contemporary vessels simply precluded a large-scale, seaborne exodus. In fact, in 1492, most refugees from Spain found temporary shelter in neighboring Portugal, the small Kingdom of Navarre and the French region of Provence, all of which could be reached overland. Others escaped to the relative proximity of North Africa. Even Italy and the Low Countries were more easily accessible than the Ottoman Empire. The significance of 1492, however, was that it uprooted a very substantial segment of Spanish Jewry.[17] Consequently, when in subsequent years Portugal, Navarre, France, and several Italian states implemented oppressive measures against their Jewish populations, or expelled them outright, new waves of migration were set in motion.[18] The diminishing possibilities for refuge in Europe and the establishment of successful patterns of immigration to, and settlement in, the Ottoman Empire had made the latter a preferred destination for increasing numbers of Jews. The migration of the Jews from the Iberian Peninsula, as well as from Italy and France, to the Ottoman Empire was, therefore, a gradual process that spanned many decades. It had begun before 1492, but greatly accelerated after that date. The most significant waves of immigration probably occurred between the years 1492 and 1512, which corresponded to the dates of the Jews' expulsion from the European countries.[19] The following two examples may serve to illustrate the slow and incremental nature of Sephardic settlement in the Ottoman Empire and some of its characteristics.

Rabbi Jacob ibn Habib was born in the town of Zamora in Castille at about 1460. In 1492, he went to Portugal together with most of the Jewish refugees of Castille. In 1497, however, the Portuguese authorities forcibly abducted and baptized Jewish children, including ibn Habib's son, Levi. Within a year, however, ibn Habib was able to gain his son's release and escape from Portugal with his family. He settled in Salonica, where he became the rabbi of Congregation Gerush and founded an important *yeshivah*.[20]

Don David ibn Yahya was born in Lisbon at about 1440. He was a wealthy entrepreneur, as well as a well-known scholar who authored several books. Following 1492, when Spanish Jews, including conversos, arrived in Portugal in great numbers, he was accused by the Portuguese authorities of having encouraged conversos to return to Judaism. Consequently, he was forced to flee Portugal, abandoning most of his wealth. He first found refuge in Naples. In 1495, however, Naples was conquered by Spain and the new authorities proceeded to implement harsh measures against the Jewish population. In 1503, David ibn Yahya was forced to leave Naples. He set out for Istanbul where his uncle, Don Gedaliah ibn Yahya, had settled in 1481. His depleted financial resources, however, enabled him and his family to travel only as far as Corfu. In Corfu he was forced to sell his belongings, including his rare book collection, to secure passage as far as Arta (Narda). From Arta he was finally able to continue to Istanbul through the financial assistance of a family friend, who was then residing in Patras. In 1504 or 1505, ibn Yahya finally reached Istanbul, where he spent the rest of his days (he died in 1524), "in abject poverty, but at peace," as Rosanes comments. His son, Rabbi Jacob Tam ibn Yahya (1475–1542), became a well-known scholar and one of the spiritual leaders of the Jewish community of Istanbul.[21]

Rosanes describes the settlement of the Sephardim after 1492 as beginning with the port cities of the southern Balkans and western Anatolia, from which areas the immigrants gradually penetrated the interior up to the Danube Valley in Europe, and to central Anatolia and Syria in Asia. In the initial stages, however, most immigrants preferred to remain in Salonica, Istanbul, Edirne, and the towns of the Morea.[22] Recent studies based on Ottoman population records have, for the most part, confirmed Rosanes' description.[23]

Indeed, by the second and third decades of the sixteenth century, Sephardic communities had become established in many Ottoman towns, which in the late fifteenth century had little or no Jewish population at all. It should be noted here that following the Ottoman conquest of Constantinople (Istanbul), in 1453, Sultan Mehmed II made the city his new capital. As part of the efforts to revitalize and repopulate Istanbul, the Ottomans transferred there large numbers of people from other parts of their empire. Among those were Jews from more than forty cities and towns in the Balkans and western Anatolia, including the majority of the Jews of Edirne. This was reflected in the names of the synagogues and congregations, which these migrants founded in Istanbul—for example, Gelibolu, Inoz, Dimetoka, Üsküp, Salonica, Tire, and so on—names referring to their original home towns.[24]

The Case of Salonica

The case of the Jewish community of Salonica, while unique in some aspects, is illustrative of this process. While Salonica had a Jewish population in the first half of the fifteenth century, the Ottomans apparently transferred the entire community to Istanbul at some point after 1453. Indeed, the Ottoman population count of 1478 indicates that at that date Salonica had no Jewish population left at all (Heath W. Lowry). By 1519, however, the city had a Jewish community consisting of 3,143 households, in addition to 930 tax-paying bachelors, comprising more than half of the city's total population.[25] In subsequent years the number of Jewish households declined somewhat, suggesting that Salonica was an important port of entry from where Jews moved to other localities. In relative terms, however, the size of the Jewish population of Salonica increased to about sixty percent of the total population, a ratio that was to continue with some fluctuations until the end of Ottoman rule (1912). Thus, Salonica, which during the sixteenth century emerged as the empire's second most important maritime center, had become a "Jewish enclave in an otherwise Muslim state," according to Lowry. The Ottoman population counts reveal another interesting aspect. The census taken around 1500 lists an Ashkenazi congregation in Salonica comprising 68 households. By 1530 the number of Ashkenazi households had risen to 97, suggesting that, side by side with the massive Sephardic influx, the trickle of Jewish immigration from central Europe persisted.

Istanbul

Istanbul had been the destination of Sephardic immigrants even before 1492. What had made the city particularly attractive to Jewish refugees after 1492 was, first, that it was the empire's capital, as well as its largest and most thriving economic center. Second, and perhaps even more important, in 1492 it had the largest and most prosperous Jewish community in the empire, by far, and the Jews of the city could be expected to, and they indeed did, assist the newcomers. For these reasons it is generally assumed that large numbers of Jewish refugees flocked to the city. These seemingly logical assumptions have found further support in some contemporary accounts, which offer excessively high estimates of the Jewish population of Istanbul in the sixteenth century.[26]

The evidence of the official Ottoman records, however, appears to support these assumptions only in part. According to an Ottoman population count in 1477, following the repopulation of Istanbul, the Jewish community consisted of 1,647 households, comprising about 11 percent of the city's total number of recorded households.[27] By the mid-sixteenth century, the size of the community established before 1492, mostly Romaniot Jews, appears to have somewhat declined. A register dating from 1540 (Table 1, column 1) lists the "old," pre-1492, congregations of Istanbul, whose taxes were assigned to the foundation (*imâret*) established by Mehmed the Conqueror. The register lists fifty congregations, including one Ashkenazi and three Karaite, comprising 1,522 households.[28] No comparable information is available for this period regarding the new congregations founded by immigrant groups following Mehmed's reign. Another register, dating from 1608 (Table 1, column 2), suggests a further decline of the older Jewish congregations.[29] The total number of households is recorded as 1,222. The number of congregations also declined to twenty-five, including one Karaite, although the majority of congregations have become larger. Of the fifty congregations listed in 1540 only seventeen remained, of which two had split and six new names were added.[30] From this period, there has survived, however, another register, dated 1603 (Table 1, column 2), which lists the "new" congregations, founded by immigrants arriving in Istanbul following the reign of Mehmed the Conqueror (1451–81), presumably after 1492. The register lists a total of seventeen congregations, comprising 973 Jewish households.[31] Whereas this data raises more questions than it provides answers, it also suggests a few tentative conclusions.

Around the turn of the seventeenth century, the total number of recorded Jewish households in Istanbul, "old" and "new," was 2,195. Of these, the Romaniot Jews still comprised more than half, whereas the immigrant congregations amounted to only about 44 percent of the total households. This suggests that Jewish immigration to Istanbul, while considerable, was not on as large a scale as generally believed. In the course of the sixteenth century, Jewish immigrant settlement in Istanbul was apparently less than a third, perhaps even less than a quarter, of that of Salonica, which in 1613 had 2,933 immigrant Jewish households, in addition to 2,270 tax-paying bachelors (Lowry). The "new" Jewish settlement in Istanbul was on about the same scale as that of Safed, which in 1596/97 had 977 Jewish households, most of them immigrant.[32] It is also obvious that, unlike other towns in the Balkans and Anatolia, in Istanbul the new arrivals did not numerically "overwhelm" the established Jewish population, one of the main reasons usually cited to explain the subsequent cultural ascendancy of the Sephardim. In fact, even among the immigrants, the eight clearly identified Sephardic congregations (Portakal. Catalan, Gerush, Shalom-Aragon, dependency of Aragon, Cordova, Señora, and Descendants of Hamon) had between them only 539 households. The register also lists four Italian congregations with 209 households; two Ashkenazi congregations with 77 households; one Hungarian congregation with 59 households; and two congregations whose origins remain uncertain with a total of 89 households. Thus, at the turn of the seventeenth century, the Sephardic congregations accounted for less than 25 percent of all the recorded Jewish households in Istanbul; and even if we were to include the two unidentified groups with the Sephardim, their combined numbers of 628 households would constitute less than 29 percent of all Jewish households. Furthermore, between the counts dated 1540 and 1608, the number of Romaniot households decreased by 216, a 16 percent loss, reflecting changes that occurred in the intervening years. Why the number of Romaniot households declined so appreciably at a time largely characterized by prosperity and general population growth[33] is not known. The numbers might reflect different methods of enumeration, or some financial arrangement between the Jewish community and the Ottoman tax authorities. Another possibility is that they represent, at least in part, a process of transfer, or defection, from the "old" congre-

TABLE 1.
The Jewish Population of Istanbul, 1540–1623

Date	1540		1608			1623		
	Number of Congregations	Number of Households	Number of Congregations	Number of Households	Percent of Grand Total	Number of Congregations	Number of Households	Percent of Grand Total
"Old" Congregations								
Romaniot Jews	46	1,368	24	1,152	52.48	24	1,147	52.45
Ashkenazim	1	25	—	—	—	—	—	—
Karaites	3	129	1	70	3.19	1	70	3.20
Total	50	1,522	25	1,222	55.67	25	1,217	55.65
(Date)	—		(1603)			(1623)		
"New" Congregations								
Sephardim	No Data	No Data	8	539	24.56	6	593	27.11
Italians	No Data	No Data	4	209	9.52	4	218	9.97
Ashkenazim	No Data	No Data	2	77	3.51	1	62	2.83
Hungarians	No Data	No Data	1	59	2.69	—	—	—
Unidentified	No Data	No Data	2	89	4.05	3	97	4.44
Total	—	—	17	973	44.33	14	970	44.35
GRAND TOTAL	—	—	42	2,195	100.00	39	2,187	100.00

Sources: Epstein, *Ottoman Jewish Communities*, pp. 178–89; Heyd, "Jewish Communities of Istanbul," pp. 299–309.

gations to the "new" ones. In that case, this would even further reduce the share of true immigrant households.

These hypotheses appear to be supported by information contained in yet another register, dated 1623 (Table 1, column 3).[34] The time span between this register and the register dated 1608 is only fifteen years, as compared with the sixty-eight-year time span between the registers of 1608 and 1540, which served as the basis for the analysis above. Still, if we compare the 1623 register with those dated 1608 and 1603, it is obvious that while the Jewish population as a whole, and most of its subgroups, remained static or even declined, the Sephardic congregations, and to a small extent the Italian ones, had gained in strength. By 1623 the Sephardim, with 593 households (a gain of 54 households, or 10 percent), rose to constitute over 27 percent of all recorded Jewish households; and with the unidentified groups their combined share rose to 31.5 percent. Having said this, it is important to note that an important reason for the growth of the Sephardic congregations, and probably also the Italian, was continued immigration. In 1612, for example, as a consequence of a commercial treaty between the Ottoman Empire and Flanders, considerable numbers of Sephardic Jews, including former Marranos, immigrated from the Low Countries to Istanbul and other Ottoman commercial centers[35]; and this immigration was to continue throughout the seventeenth century.[36]

The relatively small Jewish immigrant settlement in Istanbul in the course of the sixteenth century was probably due to one, or more, of several possible factors. First, there were the simple realities of geography and distance. To anyone traveling by sea from the western Mediterranean, from Spain, France, North Africa, and especially Italy, the ports of modern-day Albania and Greece were considerably closer than that of Istanbul. For those refugees who had to sell their last possessions to secure passage, distance and cost of travel must have been important considerations. Second, by 1492, when the large waves of Jewish immigrants began arriving in the Ottoman Empire, the reconstruction of Istanbul, begun in 1453, had been completed. The city was now a thriving administrative, financial, and commercial metropolis. On the other hand, at this time there was a clear need to develop provincial administrative and commercial centers in the Balkans and Anatolia, especially in areas that had recently come under Ottoman control, such as Serbia, Bosnia, Albania, and, particularly, the Morea. There is evidence to suggest that the Ottoman authorities actually encouraged Jews to move to areas where they were needed. Jews settling in Salonica, Trikkala (Tırhala), Patras (Balya Badra), and probably other places, were granted incentives in the form of special privileges and tax exemptions.[37] Furthermore, most of the immigrant Jews had occupational skills similar to those of the Romaniot Jews with whom they would have been in competition. The presence of a large, established Jewish community in Istanbul and the absence, or near absence, of Jews almost everywhere else meant that, for most immigrants, greater economic opportunity existed outside the capital.

It is also possible that during the reign of Bayezid II (1481–1512), when the largest migrations took place, there existed an official policy intended to control, or curb, the numbers of Jewish settlers in Istanbul. Bayezid's general attitude to Jewish immigration appears to have been favorable for the economic benefits that it was expected to yield. At the same time, however, this ruler, unlike his immediate predecessor and successors, was rigorously devout and conservative. Uncharacteristically of Ottoman practice at this age, he treated the non-Muslim population according to a strict interpretation of Islamic law. During his reign, new synagogues and churches were closed down; privileges granted to minorities came under scrutiny; and prominent Jews were pressured to, and some did, convert to Islam.[38] It is possible, therefore, that during Bayezid II's reign, when the reconstruction of Istanbul had been achieved, the government was not prepared to encourage an unchecked growth of the Jewish population in the city. Thus, through a policy that combined pressures with incentives, the flow of Jewish immigration was deflected from the capital to provincial centers.

Size and Significance of Jewish Immigration

Ottoman population counts conducted during the period 1512–30 show a considerable Jewish presence in the southern Balkans and western Anatolia, consisting for the most part of immigrant communities.[39] In addition to the major concentrations in Salonica and Istanbul, at least seven other towns had sizable Jewish populations of more than one hundred recorded households each, in addition to Jewish individuals not included in the household count. Patras (Balya Badra) had 252 Jewish households, Thebes (Istifa), 126, Trikkala (Tırhala), 181, Edirne, 231 (increasing to 553 by 1568/69), Valona (Avlonya, Vlone), 528 (but declining dramatically by the late sixteenth century), Bursa, 117 (increasing to 683 by 1571/72), and Rhodes (Rodos), 144. More than twenty additional towns recorded smaller, but still significant, Jewish populations, ranging in size from twenty-one to ninety-one households. These included Methoni (Modon) with

21 households, Koroni (Koron), 36, Mistra (Mezistre), 72, Chlomontsi (Holumiç), 38, Navpaktos (Lepanto, İnebahtı), 84 (increasing to 188 by 1597), Levadhia (Livadiya), 36, Nauplia (Anabolu), 25, Chalcis (Eğriboz), 30, Larisa (Yenişehir), 42 (increasing to 212 by 1597), Pella (Vardar Yeniçesi), 24, Serres (Siroz), 59, Gelibolu (Gallipoli), 23, Provadiya (Pravadi), 28, Plovdiv (Filibe), 32, Nikopol (Niğbolu), 91 (increasing to 177 by 1579/80), Bitola (Manastır, Monastir), 48, Berat, 25, Tire, 64, Manisa, 88, and Ankara 28. Many other towns in these areas had smaller Jewish communities with less than twenty recorded households.[40]

The Ottoman conquest of Syria, Palestine, and Egypt (1516–17) set in motion a considerable Jewish immigration to these areas, appreciably strengthening the local Jewish communities.[41] By 1548/49 Damascus had 503 recorded Jewish households[42]; Tripoli had 139 in 1594/95[43]; Safed had 713 in 1555/56 and 977 in 1596/97; Jerusalem had 324 in 1553/54; and Gaza had 115 in 1548/49.[44]

Significant Jewish communities existed elsewhere in the Ottoman Empire. For some we have data: Mardin in east Anatolia had 154 recorded households (1525/26); Mosul had 105 in 1558; Buda in Hungary had 122 (1562/63); and Kaffa (Kefe) in the Crimea had 92 (1542/43). There probably were many other sizable communities for which data have not yet become available. The sources leave, however, little doubt regarding the economic and cultural importance of the Jewish centers in Aleppo,[45] Baghdad,[46] Cairo, Alexandria, and Rashid (Rosetta).[47]

In sheer numbers, the migration of the Iberian, as well as French, German, and Italian, Jews to the Ottoman Empire in the fifteenth and sixteenth centuries constituted the most important demographic change in the structure of the Jewish diaspora at that time. The continued expansion of the Ottoman Empire in the course of the sixteenth century in eastern Europe, the Middle East, and North Africa brought additional Jewish communities under Ottoman rule. Considering the vast territorial expanse of the Ottoman Empire and the presence of Jewish populations in so many of its widely flung territories, it is impossible to avoid the conclusion, although there are no data to support it, that during the sixteenth century, more Jews lived in the Ottoman Empire than in any other state. Furthermore, both materially and culturally, the Ottoman Jewish communities emerged as the foremost Jewish centers in the world, rivaled, perhaps, only by those of Poland and Lithuania.[48]

II

THE OTTOMAN-JEWISH SYMBIOSIS IN THE FIFTEENTH AND SIXTEENTH CENTURIES

Western Perceptions of the Ottoman Empire and of Ottoman Jewry

It is legitimate to inquire what were the circumstances that made Jewish settlement in the Ottoman Empire so attractive and successful. European contemporaries observed the rise of the Ottoman Empire and its annexation of one Christian land after another with great concern and fear. European preoccupation with the Ottoman threat led to the emergence of a vast literature. Some three thousand five hundred titles were printed in the sixteenth century alone.[49] Many, if not most, of these were popular works of polemic and propaganda, hostile to the Ottomans, often portraying them as barbarous and savage. Sir Paul Rycault (1629–1700), a diplomat, author and long-time resident in the Ottoman Empire, found it necessary to admonish his readers that ". . . a People, as the Turks are, men of the same composition with us, cannot be *so savage and rude as they are generally described*" (italics added).[50] Informed writers such as Rycault were, of course, the exception. The negative stereotypes appear to have prevailed, and European Jews must have been familiar with them. In fact, they have come down to our own times. Describing the exodus of the Spanish Jews in 1492, the eminent modern historian Yitzhak Baer wrote: "Turkey was the only great power to receive the exiles with open arms and with no particular restrictions or reservations, *as befitted a barbaric conqueror* set on improving economic conditions in his new dominions and *not especially concerned with theological fine points*" (italics added).[51]

This description of the Ottoman state as "barbaric" and unconcerned with "theological fine points," is, of course, not a reflection of historical reality, but of centuries of Western bias, which also tended to reflect on the achievements of Ottoman Jewry. Since, in the view of European-centered historians, Ottoman Jews lived within a barbaric society, their achievements could not have been very considerable and their experience was not much more than a historical curiosity. This attitude has resulted in a problematic dichotomy in modern Jewish historiography. There exists a rather large corpus of studies, much of it in Hebrew, dealing with the important religious and intellectual movements centered in Palestine and other Ottoman Jewish communities from the sixteenth to the eighteenth centuries. The careers and works of outstanding Ottoman Jewish figures have been studied in great detail. This, however, was done mainly from the perspective of their relation, and contributions, to the world of Jewish thought and scholarship in general. In the twentieth century, it has become common to study Ottoman Jewish communities in isolation, as "Egyptian," "Palestinian," "Iraqi," "Syrian," "Turkish," "Greek," "Bulgarian," even "Macedonian," and so on. There are, of course, valid political, cultural, historical, and practical reasons for this approach. The net result, however, has been that the achievements of Ottoman Jewry have rarely been examined as a unique expression of Jewish life as it was shaped by the sociopolitical realities prevailing in the Ottoman Empire. In fact, it has seldom been recognized that Ottoman Jewry formed one entity whose constituent communities were—materially, spiritually, and politically—closely linked and interconnected, in spite of their cultural diversity. Consequently, it has been rarely acknowledged that after the destruction of the Jewish center in Spain, it was Ottoman Jewry that became the hub of the Jewish diaspora.

The Ottoman Empire and Its Religious Minorities

As Sir Paul Rycault noted, the Ottoman Empire was not a barbaric state, and the thousands of Jewish refugees streaming from Europe to the Ottoman Empire in the fifteenth, sixteenth, and seventeenth centuries knew it. They found out the truth, as immigrants always have, through letters and word of mouth from earlier settlers. These reports, such as the well-known fifteenth-century letter by Rabbi Isaac Tzarfati,[52] described the Ottoman Empire not merely as a place of refuge, but also as a land of economic opportunity, where Jews could live and practice their religion in freedom and security on a level rarely found elsewhere.

* * * * *

Indeed, in the fifteenth and sixteenth centuries, the Ottoman Empire, although shrouded by myth and mystery to most Europeans, was among the most advanced and well-administered states in the world. Machiavelli, who attempted an early classification of political systems, chose the Ottoman Empire as a model of a highly centralized state.[53] Busbecq, the Hapsburg ambassador in Istanbul at the time of Süleyman (Suleiman) the Magnificent (r. 1520–66), wrote admiringly on the Ottoman system of government, including the following passage:

> It is by merit that men rise in the service, a system which insures that posts should be assigned to the competent . . . . They do not believe that high qualities are either natural or hereditary . . . , but that they are partly the gift of God, and partly the result of good training, great industry, and . . . zeal . . . . Honors, high posts and judgeships are the rewards of great ability and good service. This is the reason that they are successful in their under-takings.[54]

Compared with contemporary Christian Europe, the Ottoman Empire afforded its religious minorities an unequaled degree of toler-ance. Ottoman attitudes towards minorities were, in the first place, rooted in the Islamic tradition, that is, the Holy Law and Muslim attitudes and practices as they had developed since the rise of Islam in the seventh century. The Islamic State regarded its relations with its non-Muslim subjects as governed by a covenant of protection, known as *dhimma* in Arabic (in Turkish, *zimmet*). From this word was derived the term *dhimmi* (in Turkish, *zimmi*), which designated an individual non-Muslim subject in a Muslim state. Traditional Islam considered Judaism and Christianity as earlier and imperfect versions of the Islamic faith; and although superseded by Islam, Judaism and Christianity were regarded as still containing elements of true revela-tion. As a result of this somewhat ambivalent approach, as well as for historical and practical reasons, Muslim states acknowledged that Christians and Jews had a legal right to live securely under their protection, practice their religious beliefs, and enjoy a large measure of autonomy in the conduct of their internal affairs. For these privileges, however, the non-Muslims had to pay higher taxes, most commonly the poll tax (Arabic, *jizya*; Turkish, *cizye*), and to dem-onstrate at all times their acceptance of the superiority of Islam and of Muslims. The latter was supposed to be enforced through various restrictions of a primarily social nature. The most significant of these were that non-Muslims had to be distinguishable by means of distinc-tive clothing and other signs. They could not ride horses or camels, only donkeys and mules; they were forbidden to build new houses of worship, only repair existing ones. These were Islam's precepts. In reality, however, the application of these restrictions varied widely over time and place. Many Muslim states, for a variety of practical reasons, chose to ignore them to a greater or lesser degree. Nevertheless, even in the most liberal of Muslim societies, non-Muslims had to live with a certain measure of insecurity, as to when liberal attitudes would give way in the face of more conservative impulses, invoking the authority of the Holy Law.[55]

In its attitude towards its non-Muslim subjects, the Ottoman Empire was one of the most tolerant Muslim states ever to exist. Ottoman attitudes were in part due to the fact that the Ottomans followed the Hanafi rite of jurisprudence, the most liberal of the four Sunni rites. The Hanafis assigned greater relative importance to consensus and legal reasoning—in addition to tradition and precedent—than the other rites, and their system was, therefore, more flexible and subject to change, reinterpretation, and the adoption of new elements.[56] They also treated non-Muslims more liberally and with greater equality to Muslims. In criminal matters involving murder and bodily injury, for example, the Hanafis, in contrast to the other rites, tended to indemnify non-Muslims on the same basis as Muslims.[57]

Even more than that, however, Ottoman tolerance was due to the pragmatic strategies of government that the Ottomans had developed over the centuries. Ottoman pragmatism was born out of necessity. During the fourteenth and fifteenth centuries, non-Muslims formed a majority of Ottoman subjects. In those early centuries, new converts, and even non-Muslims, played a prominent role in the administration and the military. In fact, quite a few of the sultans had consorts and mothers who were born Christian.[58] The same was true of many other members of the ruling class. The participation of large numbers of new converts, and non-Muslims, in the highest levels of Ottoman government and society, and the sheer numbers of so many religiously and ethnically diverse non-Muslim subjects, gave Ottoman society a plural character and, on the whole, inbued it with a spirit of tolerance, liberalism, and openness. It also forced the Ottoman ruling leadership to recognize early on that, in order to govern effectively a heterogeneous society, principles had to be accommodated with reality.

In the sixteenth century, with the conquest of the Arab countries of the Middle East and North Africa, Muslims began to outnumber non-Muslims in the empire as a whole. For this, and for other reasons, by the end of the sixteenth century Ottoman society had become more conservative.[59] Nevertheless, till the end of the empire, in many important areas, most notably the Balkans, non-Muslims continued to represent local majorities, and they constituted an important segment of the population as a whole. They also continued to play an important role in the economic, political, and cultural life of the state. Consequently, the atmosphere of general tolerance, though always subject to fluctuations, persisted, on the whole, until the end of the empire. The plural character of Ottoman society was particularly noticeable in the urban centers. Almost all the major Ottoman cities, and many of the smaller towns, consisted of mosaics of religious communities (Muslims, Christians, and Jews—all of different branches and sects) and ethnic groups (Turks, Arabs, Greeks, Slavs, Albanians, Armenians, Kurds, Gypsies, Europeans, and others). In such a multireligious and polyethnic society, the tensions of majority-minority relations were more relaxed, compared with most European societies, and social attitudes and interactions more flexible and open. Ottoman pluralism must have seemed attractive to European Jews who, in their former countries, for the most part constituted the only minority confronted by a mostly hostile majority.

Life in Ottoman towns was not utopian. There was little overt social and cultural interaction among the various communities, and from time to time inter-communal tensions and crises erupted. For the most part, however, the different groups lived in peace, and even mutual respect. They conducted business relations with each other, lived as neighbors in close proximity and in many incipient ways affected each other's culture, tastes and mores, and contributed to the general Ottoman cultural synthesis (İlhan Başgöz, Pamela J. Kamarck Dorn, Esther Juhasz and Vivian B. Mann).

The Ottoman legal system reflected some of the essential characteristics of the entire sociopolitical order. As an Islamic state, the foundation of the Ottoman legal system was the Holy Law (Arabic, *Shari'a*; Turkish, *Şeriat*), considered eternal and immutable. Ottoman jurists saw the Şeriat as providing the framework and guiding principles for the entire legal system. In reality, however, much of the detail and daily management of political and societal affairs were governed by sultanic regulation, *kanun*, which produced a complementary legal system of a secular character. The system was both pragmatic and flexible. Its pragmatism derived from the fact that it took into consideration prevailing conditions, practices, customs, and traditions. It was flexible in the sense that it could be changed, and often was changed, to accommodate new circumstances.[60]

The traditional Ottoman concept of justice was different from modern principles based on a presumption of equality before the law. Traditional Ottoman society was divided into a multitude of groups—on the basis of religion, occupation, place of residence, service to the state, and other criteria—each possessing its distinctive rights and obligations. The main purpose of the Ottoman justice system was to insure that each group remained within its limits; that is to say that it fulfilled its particular obligations and received what it was due. On the whole, the system operated to perpetuate the existing dividing lines among society's various groups, although individual mobility was possible. The most important dividing line was that based on religion, separating Muslims from non-Muslims. Another important line of demarcation—and some argue that until about 1600 it was even more significant than religion[61]—was that which separated people according to their relation to the state. Those who were in the service of the state were generally referred to as *askeri*, literally meaning "military," or ruling, class. The chief privilege of this class was that its members were exempt from taxes. The tax-exempt class included not only military personnel as such, but also bureaucrats and men of religion. In the fifteenth century—and to a lesser degree in later centuries—many Christians, and a significant number of Jews, were admitted into the tax-exempt class, in spite of their religion.[62] All others, Muslims and non-Muslims, were taxpayers, known as *raya* (also *reaya*), or flocks. Jews, like Christians, could obtain a tax-exempt status for services rendered to the state as court physicians, translators, and advisors, and, more rarely, as government officials and military personnel. They could also become tax-exempt for performing certain administrative duties within the Jewish community itself.[63]

On the whole, the Jews trusted the Ottoman justice system and did not hesitate to use it, even in their own internal affairs and despite the strong remonstrances of their rabbis (Joseph Hacker). Jews did not hesitate to bring before the Muslim courts even highly placed government officials. A case in point was a lawsuit brought by a Jew against a well-known and highly placed Mamluk *amir* (officer) in Cairo, not long after the Ottoman conquest of Egypt (1517). The suit concerned a debt that was claimed by the Jew. The Ottoman Muslim court found in favor of the Jew and ordered the amir to prison until he paid his debt. This case created something of a sensation in Cairo, whose populace knew well that under the previous Mamluk regime a Jew would never have dared to sue a Mamluk officer, let alone win.[64] In, or before, 1576 a wealthy Jew from Safed, named Sevi, complained to the central government that he had been the object of extortion at the hands of the district governor (*sancakbeyi*) of Safed, named Mehmed, and his men. Sevi claimed that the governor also had him tortured and even warned him against lodging a complaint. In July 1576 the central government issued an order to Mehmed's superior, the provincial governor (*beylerbeyi*) of Damascus, and to the *kadis* of Damascus to conduct a full investigation of the complaint and punish the culprits.[65]

Jewish Attraction and Allegiance to the Ottoman State

Contemporary Jewish sources reflect that for the Jews, the most attractive aspect of life in the Ottoman Empire was the unprecedented measure of freedom that they enjoyed. They were generally free to settle wherever they wished; they could engage in almost every occupation and profession; they were able to travel freely for their business or for any other purpose; and they were free to practice their religion, to establish their own educational and social institutions and to organize their community life with minimal interference on the part of the authorities. Rabbi Samuel de Medina (1506–89), a leading sage of Salonica, repeatedly extolled in his writings the freedom that Ottoman Jews enjoyed: "This realm is wide open without a wall . . . and everyone anxious to do so may come in and attend to his business."[66] And again: "[In the Ottoman Empire] we Jews live under [a] sovereign who imposes no restrictions on travel or on commercial activities on any of his subjects."[67] And Samuel Usque, a former Portuguese Marrano (sixteenth century) concurred: "Here the gates of liberty are always wide open for you that you may fully practice your Judaism."[68]

The unification of the larger part of the Mediterranean lands and the Middle East under Ottoman rule in the sixteenth century enhanced the Jews' freedom of movement, with important consequences for their material and cultural efflorescence. The establishment of a Pax Ottomanica, with its familiar administrative and legal institutions, throughout these widely-flung territories, facilitated the emergence of Jewish commercial networks and provided a safe haven from which Jews could trade not only within the Ottoman Empire,

but also with Europe, Iran, and India. Economic prosperity and freedom of movement, also facilitated the emergence of major Jewish
cultural centers, which attracted scholars from various parts of the
Ottoman Empire and beyond, and from which education and culture
radiated to the smaller communities. The careers of many renowned
rabbis reflect an unusually high level of mobility, which permitted
them to seek the best opportunities for their educational advancement
and, in the process, for the enhancement of Jewish scholarship and
culture in general.[69] The career of Joseph Caro (ca. 1488–1575), author of the *Shulhan Arukh,* the widely accepted code of Jewish law,
and one of the greatest Talmudic scholars of all times, may serve to
illustrate this point. Born in Toledo, or Portugal, he was brought by
his family to Istanbul as a child at about 1497, and probably acquired
there his rabbinic training. Around 1522, he obtained an appointment
at Edirne and later moved to Nikopol, where he met, and was influ-
enced by, Solomon Alkabetz (ca. 1505–84), the renowned kabbalist
and mystical poet. Caro later moved to Salonica, where he studied
with the well-known scholar, Rabbi Joseph Taitatzak (ca. 1487–ca.
1545). Around 1536, after a brief sojourn in Egypt, he moved to
Safed, where he studied under Rabbi Jacob Beirav (also Berab; ca.
1474–1546). As of 1538, and until his death, Caro was recognized as
the foremost rabbinic authority in Safed. He served as the head of
the local Jewish court; he directed a large yeshivah and was apparently
also the head of the community council.[70]

Another aspect that attracted Jews to the Ottoman Empire was,
first, its proximity to the Holy Land, and, after 1516, the incorporation
of Palestine within Ottoman boundaries. This afforded Jews the opportunity to go on pilgrimage to the Holy Land and even settle there
out of religious motives and messianic expectations.[71] Already in the
fifteenth century, Rabbi Tzarfati's letter urged European Jews to settle
in the Ottoman Empire, because through it "the way to the Holy Land
lies open to you."[72] The drive to settle in Palestine had been particularly strong among Iberian Jews, following an early wave of attacks,
massacres, and forced conversions, which took place in 1391. As a
result of Sephardic immigration to Palestine, already by the 1460s
and 1470s, Sephardim assumed leadership positions within the Jewish
community of Jerusalem. The expulsion from Spain in 1492 and the
Ottoman conquest of Palestine in 1516 set in motion new waves of
Iberian immigrants to the Holy Land.[73] The rebuilding of the city
walls of Jerusalem by Süleyman the Magnificent between 1536 and

1542 also made a great impression throughout the Jewish diaspora and further strengthened messianic expectations. A contemporary Jewish chronicler, Joseph Ha-Cohen (ca. 1496–1575), wrote: "God aroused the spirit of Süleyman . . . and he set out to build the walls of Jerusalem, the Holy City in the Land of Judea. He sent officials who built its walls and set up its gates as in former times . . . . And his fame increased throughout the land for he has done a great deed."[74]

Indeed, more than a century after Rabbi Tzarfati's letter, Rabbi Samuel de Medina attested: "In our time, we see many people travelling to the Holy Land and the journey involves no risk, especially since both Palestine and our country are under the same ruler."[75]

These realities did not fail to generate among the Jews sentiments of gratitude and loyalty toward the Ottoman state. In his writings, Rabbi Samuel de Medina repeatedly refers to Ottoman generous hospitality and to the opportunity that the Jews had found in the Ottoman Empire to live happily, prosperously, and in freedom. When Medina found out that some Jews were illegally engaged in the trade of counterfeit currency, he angrily admonished them: "He who has no respect for the honor of our sovereign, the righteous and mighty King—may his honor increase!—it would have been better had he not been born. For it is mandatory . . . to observe his word and to perform his laws and orders in the same way that it is mandatory to perform the commandments and laws of the King of the Universe."[76]

Ottoman Preference for Jewish Settlement

As far as the Ottomans were concerned, in the early period, in the fourteenth century and the first half of the fifteenth, their expectations of the Jews were relatively simple. As Ottoman power rose and gradually expanded in western Anatolia and the Balkans, the Ottomans came to regard the Jews as a productive, urban element, politically more reliable than the local Christian Greeks and Slavs. They preferred, it appears, to repopulate and rebuild the important urban centers that fell under their control—some of which were partially destroyed and deserted—with the help of Jewish settlers. Thus, the Ottomans encouraged the Jews to settle in Bursa, their first important capital (since 1326), as well as other towns, and expected that the Jews would help in the reconstruction and economic development of these urban centers. These Ottoman expectations were apparently satisfied.[77] For when, in 1361, the Ottomans captured Adrianople (Edirne) and subsequently designated it as their new capital,[78] they again settled in the city considerable numbers of Jews, including immigrants from abroad, from Hungary, France, Italy, and Sicily.[79]

A similar development, but on a far larger scale, took place following the conquest of Constantinople (Istanbul) in 1453 and its transformation into the new Ottoman capital. To repopulate the nearly desolate city, the Ottomans transferred there a multitude of people, including Turks, Greeks, Armenians and Slavs. However, no group was concentrated in the city to a greater degree than the Jews. The Jews transferred to Istanbul came from over forty Ottoman towns. In many instances, entire communities were forced to relocate to Istanbul. In Edirne, and possibly other towns, where the continued presence of Jews was deemed highly desirable, some Jews were allowed to remain. Nonetheless, it is generally assumed that in this way the majority of Jews living then under Ottoman rule became concentrated in the Ottoman capital. Thus, although the Jews in the Ottoman Empire as a whole constituted a small fraction of the entire population, in Istanbul they numbered more than ten percent of the residents and were the third largest group after the Turks and Greeks.[80]

That the Ottomans gave preference to Jewish settlement in Istanbul is evident from their policy to permit Jewish settlers to establish new synagogues in the city, a measure that stood in clear violation of the Holy Law. It was also in marked contrast to contemporary Ottoman practice with respect to Christian houses of worship, a number of which were closed down after the city's conquest. Similarly, in the sixteenth century, Jews were permitted to establish new synagogues in Salonica and other Ottoman towns. During the reign of the conservative Bayezid II (1481–1512), however, restrictions were imposed on the construction of new synagogues, and some houses of worship, built in Istanbul after 1453, were closed. Jews were not, however, prevented from practicing their religion, although they had to be more circumspect in the choice of places of worship. Bayezid's restrictions proved to be temporary and they were lifted following his death.[81]

Indeed, in the second half of the fifteenth century, the Jews made an important contribution to the development of Istanbul into a major imperial and economic center. Jews were engaged in a wide range of crafts and professions, but their greatest contribution was in the development of the city's internal commerce and international trade. It appears that by the 1470s, the Jews had come to dominate the city's commercial life, and many of the successful merchants had moved on to play a role in a wide range of large-scale entrepreneurial ventures.[82] Jews played a major role in the operation and administration of the customhouses and the docks, and they formed partnerships to outbid rivals for tax-farming contracts and government monopolies. In fact, around 1480, almost all the important tax farms in the area of Istanbul were held by Jews. Minting of coins was another area in which Jews had become very active. Available documents indicate that in the 1480s a large number of the mints in Istanbul and throughout the country was being operated by Jews.[83] Jews also dominated the distribution and recall systems of coinage. It thus appears that within a relatively short period of twenty to thirty years following the conquest of Istanbul, the Jews were able to capture a considerable share of the major financial and commercial activity in the capital, which had previously been dominated by Greeks and Europeans. In the process, the Jewish community had become prosperous. Of course, Greeks and Europeans—joined now by Muslims and Armenians—continued to be active in these same areas, but the Jews appear to have captured a disproportionately important position in the city's economic life.[84] It should be pointed out that these activities were not merely of a financial and economic nature. They also constituted administrative services of great importance and sensitivity to the state. In fact, in some other states, these same operations were carried out directly by the authorities. It is true that the Ottomans generally granted tax farms and other concessions on a competitive basis to the highest bidders. Considering, however, the political sensitivity and importance of these activities, and the Jews' ability to capture such a disproportionate share of them, it is difficult to avoid the conclusion that this was due, in part at least, to official Ottoman encouragement and preferential considerations.

Jewish Immigrant Contributions to Ottoman Expansion and Economic Development

In the second half of the fifteenth century and through the sixteenth, as its power continued to expand in southeastern Europe, the Middle East, and the Mediterranean, the Ottoman state was transformed from a regional power to a world empire. By the end of the sixteenth century, the sultans ruled a vast domain, whose boundaries extended from Hungary and Transylvania in the north to Yemen in the south, and from the borders of Morocco in the west to the Iranian plateau in the east. The administration of such a vast empire created new, and more complex, needs, as well as opportunities. The newly acquired territories required virtually legions of bureaucrats and entrepreneurs to govern and administer them and to exploit their resources in order to meet the ever-increasing financial needs of the state. Additionally, by virtue of its new position and power, the Ottoman Empire sought, and was indeed required, to play a central role in international affairs and the world economy.[85]

The importance that the Ottomans attributed to commerce, in general, and to international commerce, in particular, is reflected in the following advice, which the scholar and statesman Sinan Pasha (ca. 1440–86) offered the sultan in the second half of the fifteenth century:

> Look with favor on the merchants in the land; always care for them; let no one harass them; let no one order them about, for through their trading the land becomes prosperous, and by their wares cheapness abounds in the world; through them the excellent fame of the Sultan is carried to surrounding lands, and by them the wealth within the land is increased.[86]

* * * * *

Several factors coincided to contribute to the successful settlement of large numbers of European Jews in the Ottoman Empire. In the first place, it was a matter of timing. The expulsions and migrations of the European Jews coincided with the great Ottoman expansion, which created vast new economic opportunities. The established Romaniot Jewish population was relatively small and for the most part concentrated in Istanbul. In the outlying provinces, however, there was a great demand for people with managerial and entrepreneurial skills. The Ottomans could look back with satisfaction on a record of Jewish cooperation of some two centuries. They were, therefore, pleased to provide Jewish refugees with a safe haven, expecting in return Jewish cooperation in the development of their empire. Indeed, the Ottoman government took an active role in directing Jewish immigrants to those areas where they were most needed and where, in all probability, economic opportunities were available. This the Ottomans did, at times, by forceful settlement (*sürgün*), but, more commonly, through the offer of various incentives. This may explain, in part at least, why relatively few European Jews settled in Istanbul whereas the great majority settled in provincial towns. Thus, the arrival of large numbers of Jewish immigrants from the West resulted less in competition with the local Jews, but rather added to a pool of human resources that the Ottomans needed to develop their new provinces.

Additionally, the European Jews, even more than their Romaniot coreligionists, possessed knowledge, experience, and skills better suited to meet the new needs of the rising Ottoman Empire. Like the Romaniots, many of the Iberian Jews had extensive experience in banking, commerce, tax-farming, management of ports and customhouses, and the purveying of large quantities of foodstuffs, clothing, and arms for the government and the army. It has been estimated that in fifteenth-century Spain, Jews controlled about two thirds of the kingdom's indirect taxation and customs systems. A network of Jewish tax farmers and collectors had operated throughout the country under the leadership of a Jewish chief tax farmer, who also served as banker to the king.[87] The Iberian Jews had also been prominent in international commerce and banking. Moreover, it was their very misfortune—namely, their expulsion and dispersal across the Mediterranean lands, the Atlantic seaboard, and the New World—that presented them with the opportunity, or forced them, to forge more widely flung commercial and banking networks and propelled some of them to new heights of wealth and fortune.[88] Especially prominent among the latter were the Marranos, who initially adopted Christianity and weathered the early expulsions. When they later escaped, they succeeded, far better than the early refugees, to salvage considerable portions of their wealth and take it with them. Throughout the sixteenth century and the early decades of the seventeenth, Marranos continued to flock to the Ottoman Empire, where they almost invariably openly returned to Judaism.[89] It was this element that the Ottomans sought to attract in their quest to become a leading center of international trade.[90]

Indeed, the European Jews made a major contribution to the development of Ottoman international trade. Within a short time of their arrival in the Ottoman Empire, they were to be found in every major center of international trade, and Salonica, with its Jewish majority, was regarded, due to the activities of the Jewish merchants, as the most important commercial city in the eastern Mediterranean.[91]

In addition to their entrepreneurial and managerial skills, the European Jews had much more to offer. They brought with them knowledge of European sciences and medicine. The well-known mid-sixteenth century travelers, Nicholas (Nicolas) de Nicolay and Pierre Bellon de Mans, came away with the impression that Jewish physicians dominated the field of medicine in the Ottoman Empire; and that they were more numerous and knowledgeable than the physicians of any other group.[92] Jews introduced new forms of the performing arts (İlhan Başgöz). They brought with them printing and a range of new technologies and methods of production, which were utilized by the Ottomans in the exploitation of mineral resources[93] and the manufacture of textiles,[94] arms, munitions, and other products. According to Nicholas de Nicolay,

> [The Jews] have amongst them workmen of all artes and handi-craftes moste excellent, and specially of the Maranes [Marranos] of late banished and driven out of Spaine and Portugale, who to the great detriment and damage of the Christianitie, have taught the Turkes divers inventions, craftes and engines of warre, as to make artillerie, harquebuses, gunne powder, shot, and other munitions: they have also there set up printing, not before seen in those countries, by the which in faire characters they put in light divers bookes in divers languages, as Greek, Latin, Italian, Spanish, and the Hebrew tongue, beeing too them naturall, but are not permitted to print the Turkie or Arabian tongue . . . .[95]

In the sixteenth century, the wool industry in Salonica employed about a thousand Jewish families. Each year it produced thousands of bolts of cloth for the army, the Palace, and export. Safed, too, emerged at that time as a major textile center developed by Jews, and Jews were also instrumental in developing a textile industry in Istanbul.[96] Jews from Salonica organized the exploitation of the silver mines in Sidrekapsı and the collection of gold ore excavated around Salonica.[97] In Rhodes, they were engaged in mining sulfur,[98] and at Corinth, Jews from Istanbul administered the production of alum.[99]

Jews played a considerable role in the development of the Danube basin, an area of great economic, as well as military, importance. As tax farmers, Jews managed many of the Danubian ports and cus-

tomhouses. Similarly, Jews administered several strategically important ports in the Adriatic and the Aegean seas.[100]

Jews also played a disproportionately important role in the re-
vitalization and reorganization of the economies of Egypt, North Africa, and the Fertile Crescent after the Ottoman conquests.[101] In Egypt,
a Sephardic Jew, Abraham Castro, was appointed, in 1520 or 1521,
to administer the Egyptian mint. He was at the same time also in
charge of the Beirut customhouse and perhaps also of that of Alexandria. In addition, he was engaged in international commerce. When,
in 1524, the governor of Egypt, Arnavud Ahmed, rebelled against
the Sultan, Castro refused to cooperate with him. He escaped to Istanbul and reported to the government on the rebellion's circumstances.
In the following year, the uprising was suppressed, Arnavud Ahmed
was executed, and Castro was reinstated in his former position. The
rebellion's suppression was cause for celebration in the Jewish community of Egypt, which feared the rebellious governor's vengeance. The
Jews of Egypt continued to commemorate the date of Arnavud
Ahmed's execution, Adar 28, and the restoration of Ottoman rule, as
a holiday, and called it Purim of Egypt (*Purim shel Mitzrayim*).[102]

In general, from the sixteenth to the eighteenth century, Jews
dominated the financial administration of Egypt, the operation of the
mint and the management of the customhouses. They also served as
bankers to the governors of Egypt, the local Janissary contingent and
to many of the Mamluk amirs. According to the description of the
seventeenth-century Ottoman traveler Evliya Çelebi, the official chief
sarraf (banker and money changer) of Egypt was a Jew, who headed
a network of some three hundred Jewish sarrafs. Evliya Çelebi also
reported that every tax farmer had his own Jewish sarraf, who administered his tax farm for him.[103]

Indeed, by the mid-sixteenth century, Jews had become so prominent in the Ottoman economy that to Pierre Bellon de Mans it appeared that they "have taken over the traffic and commerce of Turkey
to such an extent that the Turk's wealth and revenue is in their
hands."[104] While the statement may be exaggerated, it probably is a
reflection of the important role that the Jews had assumed in the
development of the Ottoman economy and their ability to capture, in
the process, a disproportionate share of it. That the Jews were able
to attain such a prominent position within a relatively short period of
time cannot be attributed solely to their knowledge, experience, and
skills. An equally important element contributing to their success must
have been the trust and support that they received from the state.

In fact, it appears that in the sixteenth century, the Ottomans came to regard the Jews in a class by themselves and as playing a special role in the processes of empire-building. The Ottomans considered it especially desirable to settle Jews in strategically important areas. Thus, following the conquests of Rhodes (1523) and Cyprus (1571), the Ottoman authorities issued orders to settle Jews in these islands.[105] Conversely, when in the late 1570s, the central government ordered to transfer Jews from Lepanto (İnebahtı) elsewhere, the commander of this strategically important port-fortress, and other military officers, submitted testimonies underscoring the important contributions that the local Jews had made to the defense and provisioning of the town, and requested that the orders be rescinded.[106] The orders to deport Jewish families from Safed to Cyprus were also canceled in 1578, after the kadi of Safed pointed out the considerable losses that this act would cause to the local economy and the imperial treasury.[107]

Ottoman preferential attitudes towards the Jews found their expression in official terminology. From a religious-legal perspective, both Christians and Jews were regarded as zimmis, who were equally inferior in status compared with Muslims. In practical matters, however, the Ottomans often made a distinction between Christians and Jews. In official Ottoman documents dealing with regions as far apart as Egypt, Istanbul, the Danube, and the Crimea, Christians of different branches, sects, and ethnic origins were all lumped together and referred to as *kefere*, namely infidels, whereas Jews were simply referred to as Jews (*Yahudiler* or *Yahudi taifesi*). This distinction was also made by Ottoman historians.[108] This was not intended to suggest that Jews were lesser infidels than Christians, but simply that they belonged in a different category and this fact had to be noted.

The Jewish Economic-Political Elites

It has been noted that due to their dispersal, the Jews formed widely flung, interconnected networks based on family relations. These networks spanned across the Ottoman Empire and beyond to several European countries. Such networks were most commonly utilized for commercial and business activities, but they could also provide useful political and military information, local and international. It was for this reason that highly placed Ottomans, from the sultan down, often saw in the employment of Jews an added advantage. Jews serving as physicians, financial advisors, translators, and in other capacities could offer, in addition to their professional services, political information and advice. Thus, Koca Sinan Pasha, who between the years 1580 and 1595 served three terms as Grand Vezir, employed a Jewish physician, Eliezer Eskenderi (or Iskandari), who also served as his political advisor.[109]

These facts were particularly appreciated by Ottoman officials sent to administer distant provinces. It was, therefore, not unusual for an Ottoman governor to bring with him from Istanbul a Jewish "man of affairs" (*iş eri* or *iş adamı*), who acted as his private banker (*sarraf*), agent and advisor, or to employ a local Jew in this capacity (C. Max Kortepeter). In either case, the governor's Jewish agent was likely to have relatively easy access to the local business community, where Jews often predominated, as well as to a widely flung network of correspondents.[110] Through his Jewish agent the governor could avail himself of several advantages. First, he could keep himself informed of local economic and political conditions, so as to administer his province effectively and with profit. Additionally, to assure his career, the governor had to keep abreast of political developments elsewhere and particularly at the capital. His Jewish agent could help him obtain this vital information.

Even the highly placed ladies of the imperial palace employed Jewish women as purveyors, agents, and political advisors. These women were known by the Greek title *kira* (also *kiera*, *kyra*), meaning lady. Considerable information is available on the activities of three kiras—perhaps the most prominent, although it is known that there were others. Fatma (Fatima) Kadın was apparently a Karaite from the Crimea who served Hafsa Sultan, the mother of Süleyman the Magnificent. She is believed to have died in 1548, after adopting Islam. Another kira, Esther Handali, was probably Sephardic. She served Nur Banu, the mother of Murad III (r. 1574–95) and died at about 1590. A third kira, Esperanza Malchi (or Malkhi), served as agent for Safiye, the consort (*haseki*) of Murad III, who upon his death became Queen Mother (*valide sultan*) of Mehmed III (r. 1595–1603).[111] Esperanza played some part in a correspondence between Safiye and Queen Elizabeth I of England. She herself addressed at least one letter, in Italian, to Elizabeth in 1599, in which she identified herself as a Jewess (*Hebrea*). The main subject of the letter concerned an exchange of gifts between the two queens. Esperanza suggested that in the future Elizabeth should not send jewels, but rather cosmetics and fine cloths of silk and wool, as these English products were superior to the local. She also advised Elizabeth that since these items were "articles for ladies," the Queen Mother wished them delivered only through her own hand. Individuals so close to the seat of power often raised the envy of others and they sometimes paid the ultimate price. Esperanza was reputed to have acquired great influence and wealth. In 1600, she was accused of having intervened in a senior military appointment and was killed, on 1 April, by a group of mutinous soldiers.[112]

Jewish kiras must have continued to serve the ladies of the imperial palace also after 1600. In 1622, an unnamed Jewish woman with connections to the sister of Sultan Osman II (r. 1618–22) was mentioned as having been involved in promoting the candidacy of Locadello, a wealthy Greek, to the office of *voyvoda* (governor) of Moldavia.[113] In 1709, another unnamed Jewish woman was believed to have helped the Jewish physician Daniel de Fonseca pass on information to the mother of Sultan Ahmed III (r. 1703–30) in order to bring about an Ottoman-Swedish alliance against Russia.[114]

The most prominent and best-known of the Jewish advisors were those who served the sultans. Little is known on the activities of Jews in the Ottoman court before the reign of Mehmed II (1451–81). From the reign of Murad II (1421–51), however, a few details are available regarding the presence of Jewish physicians at the court. First, there is reference to a certain Ishak Pasha, who is believed to have served as the sultan's chief physician, and whose family was granted tax-exemption privileges.[115] A much better-known figure who entered the service of Murad II and became chief physician was an Italian Jew, Jacopo of Gaeta, known in Ottoman society as Hekim Yakub (Jacob the [Royal] Physician). By the time Mehmed II ascended the throne in 1451, Yakub was already a highly influential figure at the court, where he continued to serve as chief physician. Additionally, his Western education and familiarity with European sciences and politics paved the way for him to enter Mehmed II's most intimate circle of political advisors. Yakub has been credited with having aroused Sultan Mehmed's interest in European sciences. He is also believed to have urged the Sultan to use artillery — still an experimental military branch—in the siege of Constantinople.[116] Some Ottoman accounts maintain that Yakub held high official appointments in the Ottoman administration; that he served as *defterdar* (head of the treasury) and was raised to the rank of vezir.[117] Shortly before his death in 1483, or 1484, at a time when both his health and influence were in decline,

Yakub converted to Islam. It is significant, however, that the highest achievements of his career were attained as a Jew.[118]

By the turn of the sixteenth century, the number of Jewish physicians at the court increased. None, however, was more prominent than Joseph Hamon, a native of Granada and a descendant of a distinguished family of physicians. He entered the service of the Ottoman court during the latter years of Bayezid II's reign (1481–1512) and became the personal physician of Selim I (r. 1512–20). He accompanied Selim on his campaign in Syria and Egypt (1516–17), and he died in Damascus, probably in 1518, in the course of the return trip to Istanbul. Joseph Hamon used his influence to promote Jewish interests and arbitrate internal disputes within the community. He founded a dynasty of court physicians, who served in the imperial palace for over a century. The best known and most prominent of the Hamons was Joseph's son, Moses (ca. 1490–ca. 1554), who succeeded his father as physician to Selim I and later also to Süleyman the Magnificent.

The traveler Nicholas de Nicolay wrote about Moses Hamon in 1551: "Hee which in the tyme that I was in Levant, had the first dignity and authority, amongst the order of Phisitions was of nation an Hebrew called Amon, of age aboute sixtie yeers, a personage great of authoritye, and muche estcemcd, as well for his goods, knowledge, and renowne, as for honour and portlinesse."[119]

Moses Hamon wielded a great deal of political influence at the court. During much of Süleyman's reign, life at the court was fractious and rife with political intrigue. Moses apparently was allied with the influential party led by Hürrem Sultan (Roxelana), Süleyman's favorite wife, and Grand Vezir Rüstem Pasha. Moses used his political influence to intercede on behalf of the Jewish community. He prevailed on Süleyman to issue an order protecting Jews against blood libels. He also is believed to have interceded with the sultan to exert pressure on Venice to facilitate the departure of the Nasi-Mendes family for the Ottoman Empire. Moses was a patron of learning and scholarship. Among his numerous acts of philanthropy was the maintenance of an important yeshivah headed by the renowned scholar Rabbi Joseph Taitatzak. Shortly before his death, Moses' position at the court appears to have declined. Nevertheless, both his son, Joseph (died 1577), and his grandson, Isaac son of Joseph (died in the seventeenth century), served as physicians, as well as political advisors, to the Ottoman court.[120]

Joseph Nasi

The most prominent, and best known, figure of Ottoman Jewry, however, was Joseph Nasi (ca. 1524–79).[121] He was born in Portugal as a Marrano under the Christian name Joao Micas (Miques, Míguez). His father was a prominent physician employed in the Portuguese court. In 1537, Joseph Nasi left Lisbon with his paternal aunt, Gracia Nasi Mendes, and settled in Antwerp, where he joined the commercial banking house of Mendes. The financial activities of the Mendes firm were extensive, ranging widely throughout western Europe, and their list of clients included the monarchs of France and Spain. In spite of financial success, however, in her later years, Gracia appears to have been motivated by a strong desire to return to Judaism. In 1553, she settled in Istanbul and Joseph followed her in 1554. In Istanbul, the Nasi-Mendes family openly returned to Judaism and became leading members of the Jewish community. [122]

Shortly after their settlement in Istanbul, the Nasis became heavily engaged in tax-farming activities. Their success in breaking into this lucrative field so quickly appears to have stemmed from the fact that they were in a position to make large cash advances to the treasury. In return, they were able to secure government concessions on favorable terms.[123] To operate their tax farms, monopolies, and commercial interests in the Ottoman Empire and abroad, the Nasis developed a widely flung network of agents, functionaries, and correspondents. Joseph Nasi's familiarity with current European affairs made him an invaluable advisor to the Ottoman court, and it appears that, at times, he took bold initiatives on his own. He played an important role in the peace negotiations between the Ottoman Empire and Poland, in 1562. In 1569, he encouraged the Dutch to rise against Spain, promising them Ottoman assistance. His political activities appear to have been motivated by a strong hostility towards Spain, which, at the time, was the Ottoman Empire's most formidable adversary. Nasi's political activities were interconnected with his financial and commercial affairs. His interest in good Ottoman-Polish relations was motivated, or perhaps rewarded, by the expansion of his trade with that country. Nasi exported wine to Poland. He also secured a monopoly on the importation of Polish wax to the Ottoman Empire.

Having become one of the leading entrepreneurs in the country, as well as a banker to the court and a political advisor, it was virtually impossible for Nasi not to become involved in palace politics. The latter years of Süleyman's reign witnessed a struggle for succession between princes Selim and Bayezid. Nasi had probably little choice in supporting Selim, since the latter was the candidate favored by the sultan and the court. Selim did indeed emerge victorious and following the death of his father went on to rule as Selim II (1566–74). It was during the latter's reign that Nasi's career achieved its pinnacle. He became a close advisor to the sultan and, in consequence, was able to expand his financial enterprises even further. Among various honors, he received an official appointment as governor of Naxos and the Cyclades Archipelago with the Ottoman rank of *sancakbeyi* (district governor) and the Italian title of duke. He administered the Cyclades through an agent, while he continued to live in his mansion near Istanbul. At this point in his career, he was considered one of the most powerful and influential individuals in the Ottoman court.

Both Gracia and Joseph were heavily engaged in philanthropic activities within the Jewish community. In Istanbul, Gracia founded a new synagogue named Della Señora (or Señora, in short; in Hebrew, *Shel Ha-Geveret Ha-Ma'atirah,* The Illustrious Lady). She also established a yeshivah headed by the renowned scholar Rabbi Joseph ibn Lev. Gracia, and later Joseph, secured a concession to develop the town of Tiberias, then in ruins, and its vicinity. They founded there a yeshivah, and in 1565 completed the reconstruction of the town's walls. Joseph attempted to develop Tiberias as a textile center, and he invited Italian Jewish communities to settle there. Although Jews did settle in Tiberias and its community flourished for a while, the project encountered numerous difficulties and did not fulfill its founders' expectations. The institutions founded in Tiberias were not, however, a complete failure. They continued to operate on a modest scale, and in the face of many hardships, for several generations, into the seventeenth century.[124]

Joseph Nasi also patronized Jewish scholarship in Istanbul and Salonica by supporting individual scholars and establishing a synagogue, a yeshivah and a library attached to his mansion. In the last years of Selim II's reign, and even more so following his death in 1574, Nasi's standing at the court appears to have declined, as did his health and financial activities. Nevertheless, when he died in 1579, he was still widely respected with much of his wealth intact.

Joseph Nasi's career epitomized the Ottoman-Jewish symbiosis. Although an immigrant—and an "infidel," at that—he was able, within a short time, to reach the highest peaks of economic success and political influence, and in so doing he was able to serve the interests of both the Ottoman state and his own people. Nasi's career, and those of the other successful Ottoman Jews, speak volumes of the openness and tolerance of Ottoman society, its prevailing liberalism, the pragmatic attitudes of its government, and the great opportunities it could provide those who had the skills, means, and ambition to reach out for them.

The Socioeconomic Position of the Jews

The great majority of Ottoman Jews were not, of course, wealthy bankers, tax farmers, and entrepreneurs, nor famous physicians and political advisors. In fact, most of the refugees, who arrived in the Ottoman Empire in the large, early post-1492 waves of immigration, were poor. What little wealth they had managed to take out with them was mostly lost during their travels.[125] In time, many of these early immigrants, and their descendants, had recovered and became established.[126] Still, even in the middle decades of the sixteenth century, when the condition of Ottoman Jewry was portrayed by outside observers as very prosperous, there existed, in fact, also considerable poverty. The responsa of Rabbi Samuel de Medina convey the impression that in Salonica, side by side with a "minority" of affluent and well-to-do, there existed "a large group of poverty-stricken Jews . . . and the number of the destitute was far greater than that of the affluent."[127] This must have been true for many other communities. Records for Istanbul, dating from the early seventeenth century, indicate that in the Sephardic Congregation Gerush, one of the wealthiest in the city, 57 percent of the tax-paying members belonged in the upper and middle tax brackets, leaving 43 percent in the lowest. At the same time, in the Ashkenazi congregation only 8 percent were listed in the higher two categories and 92 percent in the poorest.[128]

Some communities were better off than others. The community of Bursa, which played a prominent role in the city's voluminous international trade in silk and spices,[129] appears to have been exceptionally well-to-do. In 1598/99, 48 percent of the Jewish tax-payers belonged in the upper tax bracket, 31 percent in the middle and only 21 percent in the lowest.[130] Although the Jewish community of Jerusalem was considered by the authorities as "very poor," and all its members were assessed at the lowest rate,[131] the Jerusalem court records suggest, however, that at least some Jews were, in fact, quite affluent.[132] This information is obviously too sketchy to draw any definite conclusions, and, in fact, it raises more questions than it provides answers. It does, however, suggest what should be obvious, that even in what was almost universally considered an age of prosperity, there were considerable disparities between communities and within them.

The Jews were predominantly an urban element, and they were to be found in almost every occupation, profession and craft typical to the urban setting in which they lived. There were, however, some occupations in which Jews tended to be particularly active. Due to the Jewish requirement to observe dietary laws, food-processing was everywhere, and at all times, a major Jewish occupation. Jews worked as slaughterers, butchers, meat processors, cheese and wine makers, millers and bakers. In these occupations they usually served mainly the needs of the Jewish community, but also those of its neighbors, Muslim and Christian.[133]

The manufacture of textiles, and related crafts, was another traditional Jewish occupation. This, too, was prompted by religious requirements, and especially the prohibition against mixing wool with linen. Jews were very active in the various textile crafts, which developed in Salonica, Istanbul, Bursa, Rhodes, Safed, Izmir, Cairo, and other urban centers. In the sixteenth century, the production of textiles became the chief occupation of the communities of Salonica and Safed, encompassing all classes, from the wealthiest to the poorest. The Jews were engaged in all aspects of production, as investors, contractors, and merchants, but most of them were laborers—weavers, dyers, pressers, and an array of other manual occupations. Some phases of the production process were performed in special workshops and others in private homes, where the head of the household worked together with his wife and children.[134]

Jewelry crafts also attracted considerable numbers of Jews, who worked as goldsmiths, silversmiths, and processors, cutters, and setters of gems and precious stones.[135] Considerable numbers were also engaged in the crafts of producing soap, perfumes, and spices.[136] Additionally, Jews were to be found in a wide range of other crafts. They worked as tanners and manufacturers of leather goods, and as blacksmiths, coppersmiths, metal workers, carpenters, locksmiths, makers of buttons and toys, and bookbinders, to mention some occupations.[137]

There were also those who engaged in occupations not typically associated with Jews. Jews worked as miners and laborers in the gold and silver mines near Salonica.[138] In Salonica, Istanbul, and the Galilee region of Palestine, Jews were engaged in marine transport and fishing. They owned and operated large and small vessels, working as captains and ordinary seamen.[139] In Salonica, where Jews controlled most port activities, they also worked as porters and stevedores.[140]

It was rare, though not unknown, for Jews in Salonica, Rhodes,

Safed, Jerusalem, Alexandria and other urban centers, to own, lease, or manage agricultural property in the towns' vicinity, and sometimes to engage in farming directly.[141] In some remote provinces—the Caucasus, eastern Anatolia, northern Iraq, Yemen and North Africa—Jewish peasants and peasant communities, supporting themselves on agriculture, are known to have existed, although little information is available about them from this period.[142] In the Galilee region of Palestine, twelve villages were listed as having a Jewish peasant population. According to Ottoman records, the village of Peki'in (Bukei'a), believed to have had an uninterrupted Jewish settlement throughout the ages, had in 1555/56 forty-five Jewish households; Kefar Kanna (Kafr Kanna) had sixty-five Jewish households, ten bachelors, and one half-wit; and Kefar Yasif (Kafr Yasif) had twenty-nine Jewish households.[143] Individual Jewish peasants were found also in the Balkans, in the district of Bitola (Manastır),[144] and they probably existed in other areas as well.

From all sources it appears, however, that the main Jewish occupation was commerce, in all its forms and in all kinds of merchandise.[145] Jews were engaged in local commerce, in internal trade between various Ottoman provinces and commercial centers, and in international trade with Europe, Iran and India. They also served as middlemen and agents for foreign traders. The wealthiest merchants were wholesalers, who also competed for government contracts. The great majority, however, were engaged in retail. There were Jews who owned and operated shops; others worked as peddlers and hawkers, plying their wares in the markets and city streets, or bringing them to the villages of the countryside. In fact, Jews became so much identified with commerce that in the popular vernacular the very word for merchant or peddler, *bazirgân* (*bezirgân*), came also to denote a Jew, and as such it was often used contemptuously.[146]

From the sources it would appear that surprising numbers of Jewish women were also independently engaged in commerce and related activities.[147] We have already noted that Jewish women served as purveyors for the ladies of the imperial palace and probably also for the households of other Ottoman grandees. In addition, Jewish women were engaged in a variety of commercial and real estate activities. On the bottom of the economic ladder were Jewish women who peddled haberdashery, handkerchiefs, and napkins in the bazaars, or who hired themselves out as seamstresses and embroiderers.[148]

A woman's success in business could, sometimes, discommode her husband. In the latter years of the sixteenth century, a Romaniot Jew from Istanbul appealed the decision of the Jewish tax assessors to tax him also on the properties and business income of his wife, as it was the accepted practice to assess only heads of households. The man argued that his wife, a successful businesswoman, engaged in commerce and real estate activities on her own, kept her assets to herself, and used them to support her relatives and contribute to charities as she pleased. Since he derived no benefits from her income, he did not want to pay the taxes either. The rabbinic authorities were apparently split on this issue and some tended to exempt the husband. However, Rabbi Yehiel Basan (ca. 1550–1625), the deciding judicial authority in this matter, decreed that the husband was nevertheless liable for his wife's properties and income.[149]

Jewish Scholarship and Intellectual Life

The influx of many prominent Jewish scholars to the Ottoman Empire from different countries, representing different traditions and schools; the contacts among them and the resident scholars; the prosperity that affected considerable segments of the Jewish community; the traditions of philanthropy; and the freedom to travel, study, and publish without any hindrance, had all resulted in the cultural efflorescence of Ottoman Jewry. Since Sephardic Jews were both numerically and culturally superior to the other groups, they assumed a leadership role in this process and, thus, Iberian Jewish culture was transplanted to, and revitalized on, Ottoman soil. In the sixteenth century, Salonica, Istanbul, and Safed had replaced Toledo, Cordova, and Barcelona as major centers of Jewish scholarship and intellectual life.[150]

Salonica, which had probably the largest Jewish community in the empire, constituting a majority of the city's population, attained a special position of preeminence throughout the Jewish diaspora. The city was often compared to Jerusalem in its heyday as the spiritual center of the Jewish people. Rabbi Samuel de Medina, a confirmed partisan of his native town, stated that to settle in Salonica constituted an act of piety. He further asserted that no other city throughout the Jewish diaspora could compare with Salonica as a center of learning.[151]

Indeed, Salonica had public libraries, a Hebrew printing press founded in 1515,[152] and several renowned institutions of learning.

Among the latter was the yeshivah directed by Rabbi Jacob ibn Habib and his son Levi ibn Habib (ca. 1483–1545), as well as those of Joseph Taitatzak (ca. 1487–ca. 1545), Samuel de Medina (ca. 1506–89), and Isaac Adarbi (ca. 1510–84). The community also maintained a Great Talmud Torah, a religious primary school, where hundreds of students were enrolled, with many receiving free daily meals and clothing. The city also emerged at that time as an important center for the study of Kabbalah, Jewish mysticism. In addition to rabbinical institutions, the community also supported a school for secular studies, where medicine, astronomy, and natural sciences were taught.[153]

Salonica became an important medical and scientific center when the Marrano physician Amatus Lusitanus (Amato Lusitano; 1511–68), one of Europe's best known medical authorities, settled there in 1558. Amatus was born in Portugal as João Rodrigues and studied medicine at the University of Salamanca in Spain. He later taught at the University of Ferrara and established himself as an authority in anatomy, internal medicine, and dermatology. Among his patients were Pope Julius III and members of his family. King Sigismund II of Poland invited Amatus to become his court physician, but the latter declined the offer. In Salonica, Amatus openly practiced Judaism and became known by his Hebrew name, Haviv ha-Sefardi. From 1558 until his death in 1568, he continued his medical research in Salonica, where he trained other physicians and became the center of a circle of scientists and philosophers.[154]

Istanbul—with the second largest Jewish community in the empire, which was, however, more influential and probably also more prosperous than that of Salonica, with numerous scholars and philanthropists—rivaled Salonica as a center of Jewish scholarship. In 1493, the brothers David and Samuel Nahmias founded in Istanbul a Hebrew printing press, the first to be established in the Ottoman Empire. In 1494, it published *Arba'ah Turim* (The Four Columns), a well-known code of laws by Rabbi Jacob ben Asher (ca. 1270–1340) of Toledo. It was the first book ever published in the Ottoman Empire.[155]

Among Istanbul's best known yeshivot was that of the Romaniot rabbi Elijah Mizrahi (ca. 1450–1526), where students learned religious, as well as secular studies. Following Mizrahi's death, his yeshivah was headed by his disciple Elijah ha-Levi. Another well known yeshivah was that directed by Joseph ibn Lev (ca. 1505–80). This institution was supported by Gracia Mendes and Joseph Nasi. The famous yeshivah of Joseph Trani (ca. 1568–1639) was supported by the philanthropists Abraham ibn Yaish, Jacob Ancona, as well as others.[156]

Edirne also had several yeshivot, the most famous of which was headed by Joseph Fasi. Yeshivot were maintained also by smaller communities, such as those of Bursa, Ankara, Nikopol, and Damascus.[157]

During the course of the sixteenth century, Safed had emerged as the third largest community in the empire and the most important Jewish center in Palestine. Its yeshivot attracted scholars from different countries. Among its leading scholars was Rabbi Jacob Beirav (Berab; ca. 1474–1546), who maintained that the time was propitious to reestablish the *sanhedrin*, the supreme Jewish political, spiritual and judicial body, which had operated in Palestine during the Roman period until about 425. One of Beirav's disciples was Joseph Caro (1488–1575), the author of the *Shulhan Arukh*. Safed, however, became renowned primarily as the most important center for the study of Kabbalah. The most outstanding figures in this area were Solomon Alkabetz (ca. 1505–45), Moses Cordovero (ca. 1522–70), and Isaac Luria Ashkenazi (1534–72). The latter, known as the Sacred Lion (*Ha-Ari ha-Kadosh*), founded the Lurianic system of Kabbalah, which spread throughout the Jewish diaspora through the activities of his disciple Hayyim Vital (1542-1620). The Lurianic Kabbalah made a great impact in the Jewish world in the seventeenth century, and one of its offshoots was the messianic movement centered around the figure of Shabbetai Tzevi. A Hebrew printing press was also established in Safed, but it operated only from 1577 to 1587.[158]

The flow of Iberian scholars and Kabbalists to Jerusalem also revitalized that city as a center of Jewish scholarship. Among the great scholars who settled or taught in Jerusalem during the sixteenth century were Levi ibn Habib (ca. 1483–1545), David ibn Abi Zimra (ca. 1479–1573), Betzalel Ashkenazi (ca. 1520–ca. 1591) and Hayyim Vital.[159] At about 1560, Gracia Nasi Mendes founded an important yeshivah in Tiberias, which functioned until the beginning of the seventeenth century.[160]

Egypt's Jewry also benefitted from the migration of Iberian scholars. Among its well-known yeshivot were those headed by David ibn Abi Zimra, Jacob Beirav, Betzalel Ashkenazi, Jacob Castro (ca. 1525–1610), and Abraham Monzon (d. after 1603).[161] The fact that some scholars were active in more than one center is an indication of the mobility and opportunities available to Jewish scholars, now that the Middle East and many of the Mediterranean lands had become unified under Ottoman rule. This, in turn, was a major contribution to the efflorescence of Jewish culture.

The Jews and Ottoman Society

The Jews benefitted from many aspects that Ottoman rule brought with it, and from the generally favorable, even supportive, attitudes on the part of the authorities. Still, their lives were also affected to a very considerable degree by the particular conditions prevailing in their places of residence, and especially, by their relations with the general population among whom they lived; and these circumstances differed from one place to another and over time. It is possible to generalize, however, and say that while individual Jews might have wielded considerable influence and power, the community as a whole was perceived by other segments of society as small and weak, which indeed it was, and, hence, an easy target for attack and predation. This duality was reflected particularly in the relations between the Jews and the military. Jews played a disproportionately important role as contractors and purveyors for the military and as private bankers for senior military officers. The position of *Ocak Bazırganı,* the merchant-banker of the Janissary corps, the central branch of the Ottoman land forces, was generally occupied by Jews. The holders of this position served as chief purveyors and financiers for the Janissaries, and they must have been, therefore, on close terms with the corps' senior officers.[162] Nevertheless, Jewish and Ottoman sources record numerous instances in which Jews suffered from the predations of the Janissaries, as well as other military units. These attacks usually took place during times of unrest, and they were not directed exclusively against Jews. Nevertheless, the frequency of these acts suggests that Jews were regarded as a particularly easy target.[163]

Jews were also subject to attacks by their civilian neighbors. The Christian population, and particularly the Greeks in the urban centers of Anatolia and the Balkans, were generally hostile to the Jews. Even in the city of Salonica, where the Jews considerably outnumbered every other group, they exercised great caution not to provoke the Greeks.[164] Jews passing through Christian neighborhoods occasionally risked physical assault. From time to time, Jews were accused of ritual murder.[165] In the case of the Greeks, hostility on religious grounds was probably intensified by economic and social considerations, as the Greeks saw themselves being replaced in many areas by the Jews, who appeared to enjoy the support of the authorities and had become prosperous. As a result, Jews generally preferred to settle near or within Muslim neighborhoods, where they felt more secure.[166] Even in Muslim neighborhoods, however, Jews were not completely safe from contemptuous attitudes, verbal abuse, and occasional assault. The word *çifüt,* miser, was an insult reserved by Turks specifically for Jews.[167] In fact, the very word *Yahudi,* Jew, was often used contemptuously in popular vernacular, and when addressed to non-Jews was meant as an insult.[168]

The general impression derived from the sources is that in the Arabic-speaking provinces the attitudes of Muslims towards Jews was more hostile and contemptuous than in Anatolia and the Balkans. This may, perhaps, be explained by the fact that in the Arab provinces, where the Sephardic immigration imported a foreign language, garb and customs, the Jews, or at least some of them, were seen as culturally more alien than the Arabic-speaking local Christians and Jews. They were also perceived as a prosperous and privileged minority under the protection of, or allied with, the Turkish-speaking Ottoman rulers who, although Muslim, were also regarded as a foreign element. On the other hand, the Turkish-speaking Muslims were more accustomed to the presence of culturally diverse minority groups in Anatolia (Greeks and Armenians) and the Balkans (Slavs and Greeks), speaking their own languages and possessing their different customs.

The Jews, however, were not as defenseless as they appeared to be. To protect their interests they relied on their internal solidarity, their extensive networks and contacts, their familiarity with the Ottoman system, and on political action. Their first line of defense would normally be an appeal to the local authorities, and when this did not bring relief, they would present their case to the central government in Istanbul, with the help of the Jews of the capital. The leadership of the Jewish community in Istanbul, and especially influential individuals with access to the court and the government, thus became the spokesmen and protectors of Jewish interests throughout the empire.

The Ottoman authorities, in general, protected the Jews, and for good reason. In the first place, as an imperial power it was in their best interest to maintain law and order. Additionally, the Jewish community discharged important services of an economic and administrative nature, and it was, therefore, in the interest of the state to assure that these activities proceed uninterrupted. As in any society, however, absolute protection was not always possible. The degree of security that the Jews could expect depended, in the first place, on effective government. Wherever and whenever effective government declined, the position of the Jews became precarious.

III
THE STRUCTURE OF THE JEWISH COMMUNITY

The Ottoman *Millet* System

Community life of the non-Muslim religious minorities in the Ottoman Empire was governed by what has become known as the *millet system*. Under this order, minorities enjoyed a wide latitude of religious and cultural freedom, as well as considerable administrative, fiscal, and legal autonomy under their own ecclesiastical and lay leaders. The term millet originally meant both a religion and a religious community. In the nineteenth century, while still retaining its original meanings, it also came to denote such modern concepts as nation and nationality. The Ottoman millet system had its origins in earlier Middle Eastern states, both Muslim and non-Muslim, and it was not, therefore, an Ottoman innovation. The Ottoman contribution was mainly to regulate and institutionalize it and to pay greater attention to its proper operation.

The millet system was, in effect, an extension of Ottoman general administrative practices. In an age that lacked modern technologies of administration, communication, and control, the Ottomans, like other contemporary states, had little choice but to deal with the masses of their population corporatively, allowing each group wide latitude in the conduct of its internal affairs. The same principle was also applied to minorities. On the other hand, the impulse to control their population as much as possible brought the Ottomans to develop hierarchical governmental structures, where each man's place was precisely defined. Superiors were held accountable for the performance and conduct of those under their authority, and the discharge of governmental responsibility was closely regulated. It was, in effect, a system intended to centralize government in an age that lacked modern technologies of governance. The system appeared to be very rigid, but in reality it was not. As an imperial power, the Ottomans quickly realized that to control diverse groups of subjects, flexibility and pragmatism were important. Nowhere were these techniques better demonstrated than in the way in which the Ottomans conducted the affairs of their minority communities. Other than in certain areas of great importance to the state, such as security and taxation, the Ottomans were generally prepared to adopt a policy of laissez-faire in the internal affairs of minority communities.

Until recently it was generally believed that, following the conquest of Constantinople in 1453, Mehmed the Conqueror molded the Ottoman millet system into its definitive form. According to this traditional version, Mehmed established separate, parallel, and autonomous organizations for his Orthodox, Armenian, and Jewish subjects. These were supposedly similar, statewide structures with well-defined hierarchies, controlled from Istanbul by their respective ecclesiastical leaders, the Greek and Armenian Patriarchs and the Jewish Chief Rabbi. Recently, however, this portrayal of the millet system has been shown to be greatly oversimplified and incorrect.[169] The Ottomans, it appears, did not develop rigidly uniform structures for their minorities. Rather, their pragmatism and laissez-faire attitudes allowed for the emergence of flexible arrangements, resulting in the development of diverse structures of self-government. These arrangements took into account the needs and interests of the state, as well as the particular circumstances of each of the minority communities.

The case of the Orthodox Church came closest to the millet model as traditionally described. Mehmed the Conqueror's appointment of Gennadios Scholarios as Patriarch of Constantinople did indeed create for all the Orthodox subjects in the empire a titular head and a statewide authority. Although the Greek Patriarch of Constantinople still had to continue to contend with various centrifugal forces from within his church, under Ottoman rule, his authority was greatly enhanced, compared to what it had been in Byzantine times, in two important ways. First, in addition to religious and spiritual affairs, the Patriarch's authority was now expanded to include also administrative, financial, and legal responsibilities of a civil nature. Second, his authority was now extended over millions of Orthodox Slav communicants of the Balkans, who had previously belonged to the independent Bulgarian and Serbian churches. In the sixteenth century, his authority would be extended also over the Orthodox communities in the Arabic-speaking lands. In the case of the Orthodox church, the centralizing impulse of the state coincided with the ecumenical traditions and ambitions of the Greek clergy of Constantinople.

As for the Armenians, the realities of their organization were quite different. Prior to the Ottoman conquest, there was no Armenian patriarch in Constantinople and probably few Armenians. The two important Armenian ecclesiastical centers were in Etchmiadzin and Cilicia, both beyond the Ottoman boundaries of that period. To curtail the potentially hostile influence of these foreign centers on Ottoman Armenians, as well as to develop and strengthen the Ottoman capital, Mehmed adopted two measures. He forcibly settled Armenians in Istanbul and its environs, and he created the Armenian Patriarchate of Constantinople. Unlike its Orthodox counterpart, however, the Armenian Patriarchate of Constantinople lacked the historical and religious legitimacy to claim supremacy over other long-established ecclesiastical centers. Consequently, the authority of the Patriarch of Constantinople for a long time remained limited to Istanbul and adjoining areas. As Ottoman rule, in the fifteenth and sixteenth centuries, expanded to include additional Armenian centers, the latter were recognized as autonomous entities, not dependent on the Patriarchate of Constantinople. Thus, the Armenian Patriarch of Istanbul was initially only one of several Armenian ecclesiastical leaders. In time, however, the growing importance of the Armenian community of the capital, its proximity to the central Ottoman government and its activities as an intermediary between the Ottoman government and the outlying Armenian communities—all enhanced the position of the Patriarch of Constantinople. By the eighteenth century, although he continued to be regarded as the spiritual subordinate to the Catholicos of Etchmiadzin and the Catholicos of Sis, in effect, the Armenian Patriarch of Constantinople became the administrative head and representative of all the Armenians in the Ottoman Empire. Thus, the creation of the Armenian Patriarchate of Constantinople in the fifteenth century, and its evolution over time, represented a compromise between the Ottoman imperial imperative, on the one hand, and Armenian traditions and the changing power structure within the community, on the other.

Jewish Community Structures in the Fifteenth and Sixteenth Centuries

It is reasonable to assume that from the Ottoman perspective, the same imperial considerations, which impelled them to strengthen the Orthodox and Armenian centers in their capital, would also apply to the Jews. True, the condition of the Jews was dissimilar to that of the other minorities. In the first place, they were much smaller in numbers; there were no large Jewish communities under hostile rule in areas immediately adjacent to Ottoman territories, as was the case with the Orthodox and the Armenians in the mid-fifteenth century; unlike the Christians, the Jews were overwhelmingly an urban, peaceful element, with a proven record of loyalty to, and preference for, Ottoman rule. Consequently, the same political and security considerations, which militated in favor of creating strong centers in the Ottoman capital to attract the allegiance of the Orthodox and the Armenians, did not apply in the case of the Jews. Still, it is necessary to take into account Mehmed the Conqueror's ambition to turn Istanbul into a great imperial metropolis and the role which he assigned to the Jews in his plans. As noted above, Mehmed transferred to Istanbul large numbers of Jews. It is reasonable to assume, therefore, that the orderly administration of the Jewish community was a matter of some importance to the Ottoman government. In addition, there were immediate practical considerations. The transfer of thousands of Jews required some central authority, familiar with the Jews' language, customs, and requirements, to administer and supervise the processes of their settlement and integration in the new Ottoman capital. Beyond that, there were the general tendencies of Ottoman imperial policy to centralize government under well-defined hierarchical structures. From the Ottoman perspective, therefore, there were present important considerations favoring the establishment of a central authority for the Jewish population of the empire.

On the Jewish part, however, there were no well-defined and widely-accepted traditions of central authority and hierarchical organization. Such offices as the Exilarch of Babylonia and the Nagid of Egypt were known in Jewish history, but they emerged as a result of unique circumstances,[170] which did not apply to the realities of Jewish life in the Ottoman Empire. In medieval Europe, as of the eleventh century, in England, France, Spain, Portugal, and Germany, one encounters the positions of "chief rabbi" and "head of the Jews." These offices were generally created by the authorities for their own convenience, primarily for purposes of taxation. They were imposed on the Jews, who accepted them, sometimes with great reluctance. These offices were not necessary for the practice of Judaism or the life of the community. In fact, one authority has described the institution of chief rabbi as "not based on a true conception of Judaism, but

... a product of assimilation to the Christian concept of hierarchical organization."[171] To understand the institutions of Jewish autonomy in the Ottoman Empire, and how they evolved over time, it is necessary to look at the Jewish community structures not from the top, but rather from the bottom, from the perspective of their basic building blocks.

The most basic unit of Jewish self-government, and from the perspective of daily life also the most important, was the individual congregation (Hebrew *kahal*, sing., *kehalim*, pl.; Turkish *cema'at*). The congregation was a voluntary association of families and individuals centered around its synagogue (Minna Rozen). Congregations varied in size from a few hundred families to several dozen and even less.[172] In the fifteenth and sixteenth centuries, the Jewish congregation in the Ottoman Empire was most typically formed on the basis of place of origin. The Romaniot Jews transferred to Istanbul after 1453, formed congregations based on their town of origin, as indicated by their names: Dimetoka, Ohri, Tire, and so on. Congregations founded after 1492, by immigrants from abroad, bore names such as Portakal (Portugal), Cordova, Calabria, Ashkenaz-Alman (German), Macar (Hungarian), and so on. The reasons why place of origin was so crucial in the initial formation of congregations are easy to understand. These congregations were founded by families that were related to each other by kinship and marriage, or by business interests, friendship, and mutual acquaintance. They also shared a cultural-religious legacy of language, dialect, and particular customs connected with their ritual.

Each congregation's leadership was divided between religious and lay leaders. The lay leaders were elected by the tax-paying members of the congregation, and they formed the congregation's executive council (often known as *ma'amad,* meaning deputation or assembly). Since taxation in the Ottoman Empire was based on wealth, with three categories of "high," "middle," and "low" tax brackets, the executive council often consisted of representatives of all three "classes." Each congregation was free to select and appoint a rabbi to serve as its spiritual leader and minister to its needs, according to its customs and traditions. Large congregations could appoint two, or more, rabbis, of which one was ranked above the others. Conversely, poor congregations could join their resources and appoint one rabbi to serve in two, or more, synagogues. The Hebrew word for rabbi was *rav* and its use was common among most Jewish groups, including the

Romaniot, Ashkenazi, Italian, and French Jews.[173] The Sephardic
Jews, however, preferred to use the title *hakham*, meaning wise or
learned man, reminiscent of the Islamic term *âlim* (Arabic, *ulamā*, pl.;
Turkish, *ulema*). Rabbis could be appointed for a limited, but renew-
able, term of a number of years, or for life. The rabbi's most important
duties consisted of the administration of justice according to Jewish
Law *(halakhah)*. In this capacity he acted as *dayyan*, or judge. The rabbi
also acted as teacher *(marbitz torah)*, thereby preserving the law by
imparting it to others. Rabbis were also expected to deliver sermons
on Sabbaths and holidays. An outstanding rabbi whose scholarship
was widely recognized could also act as *posek*, or decisor, making pro-
nouncements on difficult or controversial issues, where the law was
not always clear-cut. Above all, the rabbi served as spiritual mentor
and guide to his congregants, collectively and individually (Marc D.
Angel).

Central to every congregation was a primary school *(talmud
torah)*[174] and many congregations, and individuals, also supported advanced religious schools *(yeshivah,* sing; *yeshivot,* pl.). These schools
were generally located within, or near, the synagogue building. Each
congregation also supported various benevolent societies, for the
burying of the dead, ministering to the sick and poor, and for other
charitable purposes.

The congregation was also a fiscal entity. This was a central factor
in its day-to-day affairs, often determining its size and structure, and
the services it could offer its members. The congregation was responsible for collecting from its members state taxes, as well as internal
dues, necessary to support Jewish institutions and activities. For these
purposes, the congregation appointed tax assessors and collectors,
who operated under the supervision of its executive council. This
became, in fact, a major congregational responsibility, and the tax-col-
lection apparatus emerged as one of the congregation's most perma-
nent and regular features.[175]

On the face of it, the responsibilities of the rabbi and the lay
leaders were distinct and clearly defined: the former was to take care
of all religious and spiritual needs and the latter were responsible for
all financial and administrative matters. In reality, however, there
existed a great measure of overlapping interests and authority, with
a considerable potential for conflict between the religious and lay
leadership. The rabbi was certainly not a disinterested party when it
came to allocating funds for the support of the congregation's institu-

tions and activities, including his own salary. As judge, the rabbi was also called upon to arbitrate disputes arising from the assessment of taxes. He was also required to decide on conflicts stemming from a wide range of purely secular matters, such as business transactions, partnerships, and questions pertaining to property ownership and possession.

In principle, the lay leaders could dismiss their rabbi or not renew his contract, and some such incidents were indeed recorded. In reality, however, once appointed the rabbi wielded considerable powers. His authority derived from the fact that he was the interpreter and executor of the Holy Law and the living representation of all that Judaism stood for. The degree of his authority, however, varied, depending on his scholarship, reputation for integrity, political acumen, leadership abilities, and the popular support that he enjoyed among the rank and file of his congregants.

In towns with several congregations, the Jews generally formed a town-wide organization, which brought together all, or most, of the congregations. Congregations thus united formed an institutionalized community, or *kehillah*. The existence of the kehillah was predicated on the presence of two basic elements: supracongregational institutions (such as courts, tax committees, schools, and benevolent societies) and a unified representation vis-à-vis the authorities. Hence, the kehillah also required the presence of some form of community leadership. It was rare, though not unknown, that in one town more than one institutionalized community was present. In Istanbul, for example, it appears that two institutionalized communities emerged in the course of the sixteenth century. In a number of towns—Salonica and Jerusalem, for example—the small Ashkenazi congregations remained independent of the larger Sephardic kehillah and were recognized by the Ottomans as separate entities.[176] In the eighteenth century, congregations of European Jews, "Francos"—in Salonica, Izmir, and Aleppo, for example—did not become fully integrated into the locally organized kehillah, but maintained a degree of autonomy.[177] Even in such relatively exceptional cases, however, the Jewish groups cooperated with each other in various areas and thus formed an ad hoc community.

Jewish local organization in the kehillah was motivated, perhaps even necessitated, by Ottoman administrative and tax structures, as well as by Jewish interests. The Ottomans collected their taxes locally, by province, district, and town. For reasons of convenience, in each town the Ottoman tax officials assessed the Jewish community as a whole a total amount, based on the number and wealth of the individual Jewish tax-payers. The Jewish community then apportioned the taxes to each of its member-congregations, and the latter collected the taxes from the individual tax-payers. This pattern of tax collection also operated to the advantage of the Jewish community. For whenever disputes arose between the Jews and the Ottoman tax authorities, the collective bargaining power of the community as a whole was greater than that of the individual congregations. This was also true for other purposes requiring negotiation with the authorities, such as on matters of security, or the repair and construction of houses of worship, allocation of land for Jewish cemeteries, and the like.

Additionally, there were internal reasons why the Jews needed town-wide community organizations. The larger resources of the kehillah made it possible to maintain institutions, which the individual congregation could support only with difficulty, or not at all, such as schools and charitable societies. Additionally, disputes among members of different congregations, or among different Jewish groups and interests, necessitated the establishment of Jewish courts whose authority was recognized by the entire community. In spite of these strong incentives for close cooperation, the Jews in the Ottoman urban centers were very reluctant to surrender their congregational autonomy to the authority of the kehillah. This was due not only to the absence of strong hierarchical traditions, but also because in the important formative period, in the fifteenth and sixteenth centuries, Ottoman Jewry constituted, by and large, a heterogeneous immigrant society, hailing from different countries. Each group (*edah*, sing; *edot*, pl.) clung to its own ritual, traditions, customs, and legal practices.[178] The last aspect was of primary importance, since each edah adhered to different legal practices, especially in matters of personal law.[179] At that time, particularly sensitive legal problems arose as the result of the forced conversion of large numbers of Iberian Jews to Catholicism and the subsequent return of many of those to Judaism. The Sephardic rabbis generally demonstrated great understanding and flexibility in these matters. Sephardic Jews were concerned that rabbis from different backgrounds might be less sensitive to these issues.[180] Consequently, in areas other than tax collection, where a more or less standing organization existed by necessity, the Jewish population generally preferred to set up loose, ad hoc community superstructures, rather than establish a regular and well-defined central leadership.

This became the dominant pattern of Jewish self-government in the Ottoman Empire in the fifteenth and sixteenth centuries, and in many places it lasted well into the seventeenth and eighteenth centuries.

In Salonica, Istanbul, Safed, Lepanto, and probably other towns, delegations representing all of the town's congregations used to meet periodically to discuss issues of importance to the entire community.[181] Thus, a loosely structured local Jewish council came into existence. This council was sometimes described in the Hebrew sources as *ma'amad kolel,* meaning the general deputation or assembly. Referring to its representative structure, Rabbi Moses Almosnino, writing in the 1560s, described the Jewish community of Salonica as a "republic."[182] The organization, structures, and methods of operation of these councils must have varied from one place to another and over time. It is known, however, that their primary responsibilities were to supervise the collection of taxes and appoint committees and functionaries to administer a wide range of public affairs.

The council also appointed officials to represent the Jewish community before the Ottoman authorities. These representatives were most commonly lay leaders, who in their private lives were usually engaged in business activities. Whenever necessary and possible, these official representatives would avail themselves of the assistance and intercession of highly placed Jews. It appears that the Jewish communities generally preferred that representation before the authorities be carried out by ad hoc committees, responsible to, and controlled by, the councils. In some instances, however, the official representation of the community was carried out by single individuals, sometimes known by their Ottoman title *kethüda* (pronounced *kahya*), meaning steward. The title may suggest that these individuals attained some form of official recognition by the authorities. In those few instances in which information is available, it appears that the kethüdas tended to accumulate in their hands great power, and the relations between them and the community leaders at times became strained. The best-known case was that of She'altiel, who served as kethüda of the Jewish community in Istanbul for a long time, from the 1490s to some time after 1520. In 1518, the Jewish community dismissed She'altiel, due to complaints regarding his high-handed methods and alleged wrongdoings. A year and a half later, however, in 1520, the community decided to reinstate She'altiel after he had promised to consult more fully with the leaders of the community. It has been speculated that government pressure, or intercession, also served to convince the community to reverse its decision.[183] Similar incidents with high-handed kethüdas were recorded in the first half of the sixteenth century in Salonica[184] and Rhodes,[185] and in the 1670s in Izmir.[186] Kethüdas, and Jewish official representatives recognized by the authorities under various other titles, served also in other communities.[187] From the relatively few instances of conflict mentioned in the sources, we may perhaps conclude that, in general, the communities were able to control the activities of their official representatives to the authorities.

Another form through which the institutionalized community asserted its presence was by legislation, that is, the development of a system of internal regulations (*haskamah*, sing.; *haskamot*, pl., literally meaning agreements), which could govern a wide range of issues, both religious and secular. A haskamah could be adopted within a single congregation through some form of majority decision requiring acceptance, or acquiescence, by all its members. However, haskamot adopted by the town-wide community necessitated voluntary acceptance by each congregation, since each congregation considered itself autonomous. Haskamot dealing with matters that fell clearly within the purview of the religious law necessitated the approval of the community's rabbis only. Haskamot dealing with secular issues often had to be approved by the rabbis, as well as the lay leaders. Rabbinic sanction was, however, crucial, and a haskamah was not considered binding without it. In the mid-sixteenth century the rabbis of Salonica, Istanbul, and Safed—the largest and most important Jewish communities in the Ottoman Empire at that time—approved a haskamah that absolutely prohibited Jews to turn to non-Jewish—that is, Muslim—courts in matters of family law, such as marriage, divorce, and inheritance. Since the rabbis of these three cities were considered the preeminent legal authorities throughout the empire, this act amounted to an attempt to establish a statewide consensus, and through it to exert great moral compulsion in a matter that was of great concern to the Jewish community, but regarding which there were, apparently, numerous infractions on the part of individual Jews (Minna Rozen, Joseph Hacker, Marc D. Angel). It is most striking that the rabbis of the Ottoman Empire did not feel constrained, in this and in other matters, to challenge the authority of the Muslim courts, which were, after all, not only religious institutions, but also the official courts of the state. True, the competency of the Jewish courts in the Ottoman Empire was ill-defined and wrought with many uncertainties. Cases of intervention by the Ottoman authorities in the activities of the Jewish courts were not infrequent. Still, the ability of the Jewish communities to legislate for themselves town-wide, and, admittedly very rarely, even statewide, regulations, was an indication of the great relative freedom and sense of security in which they lived. In spite of many uncertainties, compared to conditions in most European countries, the Jews of the Ottoman Empire enjoyed wide judicial autonomy and the privilege to be tried by their own authorities and according to their laws in a wide range of areas.

From time to time, certain individuals were recognized as holding particularly important leadership positions within the community. In Salonica, for example, in the early years of the sixteenth century, three rabbis were considered as the community's leading spiritual authorities, and it is possible, as Rosanes suggests, that around 1514 they were formally so recognized.[188] They were Jacob ibn Habib of Castile (ca. 1445–1515/16), Solomon Taitatzak of Portugal (dates unknown),[189] and Eliezer (or Elazar) Hashim'oni (died ca. 1530), an Ashkenazi rabbi. Of the three, Jacob ibn Habib was the best-known scholar, and his responsa were cited at great length in the works of his contemporaries. He served as rabbi of Congregation Gerush, one of the largest in Salonica, and he also headed an important yeshivah.[190] Hashim'oni, although an Ashkenazi rabbi, served as spiritual leader to both the Ashkenazi congregation and the Sephardic Congregation Catalan, also one of the city's largest.[191]

In the second half of the sixteenth century, a towering figure in Salonica was Rabbi Samuel de Medina (1506–89), also known by the Hebrew acronyms Rashdam and Maharashdam. He was considered one of the most prominent Ottoman Jewish scholars of all times, and his responsa made a great impact on rabbinic literature in his and in future generations. He headed a major yeshivah, supported by Gracia Nasi Mendes, which graduated many disciples who went on to play an important role in Jewish scholarship and community leadership. Medina also served as the rabbi of the largest and most important Sephardic congregations in Salonica. He headed delegations sent to Istanbul by the community to plead its case before the Ottoman government. His authority as judge was widely accepted and he was called upon to arbitrate some of the most difficult disputes, which arose in Salonica and other communities.[192] This was probably the highest position an individual could attain at that time within the community. It is clear, however, that Medina's authority derived from his personal reputation for scholarship and integrity, that it was accepted voluntarily and was limited. As a community leader, Medina exercised essentially moral authority, but he was not in any sense the official head of the community. Nor was anyone else.

From the fifteenth to the seventeenth centuries, Ottoman Jewry was able to support a wide range of community activities in the religious, legal, educational, and welfare spheres, while maintaining a vigorous intellectual and spiritual life, for the most part without well-defined structures and a strong executive leadership beyond the level of the individual congregation. These fluid and completely decentralized structures were chaotic in appearance and sometimes outright unmanageable. They also contained, however, many strengths and benefits. In Baron's words, "in the long run Ottoman Jewry learned to live with an increasing variety of groups and approaches and, perhaps because of that plurality, was able to develop an even more flourishing and pulsating cultural life."[193] It needs to be remembered that such a state owed much to the Ottoman policy of laissez-faire, the minimal pressure that the authorities exerted on the community, the relatively few instances of intervention in its internal affairs, and the overall sense of security in which the community lived.

The Question of the Chief Rabbinate in the Fifteenth and Sixteenth Centuries

There are indications that in the fifteenth and sixteenth centuries, the Ottoman authorities tried to encourage, or impose on, the Jews hierarchical structures. The nature of all these reports is vague and uncertain. The most that can be said with some degree of confidence is that on the Ottoman part there was a motive and an interest in forming such institutions, while on the Jewish side there was reluctance and perhaps even resistance. At the end, however, the Ottoman policy of laissez-faire allowed for internal developments within the Jewish community to determine the nature of its own institutions.

The generally well-informed Rosanes has stated that already in the first half of the fifteenth century, during the reign of Murad II (1421–51), the authorities appointed Rabbi Isaac Tzarfati as chief rabbi in Edirne, then the Ottoman capital.[194] This claim has remained unsubstantiated by contemporary sources. From an Ottoman perspective, however, such an appointment would have been desirable for a number of reasons which later developments have made more apparent. First, there was the Ottoman imperial impulse to centralize authority and establish well-defined hierarchical structures. Second, the Jewish community of Edirne consisted at the time of three distinct groups, which founded their separate congregations: established Romaniots and newly arrived Ashkenazi and Italian Jews. It would have been in the Ottoman interest to deal collectively with these disparate groups. This same condition, however, would have militated against the emergence of a well-defined central authority, because it would have been unlikely that the different Jewish groups would have submitted to a strong central authority; and considering the general Ottoman attitudes of laissez-faire, it is doubtful that the authorities would have insisted on imposing such an institution on an unwilling community. At the present stage of our knowledge, it may be prudent to accept the view that Tzarfati was a leading, perhaps even the preeminent, rabbi of the community, but not its "chief rabbi," namely its head in spiritual and civil matters.[195]

Next, and of greater significance, is the question of the appointment of Rabbi Moses Capsali as chief rabbi following the conquest of Constantinople. The existence of such a position appears to be supported not only by contemporary Jewish sources,[196] but also by at least one entry in the official Ottoman records, which identifies Capsali as "rabbi and metropolitan (*rav ve metropolid*) of the Jews of Istanbul."[197] The sources, however, are not without their ambiguities, which has resulted in uncertainty and controversy as to what exactly did the responsibilities of Rabbi Capsali entail.

The main references in the Jewish sources describe Rabbi Capsali in the following terms: "The rabbi who leads (*ha-rav ha-manhig*) all the congregations [of Istanbul]"; "*ha-rav ha-shofet*," which could be understood either as "the rabbi who administers justice" or "the ruling rabbi"; "head of the court of justice" (*rosh beit din*); and "he who decides all the city's regulations (*tikkunim*) and practices (*minhagim*)."[198]

It has been argued that the term *haham başı*, meaning chief rabbi in Turkish, does not occur in the contemporary sources and, therefore, the office did not exist.[199] This argument overlooks the simple fact that the term haham başı represents a much later nomenclature. It came into official use only in the nineteenth century.[200] Only the Sephardic Jews referred to their rabbis by the title *hakham*, which served as the basis for the Turkish term. However, the Romaniot, Ashkenazi, French, and Italian Jews all used the Hebrew title *rav*. Thus, in the mid-fifteenth century, before the mass influx of Sephardic Jews, the common Hebrew term for rabbi was *rav*.[201] Consequently, the absence of the title haham başı in the fifteenth century cannot be taken as an indication that the office of chief rabbi did not exist under a different nomenclature.

Indeed, the Jewish sources make it clear that Capsali was the leading rabbi of all the congregations in Istanbul, the community's chief justice and the final authority who decided on all rules and regulations. From the Jewish perspective, these were the most important responsibilities of a spiritual and civic leader. Furthermore, at this time only Capsali is known to have been granted official recognition by the government, which apparently also placed at his disposal a small police detachment to help him enforce his authority.[202] Indeed, the Jewish sources depict Capsali as rushing about town, settling disputes, and trying to solve problems arising from the resettlement of the Jews in the Ottoman capital. In view of all this, it is difficult to see how else to describe Capsali other than as chief rabbi.

True, the Jewish sources are unclear as to Capsali's responsibilities in two important areas: tax collection and representation of the community before the authorities.[203] This may be explained by the following arguments. First, the responsa literature and the Jewish sources, in general, were primarily concerned with the internal life of the community and were vague on matters pertaining to its external relations. Second, Rabbi Capsali could have been held accountable in these areas, but delegated his responsibilities to subordinate officials dependent on him.[204]

Another issue that needs to be clarified is whether the authority of Capsali was statewide, as most historians believed until recently,[205] or was it limited to Istanbul only. The references in the foregoing contemporary Jewish sources, as well as other examples, strongly suggest that Capsali's authority was limited to Istanbul and its environs only.[206] This is further supported by the term "metropolitan," which the Ottomans used as Capsali's title. The absence of a Jewish religious hierarchy meant that there was also no accepted nomenclature to define the position that the Ottomans sought to create. Perhaps in order to streamline, and create parallel structures for, the administration of their religious minorities, the Ottomans borrowed the term metropolitan from Greek usage. The Greek Patriarch was the head of the Orthodox Church throughout the empire and a metropolitan was the spiritual leader of a province or a city.[207] Thus, the Ottoman term and, in fact, the entire tenor of the entry, seem to further support the hypothesis that the Ottomans recognized Capsali's authority as limited to Istanbul only, and it was not statewide. This is what most scholars believe today.[208]

It has been argued that, whereas Mehmed the Conqueror transferred to Istanbul the majority of the Ottoman Jews, no other Jewish leader enjoyed a status comparable to that of the head of the Istanbul community. Consequently, Capsali "was recognized by the Ottoman government as the unqualified leader of the Ottoman Jewish community."[209] While it is true that until the end of Capsali's life (he died in the late 1490s), the Istanbul community was by far the largest and most important Jewish center in the Ottoman Empire, this argument overlooks the fact that, during the second half of the fifteenth century, the Ottoman Jewish population increased considerably, largely outside Istanbul, in two ways. First, through new Ottoman conquests in Greece, the northern Balkans, Anatolia, and the Crimea, a significant number of additional Jewish communities were incorporated under Ottoman rule. Many, if not most, of these were not transferred to Istanbul. The second source of Jewish population growth was through immigration, which increased in the 1480s and peaked after 1492. Even more important than the question of numbers is the substantive issue. Did the Ottomans aim to support a statewide Jewish authority, as in the case of the Orthodox Church, or did they intend to establish a strong center in the capital only, as in the Armenian model, and allow the internal dynamics within the community to determine its future development? The case of the Jews appears to approximate that of the Armenians, namely, the creation of a local center. This was important for the future development of Ottoman Jewry. Rabbi Capsali, like his Armenian counterpart, attempted to extend his authority beyond the confines of Istanbul. However, in the absence of a strong hierarchical tradition in Judaism, and perhaps more important, without active government support, his efforts met with little success. In a well-publicized dispute with several Sephardic leaders from Salonica, the latter flatly rejected Capsali's demands that they accept his authority.[210]

Following the death of Moses Capsali in 1496 or 1497, Rabbi Elijah Mizrahi emerged as the leading rabbi of the community in Istanbul. During his time large numbers of immigrants, primarily Sephardic and Italian Jews, settled in Istanbul, introducing change and new tensions in the established order. These are believed to have further strengthened the centrifugal forces within the community and undermined the chances for the continuity of a strong central authority. Mizrahi was a renowned legal expert and much is known about his scholarly activities.[211] The information on his official leadership responsibilities is, however, sketchy. It is generally believed that Mizrahi's position as a community leader was considerably weaker than that of Capsali. This assumption is based primarily on the fact that during Mizrahi's time, the responsibilities for the community's fiscal administration and representation before the authorities were assumed by the Kethüda She'altiel. Due to She'altiel's long tenure of office, and because of his intimate relations with the authorities, he commanded great power within the community, which eclipsed Mizrahi's position.[212]

The rabbinic literature of the period makes it abundantly clear that Mizrahi was considered the preeminent spiritual leader and legal scholar in Istanbul. He also labored energetically to help in the resettlement of the Sephardic refugee influx, which peaked during his tenure of office.[213] For all these reasons, even the newly arrived Sephardic rabbis accepted his authority in legal matters.[214] It is known that he acted, at least periodically, as the head of the highest Jewish court in the city. He was called upon to arbitrate difficult disputes, which arose between different congregations, and to pass judgment on public issues that concerned the entire community. The rabbinic literature is replete with references to him as a great scholar. Still, the Jewish sources do not refer to him in such terms, as in the case of Capsali, that would suggest that he held an official appointment as chief rabbi. Neither has there been discovered any evidence in the Ottoman records. It is not even certain that he acted as chief judge on a regular basis. It is possible, therefore, that his position as the leading rabbi in Istanbul rested only on his reputation for scholarship and personal integrity and not because he held an official appointment.[215]

Following Mizrahi's death in 1526, no single individual emerged as holding a position of sole leadership in the community, either on the model of Capsali or on that of Mizrahi. The two most respected scholars in Istanbul after 1526 were Mizrahi's disciples, Rabbi Elijah ha-Levi and Rabbi Tam ibn Yahya. After them, other scholars assumed leading positions and each of them had their own following, but none was recognized as the sole spiritual leader of the entire community.[216]

To sum up, the current state of our information suggests that

between approximately 1454 to 1526, the case of the Jewish community of Istanbul was atypical of Jewish structural patterns throughout
the Ottoman Empire. Following the conquest of Constantinople, the
state appears to have intervened and imposed on the Jews an ecclesiastical authority reminiscent of the Armenian model. Rabbi Capsali
served as an officially-appointed chief rabbi of Istanbul, that is, the
religious and probably civic head of the community, most likely until
his death in 1496 or 1497. Rabbi Mizrahi, on the other hand, was
acknowledged by the community as its spiritual leader, but the question of his civic responsibilities and official appointment by the authorities remains moot. In the meanwhile, the influx of European
Jews changed the power structure within the community. The distinctiveness and individualism of the single congregations, and the centrifugal forces inherent in them, successfully countervailed the centralizing imperial impulse of the Ottoman state. After 1526, the organizational structures of the Jewish community of Istanbul resembled
those of Salonica and other Jewish communities; namely, the individual congregations enjoyed a great measure of autonomy, and there
was no strong central authority, but only loose community superstructures. Jewish tradition, and the internal dynamics within the community, channeled the development of Jewish structures of self-government towards a high degree of decentralization, a model totally different from those prevailing in the Orthodox and Armenian communities.

The Ottoman authorities accepted the new status quo in Istanbul,
as they had done elsewhere in the empire. They no longer granted
official sanction to the appointment of any specific individual as chief
rabbi, but they continued to recognize the principle of Jewish autonomy and self-government. For the privilege to conduct their own
internal affairs and maintain their autonomous legal and administrative institutions, under their self-designated leadership, the Jewish
communities of Istanbul and other towns had to pay a special tax,
known as the rabbi's tax (*rav akçesi* or *cizye-i rav,* in Turkish). This tax
was similar to a payment made by Christian church officials, known
as *pişkeş* (*peşkeş*), at the time when their appointment was officially
confirmed by the Ottoman government. There was, however, an important difference. In the case of the Christian prelates, the payment
was linked to the appointment of a specific individual. In the case of
the Jews, it was probably originally linked to the appointment of Rabbi

Capsali, but with the demise of the office of chief rabbi, it was paid simply in return for the privilege of self-government and it became, apparently, an annual tax.[217]

Jewish Acculturation and the Consolidation of Community Structures (Sixteenth to Eighteenth Centuries)

In fact, it appears that during the sixteenth century, the Jews of Istanbul coalesced into not one, but two loosely organized communities, each with its own distinctive leadership and institutions. This development seems to have been the result of two factors. First, it was due to the tax arrangements, which the Ottoman authorities had imposed on the Jewish population; second, it was the outcome of internal processes of acculturation and integration affecting the Jewish community from within.

Apparently, during the reign of Mehmed the Conqueror (1451–81), the poll tax payments of all the Jewish congregations of Istanbul were assigned as income to support a charitable foundation (*imâret*), which the sultan established to develop Istanbul.[218] This included the taxes of the Byzantine Jewish congregations found in the city at the time of the conquest, as well as those communities transferred there from other towns under a *sürgün* (transfer) order.[219]

However, the taxes of Jewish congregations largely founded by immigrants from abroad after 1481 were kept apart and earmarked for other purposes. This fiscal separation was maintained at least until the latter part of the seventeenth century.[220] In time, however, to simplify matters, in official documents the Ottomans began identifying all the Romaniot congregations of Istanbul, including the former congregations of Byzantine Constantinople, as *Sürgün* (or *Sürgünlü*), namely "transferred." At the same time, the new congregations were designated as *Kendi Gelen,* literally meaning "those coming of their own free will," or immigrants.[221] It has been noted that meeting the tax obligation was a major responsibility of the institutionalized Jewish community, leading to the establishment of the strongest regular supracongregational organization within it. Hence, the fiscal separation between the "transferred" and "immigrant" congregations contributed to the foundation of two institutionalized Jewish communities in Istanbul, each with its own tax collection apparatus. The second factor had to do with socioeconomic and cultural processes that operated within the Jewish population.

One of the most important reasons usually cited to explain the rise of the Sephardic Jews to a position of predominance within Ottoman Jewry and the adoption of Judeo-Spanish culture by most other groups is the numerical argument. The Sephardim, it is said, overwhelmed the local Romaniot Jews by sheer numbers.[222] This may have been true for the Ottoman Empire as a whole, and especially in the Balkans, western Anatolia, Palestine, and perhaps even Cairo, Aleppo, and other Syrian communities.[223] It has been noted, however, that Sephardic immigrants constituted a minority among Istanbul's Jewish population as late as 1623. Thus, the argument of numerical superiority must be supplemented by other factors.

The most important cause for the ascendancy of the Sephardim appears to be that they brought with them higher educational and cultural standards. The majority of the most respected rabbis and legal scholars active in the Ottoman Empire in the sixteenth and seventeenth centuries appear to have been of Sephardic origins. The same was true with respect to the most distinguished Jewish physicians, scientists, entrepreneurs, and courtiers. In addition, throughout the sixteenth and seventeenth centuries, the Sephardim were strengthened by a continuous flow of immigration from abroad and their numbers steadily increased. The later immigrants, many of them Marranos, were a particularly cultured and dynamic element. Consequently, the Sephardim were able to capture a dominant economic position within the community, as reflected in the Ottoman tax registers.[224] Thus, the higher social, cultural, and economic position of the Sephardic congregations attracted members of other groups.

Nevertheless, there was also resistance to Sephardic domination. This was supported by the general conservatism of the society and the desire of each group to maintain its unique heritage and identity and pass them on to the next generation. To these were added also important financial considerations. Since each congregation also acted as a fiscal unit, responsible for the collection of state taxes, as well as internal dues, the defection of its members was likely to impose a greater financial burden on the remaining congregants. This could place in jeopardy the group's ability to maintain its institutions and activities. For this reason, the Jewish leadership generally frowned upon, and outright discouraged, the defection of members from one congregation to another, and several important regulations were issued to that effect (Minna Rozen).

While the foregoing reasons encouraged resistance to Sephardic domination on the part of all other Jewish groups equally, the Romaniots of Istanbul were supported by a number of particular factors. In the first place they, and their descendants, formed until well into the seventeenth century the largest group of the city's Jewish population. Additionally, they took great pride in the fact that they were the "native sons," so to speak, of the country, who welcomed, and assisted in the settlement of, all the others.[225] This pride of origin was strengthened by the fact that Greek was a popular language in Istanbul (and elsewhere). It was spoken by the large Greek community, which was particularly prominent in commerce and finance, areas of prime economic importance for the Jews as well. This encouraged the Romaniots to hold fast to the use of their Judeo-Greek language, and they offered the Sephardim the greatest degree of resistance.[226]

Consequently, Sephardic influence in Istanbul first spread among the other immigrant groups, the Italian and Ashkenazi Jews. This pattern was facilitated, or perhaps even determined, by Ottoman tax arrangements, which forced all immigrant congregations to come together in order to discharge their tax obligation. Consequently, in the course of the sixteenth century, two Jewish communities, each with its distinct leadership and institutions, coalesced in Istanbul. On the one hand were the long-established Romaniots, identified in Hebrew as *Benei Romania* and in Turkish as *Sürgün* (or *Sürgünlü*); and on the other hand were all the immigrant congregations, united under the leadership of the Sephardim and identified in Hebrew as *Benei Sepharad* and in Turkish as *Kendi Gelen*.[227] Thus, both Jews and Ottomans created the nomenclature, which reflected the dual character of the Jewish population of Istanbul.

The Jews considered each community autonomous and coequal. Each community had its own spiritual leadership, courts, schools, and charitable societies.[228] However, because all the Jewish groups lived intermingled with each other, problems of daily life forced the two communities to cooperate among themselves. Regulations applicable to the entire Jewish population of Istanbul had to be approved by the religious leadership of both communities. Indeed, in 1576/77, the religious leaderships of the two communities approved a major internal regulation (*haskamah*) governing real estate transactions and forbidding Jews to take their disputes in these matters to Muslim courts.[229] To implement this regulation, the two communities appointed magistrates (*memunnim shel ha-hazakot*), with authority over all the Jews of Istanbul. In addition, the two communities appointed joint "morality boards" (*memunnim shel ha-aveirot*) to oversee the proper religious practice and ethical behavior of the entire Jewish population.[230] Still, each community maintained its administrative and religious autonomy. The leading rabbinic authority in Istanbul at that time was Rabbi Elijah ben Hayyim (ca. 1530–1610), a native of Edirne who moved to Istanbul in the 1570s. He apparently became the spiritual leader of the Sephardic congregations.[231] He was asked to intervene in an internal dispute that erupted within the Romaniot community, but he refused. As is reported, he explained his position, saying: "Should an outsider intervene in the affairs of the [Romaniot] community (edah), he will prove to be not only unhelpful, but he may even cause outright damage and disunity."[232]

The forces of acculturation and integration were, however, at work almost from the beginning. In the first place, the various Jewish groups lived intermingled with each other and there was considerable intermarriage among them.[233] These processes, while operating to integrate growing segments of the Jewish population, also presented numerous problems for the Jewish courts, since the various groups followed different legal practices in matters of family law and inheritance. Consequently, there was a growing need to adopt some standardized legal practices.[234] The predominance of Sephardic rabbis, both numerically and qualitatively, probably operated to favor the gradual adoption of Sephardic practice and ritual. Additionally, general processes of change, or "the flow of time," as Rosanes phrased it,[235] also favored the gradual submersion of the Romaniots within Sephardic society and culture, as of the seventeenth century.

Devastating conflagrations (in 1633 and 1660, for example, which destroyed old neighborhoods[236]), the construction of new roads and quarters, and urban growth and development, in general, resulted in considerable internal migration of Istanbul's Jewish population. The old order, in which congregations were primarily organized on the basis of their ancestral country or city of origin, gradually gave way to a new order, in which congregations formed increasingly on a spatial basis of neighborhood, quarter, and the actual place of residence. These processes broke down the old congregational barriers even further. Congregations continued to maintain their old names, but their membership had become mixed, and this further accelerated the ascendancy of Sephardic ritual and culture. This was obviously a slow and gradual process whose date of completion cannot be established with certainty. It probably accelerated in the early decades of the seventeenth century,[237] but continued well into the eighteenth and even nineteenth centuries.[238] Although the population had become much more integrated and homogeneous in its culture and outlook, a certain awareness of its diverse origins still persisted for a long time.[239] It is significant that, well into the nineteenth century, the Jewish court of Balat maintained two separate lists of congregations identified as *Sürgünlü*, namely, Romaniots, and *Kendi Gelen* (in Hebrew, reflecting the Jewish pronunciation, *Kendi Yelen*), or Sephardim. These lists were intended to assist the courts in deciding cases of inheritance in accordance with the customs of the individual congregations.[240] Additionally, in some Romaniot synagogues in Istanbul (as well as in Edirne, Sofia, and possibly other places) elements of the old Romaniot ritual remained until the turn of the twentieth century.[241]

* * * * *

Due to its size, but more importantly, because of its large Romaniot element, the Jewish community of Istanbul was not typical of the great majority of Jewish communities in the Balkans and Anatolia. Still, the processes described before for Istanbul, probably reflected in their broadest lines the sociopolitical dynamics experienced by other Jewish communities. These changes varied, no doubt, in substance and pace, from one community to another, depending on the make-up of its various components, the balance between them, and other local factors. On the whole, the processes through which Sephardic ritual and culture gained ascendancy throughout the Balkans and Anatolia appear to have proceeded at a faster pace than in Istanbul. This, however, was not uniformly so. In some Greek-speaking areas, the Romaniots emerged as the dominant element, and the Sephardim were absorbed by them. In the communities of Kastoria, Yanina, Arta, and Chalcis, for example, Judeo-Greek, supported by the local language and culture, became dominant and was used by all segments of the community, including the Sephardim.[242] Some small Ashkenazi communities of central and east European origins were also successful in preserving their distinctive character. As of the late seventeenth or early eighteenth century, small Italian-speaking groups, known as Francos (consisting of Italian and other West European Jews), were also to be found in some of the main commercial centers of the empire (Salonica, Istanbul, Izmir).[243] Nevertheless, in the core territories of the Ottoman Empire, in the Balkans and western Anatolia, the Sephardim had gradually established themselves as the dominant element.

Under the Sephardic patina, however, there was, in fact, an amal-
gam that represented, in varying degrees, the contributions of the
different Jewish groups. Judeo-Spanish became the dominant language in most Jewish communities, but it absorbed some of the Judeo-
Greek vocabulary of the Romaniots.[244] In fact, spoken knowledge of
Greek continued to be widespread among Ottoman Jews until the
twentieth century. To the diverse Jewish components that contributed
to the emergence of this new cultural synthesis were added elements—
Turkish, Greek, Slav—which the Jews absorbed from the local environment. These affected their language, cultural tastes, and daily life.
Thus, in the course of the sixteenth and seventeenth centuries, out
of this fusion of diverse Jewish elements and the impact of the local
environment, a new society emerged, whose culture, institutions, and
outlook on life were uniquely Judeo-Ottoman. (Pamela J. Kamarck-
Dorn, Esther Juhasz, Vivian B. Mann, Marie-Christine Bornes-Varol).

* * * * *

In the Ottoman Arabic-speaking provinces, the impact of the
Sephardic immigrants was at first considerable, but with few excep-
tions, it eroded over time. In the sixteenth and seventeenth centuries,
Sephardic Jews often occupied leadership positions in these communities, and they were able to preserve their culture. With time,
however, they became culturally absorbed by the local Arabic-speaking
Jews (known as *Musta'riba* in Arabic and Turkish; *Mista'arvim* in Hebrew). The Sephardim gradually gave up speaking Judeo-Spanish and
instead adopted Arabic. As in the case of Romaniot domination in
some Greek-speaking areas, this was probably due to the fact that
Arabic-speaking Jews had become largely integrated into the local
majority culture and were supported by it in their cultural confronta-
tion with the Sephardim. In some cities, such as Cairo, Damascus, and
Aleppo, which due to their commercial importance experienced for
a long time a more or less steady trickle of Sephardic settlers, the
Sephardim were able to maintain their distinctive character well into
the eighteenth century. In the towns of Palestine, however, in
Jerusalem, Safed, Tiberias, and Hebron, due to an almost continuous
flow of Sephardic settlers over the ages and their contacts with, and
dependence on, the large Jewish centers in the Ottoman Empire, the
Sephardim emerged as the dominant element, and the Arabic-speaking Jews tended to adopt their language and culture.[245]

* * * * *

It has been noted that it was in the interest of the Jewish population itself to form local institutionalized communities with town-wide structures. What prompted the Jews to keep these structures as loose as possible, from the fifteenth to the seventeenth centuries, was the reluctance of the various groups, organized in different congregations, to surrender their autonomy, and with it their distinctiveness, to the authority of the town-wide community, the *kehillah*. By the seventeenth century, however, in many communities the processes of acculturation and social integration had become sufficiently advanced that these considerations were no longer valid. At the same time, the Jewish community was coming under increasing pressure from both the state and general society.

Since the latter part of the sixteenth century, when the Ottoman Empire first began experiencing a revenue crisis, it responded by gradually increasing the burden of taxation imposed on the general population. The Jewish communities, as well as the other segments of society, were now faced with rising tax obligations.[246] This was coupled with a slow process of general Ottoman economic stagnation and decline and the gradual impoverishment of society as a whole. These processes also affected the Jewish population and they placed on the Jewish community additional burdens to care for the growing numbers of the poor. Additionally, as of the end of the sixteenth century, unrest and disorder began to spread to increasingly wider areas of the empire, also adversely affecting the Jewish community's security and economic stability. In the face of rising external pressures, on the one hand, and diminishing resources, on the other, greater unity became imperative: first, in order to administer the existing levels of community services more effectively; later, to supervise necessary cuts and savings; and, finally, by the end of the eighteenth century, to maintain those basic services and institutions without which organized community life could not survive.[247] As a result of all these changes, more centralized community structures began to make their tentative appearance.

It would appear that it was relatively easier for compact and homogeneous Jewish communities to integrate and form more centralized structures. This process was often linked to the presence and actions of especially forceful personalities. The transformation, however, was often hesitant and tentative, characterized by fits and starts.

In the mid-sixteenth century, the town of Patras (Balyabadra) had a Jewish population of close to three hundred households,[248] divided into four congregations: two Sicilian, one Sephardic, and one Romaniot. It appears that at some point in the mid-sixteenth century, the four congregations agreed to recognize Rabbi Moses Hanin as spiritual leader and chief judge of the entire community. In the early 1560s, upon the death of Hanin, Rabbi Joseph Formon attempted to take over the same position. The two Sicilian congregations, as well as the Sephardic one, recognized Formon as their spiritual leader, but the Romaniot congregation refused to acknowledge his leadership. This resulted in bitter disputes within the community, which lasted for many years.[249]

In Bitola (Manastır), the two small Sephardic congregations[250] agreed in 1575 to join forces financially and administratively, but to continue to maintain two separate houses of worship. The immediate motive for this union appears to have been a fire, which burned down both synagogues and imposed a heavy financial burden on the community, which was required to rebuild them. It is not clear, however, whether this union was long-lasting.[251]

Around 1614, the two congregations of the Town of Rhodes agreed to appoint Rabbi Moses Hacohen, originally from Salonica, as spiritual leader of the entire community for a period of ten years. His most important civic duty was to serve as sole judge of the entire community. A few years following his appointment, however, Hacohen became involved in disputes with some local rabbis, and he left Rhodes before the expiration of his contract.[252] Sometime later, the community appointed Rabbi Moses de Vushal to the same position. Vushal was born in Sidon and grew up in Safed. His tenure of office was apparently more peaceful and lengthy than that of his predecessor. He died while in office in the second half of the seventeenth century.[253]

The community of Izmir, which became one of the most prominent Jewish centers in the Ottoman Empire, was unique from several important aspects. First, it developed only in the seventeenth century, when Izmir emerged as a major Ottoman port and commercial center. In other words, it rose a century, or more, after the establishment of the other major Jewish centers. Second, unlike the older Jewish communities, most of the Jewish settlers in Izmir were not immigrants from abroad (although some were), but internal migrants, coming from other Ottoman towns. Stated differently, these were primarily acculturated Ottoman Jews; and although they were undoubtedly distinguished from each other by customs and traditions, which they had brought with them from their particular places of origin, these were much less pronounced than those differences that characterized the older Jewish centers during the early stages of their development. It is perhaps due to this greater degree of acculturation that, of the main Jewish centers, Izmir became the first Jewish community to develop centralized structures, which later served as general models for other communities. This development was undoubtedly due also to the activities of some key individuals.[254]

Around 1630, Izmir's two most distinguished rabbis, Joseph Eskapa and Azariah Yehoshua, agreed to form a joint spiritual leadership. In the 1640s, when the city had six congregations, each of them controlled three. In addition, regulations pertaining to the entire community required the approval of both. Thus, in effect, a joint chief rabbinate for the community of Izmir was established. The two chief rabbis probably did not receive official sanction from the Ottoman government. Their authority simply rested on a consensus reached voluntarily by the Jewish community itself, and, once again, the Ottomans did not interfere in the community's internal affairs. Later, other major communities adopted similar leadership structures. The Hebrew term increasingly used now to designate the new institution of chief rabbi was *rav ha-kolel* (or *rav kolel*), literally meaning the rabbi of the entire community,[255] as distinguished from lesser rabbis.

The emergence of patterns of shared leadership suited the Jewish population, because it permitted for the representation of various interest groups within the community, and that was a prerequisite for attaining an internal consensus voluntarily. At the side of the chief rabbinate operated a committee of lay leaders, whose responsibilities included overseeing the relations with the authorities, tax collection, and administering the community's institutions. This committee was often known as *kolelut*,[256] a term which was used also to designate the entire community leadership, religious and lay. For this period, the information on the structure and activities of the lay leadership is even more sketchy than that which is available regarding the religious leadership. What is clear, however, is that during the seventeenth and eighteenth centuries, the Jewish communities exhibited unmistaken trends toward administrative centralization.

In Izmir, the joint leadership of Rabbis Eskapa and Yehoshua lasted until the death of Rabbi Yehoshua in 1648, when Rabbi Eskapa became sole chief rabbi of the entire community, until his death in 1661. As sole leader, Rabbi Eskapa introduced community-wide regulations, dealing not only with religious matters, but also with a wide range of secular issues, including taxation and real estate. The impact of this legislation was to shift power from the individual congregations to more centralized community authorities. The organizational patterns laid down by Rabbi Eskapa were amended and changed over the years, but they served the community until the end of the Ottoman era. Following the death of Eskapa in 1661, the chief rabbinate was again shared by two rabbis. For the most part, the chief rabbinate of Izmir, as in other communities, continued to be held jointly by two, and sometimes three, rabbis until the nineteenth century (Jacob Barnai).

In Salonica, an early attempt in the mid-seventeenth century to establish a regular rabbinic council to administer the community had failed.[257] It was only in the last quarter of that century, perhaps in response to the crisis caused by the Shabbatean controversy, that a chief rabbinate finally emerged in the form of a three-member rabbinic council. Each of the three was designated as chief rabbi (*rav ha-kolel*) and his appointment was for life. A new rabbinic council was installed only following the death of the last member of the previous triumvirate. Consequently, the number of chief rabbis in Salonica varied between one and three. This arrangement appears to have lasted until the nineteenth century.[258]

The first reliable information regarding the existence of a chief rabbinate in Edirne is from the early eighteenth century, although there had been earlier attempts to establish such an institution. In 1722, Rabbi Abraham Geron and Rabbi Menahem Ashkenazi formed a joint chief rabbinate, dividing between them the control of the city's thirteen congregations. These two rabbis founded "dynasties," whose descendants continued to share the chief rabbinate until late in the nineteenth century.[259]

Similar trends for a stronger leadership appeared also in other Jewish communities throughout the empire in the course of the seventeenth and eighteenth centuries. Details on the activities of a *kolelut* are available for Aleppo, beginning with the second half of the seventeenth century[260]; for Jerusalem, since the latter years of the seventeenth century[261]; for Safed, in the eighteenth century.[262]

There is some evidence to suggest that in Istanbul, too, a unified community under one central leadership emerged as early as the second half of the seventeenth century.[263] It was certainly true for the eighteenth century (for which period more details are available). At that time the community had a unified religious leadership, consisting of a collective chief rabbinate of three, and sometimes four, members. Each held the title of *rav ha-kolel*, although one had precedence over the others. Financial and administrative matters, and the representation of the community before the authorities were supervised by a central committee of lay leaders, which usually numbered seven officials. In addition, there existed a *ma'amad*, a general assembly of representatives of the various Jewish quarters and neighborhoods, rather than congregations. The responsibilities of the ma'amad included the election of committees to administer various aspects of community life.[264] The membership of the ma'amad reflected the new spatial organization of the community. Neighborhood institutions now occupied an intermediate level between the individual congregations and the city-wide community leadership. In each of the Jewish quarters operated a local rabbinate, in addition to the rabbis serving in the individual congregations of the quarter. The local rabbinates, with the help of lay leaders, coordinated and supervised matters affecting all the Jews in their quarters. In principle, the local rabbinates were under the authority of the chief rabbinate, although they appear to have enjoyed considerable autonomy. The local Jewish administrations in the quarters established their own networks for collecting funds for the support of charitable foundations within the quarters. These operated side by side with the central, and traditional, networks managed by the community's central leadership for the collection of state and community taxes from the individual congregations. Jewish courts operated in each of the two largest Jewish quarters, Balat and Hasköy. Above them was a superior court (*beit din rabba*) with authority over the entire community.[265]

Thus, by the eighteenth century, the Jewish community of Istanbul had become more homogeneous, better integrated, and more tightly organized. It also developed institutions that were uniquely adjusted to the topography, administrative structures, and general character of the city. From the fifteenth to the eighteenth century, the population of Istanbul increased several times over and with it came a great urban expansion. The metropolitan area of Istanbul, dissected by several bodies of water and with a steep, hilly terrain, comprised widely flung quarters and suburbs, where daily life centered around strong neighborhood institutions.[266] The Jews who lived in many of the city's quarters adjusted their community institutions to the city's general structures. The local Jewish representatives in each quarter communicated with the quarter's authorities on local issues. They were also accountable to the central administration of the Jewish community, which, in turn, represented the entire community before the Ottoman government.[267]

IV
THE ERA OF STANDSTILL
AND DECLINE
1580–1826

Causes and Manifestations of Ottoman Decline

In the last decades of the sixteenth century, the Ottoman social and political fabric began to exhibit signs of fatigue, and the empire entered a long period of standstill, followed by decline. It needs to be emphasized, however, that post-1580 Ottoman history cannot be regarded simply as one long, monotonous process of disintegration. The general curve of decline was punctuated by extended periods of stability, recovery, and even temporary ascent. Osman II (r. 1618–22), Murad IV (r. 1623–40), the famous grand vezirs of the Köprülü family (second half of the seventeenth century), and other Ottoman rulers made numerous attempts, many of them temporarily successful, to rejuvenate, reform, and change various sectors of the body politic. Consequently, the Ottoman state remained a great imperial power until the end of the seventeenth century. Only after 1683, with the failure of the second Ottoman siege of Vienna and the retreat that followed, did it become apparent that the balance of power had shifted against the Ottomans. Still, the Ottoman Empire continued to offer a determined resistance to its two major enemies, Austria and Russia, for another century. The nadir of Ottoman military weakness was reached only at the end of the eighteenth century and the early decades of the nineteenth. At that time, also the internal disintegration of the state had approached a critical point and the central government lost effective control over many of its provinces. The lot of Ottoman Jewry was always closely interwoven with that of the Ottoman state. Where Ottoman fortunes declined, so did those of its Jewish population. For this reason it is necessary to review here the main aspects of Ottoman standstill and decline.[268]

The decline of great powers has almost always been the outcome of a complex and interrelated web of causes, which do not lend themselves to easy unravelling and analysis. The Ottoman Empire was no exception. If, however, one has to start somewhere, the military aspect seems appropriate, because Ottoman economic and social dynamism appears to have been for a long time predicated on conquest and territorial expansion. It was a paradox of history, experienced by other great powers as well, that the Ottomans' very military successes and great territorial conquests confronted them with ever more difficult problems of logistics and military strategy. As distances between frontiers increased, the mobilization and deployment of forces became more difficult and costly. In the course of the sixteenth century, almost everywhere the Ottomans came face to face with more determined and powerful enemies: Austria, Poland, and Russia in central and eastern Europe; Spain and Venice in the Mediterranean; Portugal in the Red Sea and Indian Ocean; and Iran in the east. The Ottoman capture of Cyprus (1571) and the definitive reconquest of Tunis (1574) marked the end of the era of great territorial expansion. Although Ottoman military victories and new conquests continued well into the seventeenth century (see Chronology), the pace had now slowed down considerably. The wars had become more difficult and costly, imposing an ever-increasing burden on the treasury and the economy.

The great Ottoman expansion in the fifteenth and sixteenth centuries had resulted in the emergence of a vast administrative-military establishment, which, in the new circumstances, became an additional burden on the economy. As the great expansion slowed down and opportunities for career-advancement became more limited, this establishment also appears to have become gradually more conservative and resistant to change, at a time when change and innovation were needed more than ever before, to cope with the economic and technological advances of the West and their variegated ramifications.

The great geographic discoveries and Europe's expansion to the Americas, Africa, and Asia resulted in a decline—slow at first, but more rapid after 1600—in the Ottoman Empire's share of the world's trade. The Middle East was no longer as central in international trade as it had been for millennia, when it served as the main bridge between the three continents of the Old World. New important centers of international commerce emerged in western Europe and the Atlantic seaboard. Although for a long time after 1600 the old trade routes from the Indian Ocean to the Mediterranean, continued, for the most part, to traverse the Middle East, they were now increasingly controlled by the maritime European powers, first the Portuguese and later the French, British, and Dutch. Even the internal carrying trade between Ottoman ports now gradually fell to European interests. These changes deprived the Ottoman state of valuable income and resources, and they reduced entrepreneurial opportunities for its commercial elites.[269]

The difficulties of Ottoman international traders were compounded by Europe's increasingly state-controlled mercantilist policies, which sought to increase exports and limit imports. European markets became progressively more difficult for Ottoman traders to penetrate. Furthermore, European accumulation of capital, coupled with technological advances, led to the emergence of new industries with which the Ottomans could not compete. Spurred on by mercantilist economies, the new European industries aggressively sought overseas markets for exports. On their part, the traditional Ottoman economic concern was to assure the internal market an abundance of commodities, and, consequently, no limitations were placed on imports. It was, therefore, relatively easy for the superior European manufactured products to penetrate the unprotected Ottoman markets. This had several adverse effects on the Ottoman economy. In the first place, it further increased the European merchants' share of the Ottoman international trade. It also weakened the Ottoman craft industries, particularly in the areas of textiles and metallurgy.

At the same time, Europe's rising population and expanding industrial production created a growing demand for grains and raw materials. The high prices that these commodities commanded on the European markets resulted in their massive flight from the Ottoman Empire to Europe. The Ottoman government attempted to block the exportation of grains and raw materials. However, the profits to be made from this trade were so great that merchants and government officials alike, more often than not, conspired to subvert government orders. This resulted in shortages in basic foodstuffs and raw materials needed for the local population and craft industries; prices were pushed up and inflation set in.

The government attempted to control prices, but with little success. To meet its own rising expenses and growing need for ready cash, over time, the government resorted to a number of methods. It increased old taxes and raised new ones; it converted a growing number of state revenues into tax farms, yielding immediate cash; it debased the currency and attempted to hold back salary increases for state officials and soldiers.[270]

These measures had, however, a devastating impact on the society at large, although many individuals were able to profit from them. To begin with, the effectiveness of the administration and the military slowly eroded. To compensate for the reduction in their real income, state officials and soldiers began to take bribes, if they could, or seek additional employment and other sources of income. The bureaucracy gradually became corrupt and venal, and the military less and less disciplined and effective. In the economic sphere, the oppressive burden of taxation, the increasingly extortionist fiscal policies employed by the tax farmers, and the intrusion into business by an often corrupt bureaucracy stifled initiative and hampered the accumulation of capital necessary for industrial modernization and commercial enterprise.

Shortages in basic commodities, inflation, the crushing burden of taxation, and widespread misrule led to popular discontent, unrest and disorder. As of the late sixteenth century, the Ottoman Empire began experiencing mass uprisings. On the periphery of Ottoman power, renegade officials, tribal chieftains, and local strongmen capitalized on the government's difficulties and began to rise in rebellion and challenge the sultan's authority.

The Impact of Ottoman Decline on the Jewish Communities in the Seventeenth Century

As in the case of the Ottoman Empire as a whole, the decline of its Jewry was also the subject of misconception and misrepresentation. The pace and degree of this trend have been greatly exaggerated by Jewish historians, who have focused primarily on the rising Jewish communities of Europe. It is true that the period from about 1580 to 1826 was, on the whole, characterized by economic and spiritual impoverishment, but that process was slow, incremental, and interspersed with periods of stability and even prosperity. The decline of Ottoman Jewry also represents an uneven pattern in the sense that at the same time as some Jewish communities weakened, others prospered. In general, Jews continued to play an important, although diminishing, role in Ottoman economic, political and cultural life well into the eighteenth century. On the whole, the decline of Ottoman Jewry mirrored the dynamics that affected Ottoman society as a whole, except that the Jews were more susceptible than others to some of the changes. Consequently, in some respects, their position suffered greater deterioration than that of other segments in the society. The fate of the Jews appears to have been linked particularly to the fortunes of the central government. Where the authority of the sultan waned, so, almost invariably, declined Jewish fortunes. The nadir of the Jewish experience in the Ottoman Empire was from about 1770 to 1826, when the authority of the central government also was at its lowest point and the very survival of the Ottoman state was in doubt (see Chronology).

* * * * *

In the "golden age," the Jewish economic elite consisted of a wealthy entrepreneurial class engaged in large scale commerce, banking, tax-farming, administration of state monopolies, and the purveying of goods and services for the court, the military, the government and the households of the Ottoman elite. In addition, there were significant numbers of Jewish physicians, experts, and advisors who served the Ottoman court and the highest-ranking officials. Different aspects of Ottoman decline adversely affected, or curtailed, Jewish activity in almost every one of those areas. The decline of the Ottoman Empire as a world trading center, and the growing control that Europeans now came to exercise over the empire's international trade, and even on some aspects of its internal trade, must have resulted in diminishing opportunities for Ottoman traders. Since Jews played such a disproportionate role in the empire's commerce, it is reasonable to assume that these processes affected Jews more than others. This is not to say that Jews were completely eliminated from large-scale trade. Jews were able to maintain a significant position in Ottoman international commerce to the end of the eighteenth century and the beginning of the nineteenth (Thomas Philipp; C. Max Kortepeter). That role, however, became far more limited than what it had been in the sixteenth century. Furthermore, in trade, as in other areas, the Jews increasingly encountered competition on the part of the local Christians, with whom the Europeans generally, though not exclusively, appear to have preferred to deal. Consequently, Jews were forced out from positions as principals in large-scale trade to secondary occupations as agents, brokers, and interpreters. This resulted in a considerable diminution of the wealthiest Jewish group.

In the area of tax-farming, the Jews also lost important ground. As has been noted, the revenue crisis that the government began to experience in the last decades of the sixteenth century, forced it to convert an increasing number of state revenues into tax farms as a quick measure to obtain liquid funds. At the same time, however, tax-farming attracted new groups of investors, mainly highly-placed bureaucrats, soldiers, and ulema. The latter were both forced into tax-farming and attracted by it for several reasons: senior government positions became more difficult to obtain, and officials had to wait long periods between appointments; even when they received an appointment, these bureaucrats and soldiers found that, due to inflation, their official salaries were inadequate. At the same time, inflation made tax-farming increasingly lucrative. As of the end of the sixteenth century, merchants and bankers were no longer the sole purchasers of tax farms, but they had to compete with these new groups of investors, who generally were better connected to the government and the state treasury.[271] The case of Bursa may serve to illustrate this point. In the beginning of the seventeenth century, Jewish entrepreneurs virtually controlled tax-farming activities in Bursa. About half a century later, they were almost completely eliminated from this lucrative sector. The Jews were now gradually reduced to secondary positions, typically as agents or managers of tax farms. These tax farms were held by government officials and soldiers, who reaped most of the profits.[272]

The worsening economic conditions also operated to reduce the number of Jewish physicians and advisors at the court. As financial constraints necessitated reductions in the size of the imperial medical staff, and competition over the remaining positions intensified, growing pressures were exerted to reduce first the number of Jewish physicians. When a Jewish court physician died toward the end of the sixteenth century, at the request of the Chief Physician, he was replaced by a Muslim. The Chief Physician argued that there were already too many Jewish physicians, compared with Muslims.[273] Indeed, around 1600, there were forty-one Jewish physicians in the service of the court, as compared with only twenty-one Muslim physicians. By the mid-seventeenth century, however, the medical staff was reduced to fourteen Muslim physicians and only four Jews.[274] Still, individual Jews continued to serve as physicians to the court, or in the service of the government and the households of vezirs, until the second half of the eighteenth century and even in the beginning of the nineteenth.[275]

Some of these Jewish physicians were foreign-born and educated, and a few became prominent as political advisors to the court. Solomon Ashkenazi (ca. 1520–1602) was born in Udine, Italy, and studied medicine at Padua. He settled in Istanbul in 1564 and was instrumental in the diplomatic negotiations, which led to the peace treaty between the Ottoman Empire and Venice in 1573. He continued to wield considerable influence in Ottoman foreign relations into the 1590s.[276] Israel Conegliano (Conian; ca. 1650–ca. 1717) was born in Padua and settled in Istanbul in 1675. He became the physician of Grand Vezir Kara Mustafa Pasha (held office 1676–83) and was also consulted by Sultan Mehmed IV (r. 1648–87). In 1694, during the Ottoman war with the Holy League, all Venetian subjects were expelled and he, too, had to leave Istanbul. He took a somewhat prominent part in the negotiations at Karlowitz (1698–99), which led to the peace treaty between the Ottoman Empire and the European powers, but as physician and secretary to the Venetian envoy Carlo Ruzzini.[277]

One of Conegliano's students and colleagues was Tobias Cohn (Tuviyyah Cohen; ca. 1652–1729), a native of Metz. He received a traditional Jewish education and also studied medicine at Frankfort on the Oder and at Padua. After settling in Istanbul, he entered the service of Rami Mehmed Pasha, who served as grand vezir in 1703. He later became the physician of Sultan Ahmed III (r. 1703–30). Cohn was also a Hebrew scholar and author. His *Ma'aseh Tuviyyah,* first published in Venice in 1707, is an encyclopedic work dealing mainly with medicine, but also with theology, astronomy, geography, botany, and other subjects. The book also contains a Turkish-Latin-Spanish dictionary of scientific terms. It was deemed by contemporaries to have considerable medical significance because of the advanced theories it presented, especially in pediatrics, and it was issued in five editions. At about 1714, Cohn left the imperial service and retired to Jerusalem, to dedicate his life to religious studies, and there he died.[278]

Cohn's place at the court of Ahmed III was taken over by another European Jew, Daniel de Fonseca (ca. 1668–ca. 1740). Born in Oporto, Portugal, as a Marrano, he studied medicine in Bordeaux and resided for a while in Paris. In 1702, he settled in Istanbul, where he openly returned to Judaism. He served as a physician to the French Embassy, as well as to several Ottoman dignitaries. In 1714, he became the physician of Ahmed III and served in that capacity until the latter's deposition in 1730. De Fonseca also became somewhat prominent in Ottoman diplomacy. In 1709, he supported the Swedish-Ottoman alliance against Russia. After the fall of Ahmed III, de Fonseca settled in Paris.[279] In addition to European Jews, the Ottoman court continued to employ also local Jewish physicians, although they, as far as is known, did not play a political role. The following Ottoman Jews are mentioned as having served as court physicians during the reigns of Mahmud I (1730–54) and Osman III (1754–57): Isaac Çelebi, Joseph ha-Rofeh, David ha-Levy Ashkenazi and Judah Handali.[280]

In spite of these examples, it is evident that as of the mid-seventeenth century, the number of Jewish physicians in the service of the Ottoman court, and in the medical profession in general, had sharply declined. This was symptomatic of Jewish decline in a wide range of areas.

A major factor which had contributed to the Jews' success in the Ottoman Empire in the fifteenth and sixteenth century was their knowledge of European sciences, economy, languages, and the ways of Europe in general. In the second half of the seventeenth century, and even more so in the eighteenth, Ottoman Jewry's connections with Europe, and its Jewish communities, appear to have weakened.[281] Jewish immigration from Europe declined and the Ottoman Jews' knowledge of Europe gradually faded and became outdated. At this very juncture, they were faced by a growing challenge on the part of the Greeks, and, subsequently, the Armenians and other local Christians, who began to educate their children in European schools, acquiring thereby the kinds of skills and knowledge that the Jews had previously possessed. To some extent, the Christians now emulated the career patterns followed by the Jews in the sixteenth century. The Phanariote Greeks sent their sons to Italy, where many of them studied medicine. They returned to the Ottoman Empire to serve as physicians to high government officials. The first two Greeks to hold the influential office of translator to the Grand Vezir's Council first served as physicians to Grand Vezir Köprülü Ahmed Pasha (1635–76). Gaining entrance to the upper levels of the Ottoman bureaucracy gave Greeks the opportunity to increase their wealth and to advance to other political positions.[282] Soon, they were able to displace the Jews, not only as physicians and translators, but also as financiers and international merchants. In their competition with the Jews, the Christians enjoyed several advantages. In the first place, they were far more numerous than the Jews and could rely on stronger local networks. They could also count on the support of their churches, which were more tightly structured than the loosely organized Jewish communities. Finally, as European companies began to make ever-increasing inroads on Ottoman trade, the Jews' advantage, based on their overseas networks, further declined. Moreover, in commercial transactions, European companies generally preferred to deal with the local Christians, rather than the Jews, although they did not hesitate to cooperate with Jewish merchants when it was to their advantage (Thomas Philipp; C. Max Kortepeter).

The foregoing socioeconomic changes combined to produce a twofold negative impact on the Jewish community. First, the wealth of the highest Jewish economic class was gradually reduced; and second, the community as a whole was deprived of spokesmen and intercessors at the highest levels of government. These changes produced a chain reaction that deeply affected other segments of the community. The Jewish economic elite had been the main initiator of entrepreneurial activities; these activities benefited other classes within the community. This elite was also the main supporter of scholarly and educational institutions. Thus, the decline of the Jewish economic upper class resulted in the gradual impoverishment, materially and spiritually, of Ottoman Jewry as a whole.

The decline of Ottoman crafts and their inability to compete with European-manufactured products must have had an adverse impact on a broad spectrum of the urban economic classes. This was particularly true with respect to the textile craft industry, which had been a major area of Jewish economic activity and which was also one of those most adversely affected by European competition. Extortionist taxation, coupled with inflation, placed the local craft industry at a considerable disadvantage compared with European manufacturers. Ottoman entrepreneurs did not have adequate means to modernize their industries and introduce the necessary new technologies, tools and equipment. They also could not compete with European merchants, who paid with stable foreign currency, for raw materials grown locally. Moreover, the failure of the Ottoman government to protect its markets from the superior foreign-manufactured products led to the decline of the local industry's share of its own home market. As of 1600, and probably even earlier, Salonica textiles could no longer compete in quality with those of England, France, Italy, and Holland. The crisis in the textile craft industry affected all classes involved in it, from the wealthy entrepreneurs and merchants to the humble artisans and laborers. The Jewish communities of Salonica and Safed, which were particularly dependent on this industry, appear to have been the most affected, and many of their members were forced to emigrate to Izmir, Rhodes, and other Ottoman towns in search of new economic opportunities.[283]

* * * * *

As of the end of the sixteenth century, the Jews, together with other segments of Ottoman society, became increasingly vulnerable to the ravages of foreign wars in the empire's frontier provinces, and to the chaos and disorder caused by internal unrest, uprisings and rebellions, which affected a growing number of regions. As primarily urban dwellers, the Jews' lot was perhaps better than that of many peasants living in the more exposed countryside. However, as a small minority with few allies, in difficult times the Jews became also very vulnerable to predation and attack, and they appear to have been among the first victims of the prevailing disorder.

In many of the Balkan provinces, where the population was largely Christian, the Jews, like their Muslim neighbors, had everything to fear from the fury of invading foreign armies and their local allies. During the Austrian-Ottoman War of 1593–1606, Prince Michael the Brave of Wallachia revolted against the sultan (November 1594) and aligned himself with the Austrian emperor. One of his first acts was to massacre, in Bucharest, all the Jews and Turks who were creditors of Romanians. During the course of the warfare, which spread south of the Danube, Michael's forces mercilessly hunted down and killed, or captured for ransom, Turks and Jews. The Jewish communities of Nikopol and Plevna were totally destroyed at that time.[284]

At times, the Jews suffered from the predations of both sides. The Jewish community of Belgrade, which prospered materially and culturally in the seventeenth century,[285] was destroyed in 1688, during the War of the Holy League. At the approach of the Austrian army, the retreating Janissaries plundered and burned the Jewish quarter. When the Austrians captured the city, their troops proceeded to kill and loot the remaining Turks and Jews. Many Jews were captured by the Austrians and were offered for ransom to Jewish communities in Austrian-controlled territories. Others managed to escape south to the safety of Ottoman territories, and when the Ottomans recaptured the city in 1690, they returned and started to rebuild the community. In 1717, however, the Austrians again seized Belgrade, and most of

1. Plan of Istanbul, 1481.

2. Sultan Süleyman the Magnificent (ruled 1520–66).

ברוך ה' אלהי ישראל

החלק הראשון

החלק הש'י

החלק השלישי

3. Introductory page of *Arba'ah Turim*, a widely-accepted code of Jewish law compiled by Jacob ben Asher (ca. 1270–1340), printed in Istanbul, 1493–94. First Hebrew book printed in the Ottoman Empire.

א יהודה בן תימא אומר

הוי עז כנמר וקל כנשר ורץ כצבי וגבור כארי

4. First page of *Arba'ah Turim*.

5. Last page of *Arba'ah Turim* with colophon naming the printers, David and Samuel Nahmias, and dating the book 4 Tevet, 5254/13 December, 1493.

פרק נשאין

סליק פרקא

פרקא

6. A page of *Sefer ha-Halakhot*, a comprehensive compendium of the Talmud by Isaac ben Jacob Alfasi (ca. 1013–1103), printed in Istanbul, 1509.

7. Front page (bearing censor's markings) of *Sefer Bereshit Rabbah*, an anthology of biblical exegesis dating from the fifth century, printed in Istanbul, 1512.

8. Title page of *Sefer Mikhlol*, a philological treatise on Hebrew language and grammar by David ben Joseph Kimhi (ca. 1160–ca. 1235), printed in Istanbul, 1532, by Gershom Soncino.

נאם דוד בן יוסף בן קמחי הספרדי

המלמד בלחם מה שיצטרך לו · וגם בם קומות וחסרים
מחצריך לו ·

ויער יי את רוחי ואמץ את לבבי לכתוב
ספר בדרך קצרה ובאתי כמלקט
שבלים אחרי הקוצר · וכמעולל אחרי הבוצר · ויצאתי
בעקבותיהם לקצר ודבריהם ולכתוב ספר · קראתי
שמו ספר מכלל · כי רצונו לכלול בו בדקדוק הלשון
ועניני על דרך קצרה · כדי שיהא נקל לתלמדים
ללמד אותו ולהבין נתיבתו · והנה בזמן בלחם בו
כל מה שיצטרכו לדקדוק ולענין · ואבתוב בתחלה
חלק הדקדוק והאחרין חלק הענין · ודרכתי בסדורו
דרך וראשונים לסדר הפעלים על סדר האותיות
שיהיה נמרץ לדורש · ונמצא למבקשי ·
ואומר בתחלה כי לשון הקדש · וכן כל לשון נחלק
לשלשה חלקים ·

שם פעל מלה

ואכתוב שער הדקדוק הפעלים בתחלה · ואף על פי
שהשם קודם לפעל · כי הפעל יצא מהשם · ואמרו
כי השם כמו הגוף נושא ומקרים · והפעל כמו מקרה
· אבל מפני אורך הכנת הפעלים אכתוב שער
הדקדוק הפעלים תחלה · ואחרין שער הדקדוק השמות
ואחרין שער הדקדוק המלים · אבל בחלק הענינים
אפרש שלשתם ביחד על סדר האותיות · ומי אשר לו
נתכנו עלילות · ולי נאוו והתהלות · אשאל העזר
לחל ולכלות ·

שער הפעלים

בבין הפעלים · בנה בשמה טולים ·

הטור האחד הוא בנין הקל · ודואו יסוד
הפעלים ונקרא כן · כי לא נוסף בו
אות על האותיות והיסודות כי אם לשמש ליצרוך
בינו לנמצא ולנסתר ולמדבר בעדו ולנקבה ולרבים
ולרבות · ואות והמשמשת אינה תוספת אחר שהיא
לצורך השמוש ולהורות על הגדבר · אבל הוא
וחמש ותוספת בבנין הפעיל · וכן בשאר הבנינים
היא תקרא תוספת כי אינם מורות על הגדבר ואינם
משמשות רק רם להכרת והבנין · והגדברים הם
בשלשה דרכם · נסתר · נמצא · מדבר בעדו · ומנהג
הלשון הוא לדבר בהם כאחד לפעמים כמו שמעו
עמס כלם ⟨ ואגלם כלם תשבו ובאו נא ⟨ לכלם ⟨
הלסרחנו ⟨ כי ייבשו מעילים אשר חמדתם ⟨
ודועסלבכם יורשים אף ישוחתנו בגה צרה והדובם לחם
⟨ ועוד נבתבם בנח הלמד בשרש מרח ⟨

יתברך ויתעלה השם רוח אדם בקרבו ·
ודעת ותבונה בלבו · להקר
ולדעת · נפש הודיעות · לידיעי שכליה · ולאחוז
מסלולית · לפלם מעגליה · ללכת בדרכי וישר ·
ונכתוב כושר · להזות בנועם יי ולבקר בהיכלו ·
ויבחר בישראל מכל האומות · ובלשון עבר מכל
הלשונות · ובו נגלה לעמו באוזר דורים · ודבר
להם עשרת הדברים · ורצה על ידי נביאו ללמד להם
מצות וחקים · ומשפטים צדיקים · ויהונ מלומדים
בנעוריהם · לשון עבר אבינם · ומזם נגלו אבותינו
בארץ לא להם · בין הגוים והם · וילמדו לשונם
וישכחו לשון הקדש עד הרגילו בניהם · ובני כניהם
עד היום לדבר לשון נברים ושפה זה · איש ללשונו
בארצותם · לפי מקומות גלותם · בקדר וארום ·
וכל לאום ולאום · לא נמצא בידנו ירק כסם שנשאר
כתוב אצלנו · עשרים וארבעה ספרים וטלים
מעטם בדברי חכמה · ועל כן צריכים אנו להזהר
על מה שיש בידינו מן הלשון להתהג כמשפטו ושלא
להשחיתו ולדבר בו דברים אשר לא כן ·

ואגבם קרמנו והזהירונו עליו וחזרונו נתיכתו
החכמים אשר הנו לפנינו · וראש
המדרים ומישרי הלשון החכם ר יהודה פאס · ובמבנה
חיזג מצאו בזמן ההוא מעוות בפי אנשים וגשחת
בלשונותם · ויחבר שני ספרים מאירים כספרים
ספר בעלי הרפוי וסמר בעלי הכפל נתיבי לשון
לומדים פוקח עינם עורית ולשון עלגים תמהר
לדבר צחות · ואחרין החזיק החכם רבי יונה אשר
בלאו לבו לכתוב ולחארין בדקריוק הלשון ובעינינו
על כל אשר לפני מאשר ראינו מדאגו ואחרין רבים
התעסקו ברקרוק הלשון · וכתבו כל אחד מהם
ספרים על סבו · ואם יבא אדם ללמד חכמת
הדקדוק ולאה ללמד כל הספרי אשר חברו והגדברים
רצטרך להתעסק כהם כל ימו · ולא טוב הות
מאדם עירי מחכמת הדקדוק אבל צריך לו להתעסק
בתורה ובמצות ובפירושים וצרכו ענינם בדברי
רזל · ולהתעסק בדקרוק על דרך קצרה כד
שיספיק לו ללמד חתומת בתיקונן ולדעת יתרון
האותיות וחסרונן ולהזהר בו כברון ובכי אורית
ובמכבן ובנרודו · וגם לזל הזהירונו בזה ואמרו
לעולם ילמד אדם לתלמדו דרך קצרה · והספרים
אשר יתעסק כהם האר למלאת רוב ספמן מן הדקדוק
הם ספרי החכם ר יהודה עם מה שהוסף עליו והחכם
רבי יונה ולדעת הענינם ספר השדרשים וכאף על פי
ששש כהם ודברים הרבה שלא ליצרוך ושלמדו

9. First page of *Sefer Mikhlol*.

10. Jewish physician, ca. 1550.

11. Jewish merchant, ca. 1550.

12.   Jewish woman of Edirne, ca. 1550.

13.   Unmarried Jewish woman of Edirne, ca. 1550.

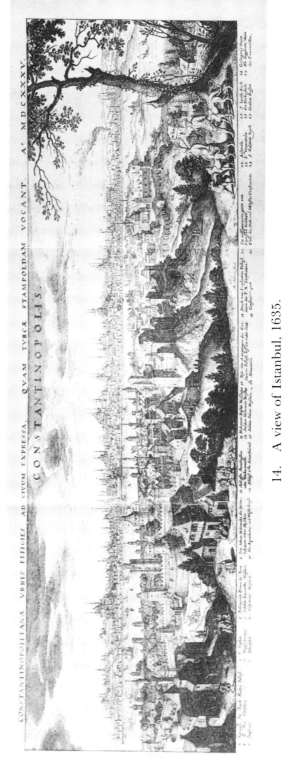

14. A view of Istanbul, 1635.

15.   Title page of the second volume of *Edut bi-Yhosef*, responsa by Joseph ben Isaac Almosnino (ca. 1648–89), printed in Istanbul, 1733, by Jonah ben Jacob Ashkenazi.

16. Title page of *Sefer Yad Aharon*, a compendium of responsa literature by Aaron ben Moses Alfandari (ca. 1690–1774), printed in Izmir, 1735, by Jonah ben Jacob Ashkenazi and David Hazzan.

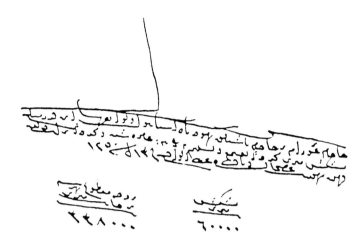

17. Recorded copy of an imperial edict (*ferman*) instituting the office of *haham başı* (chief rabbi) and conferring it on Abraham Levi, dated 21 Ramazan, 1250/21 January, 1835. Başbakanlık Arşivi, Istanbul (henceforth BA), *Gayr-ı Müslim Cemaatlere Ait Defterler* (henceforth GMC), vol. 17, p. 95.

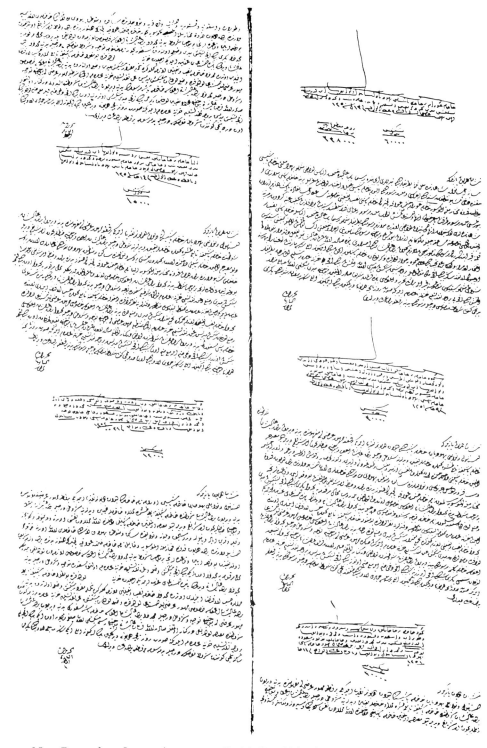

18. Records of appointment of chief rabbis for Istanbul, Izmir, Salonica, Bursa, and Edirne, dated 1835–36 (size greatly reduced; fig. 17 is at top right). BA, CMC, vol. 17, pp. 95–96.

19. Official seal of the chief rabbi of Istanbul, Jacob Avigdor (Yako Avidor), dated 1276/1860. BA, GMC, vol. 18, p. 4.

20. Official seal of the head (*cemaat başı*) of the Karaite community (*millet-i kara'i*), Elijah (Iliya), dated 1291/1874. BA, GMC, vol. 18, p. 4.

21. Circular letter in Turkish, Hebrew, and Judeo-Spanish in Hebrew characters, from the chief rabbi of Istanbul, Hayyim Moshe Fresco, to Jewish communities throughout the Ottoman Empire, urging the study of the Turkish language. Dated 1 Heshvan, 5601/28 October, 1840. American Jewish Historical Society, Waltham, Massachusetts, no. I–238.

ספר

שם חדש

ח"א

שם גדול טובב הולך על ס' **יראים** לחד מן קמאיי חכמי עליה התיר הגדול **רבינו אליעזר ממיץ** זלה"ה הנוקמאמר, עמוקי
ספר עבוד פרישה טופ שפיר מאשרי שופרי : דולה ומאשקה מים מבורות
גופי הלכות הלכתא גברוותא פנימיותא ומסתרתא וכולהו תניי חכו כאן שנה רבי מסרפא וסרי : לא היים דבר קטון ודבר גדול קלוט
וחמורות לחבין ולהורות את מי יורה דעה ואת מי יבין אמוטפה כל חיבה הטריכה לגמ"ד והיה סבל"מה : עמד בפ"ד רב כל חמיי"רא
יסם חו"ר כו ונסתרא פתייס סרי : משאחתו קב וזנקי זך וישר פעלו לאשמיון שמחתתא אליבא דהלכתא הלכתא כרב באיש"רי : מחדש
חדש בכל יום חמיי רחא זה

שם טוב קנה לעצמו טודע בשערים שמו כל הטאם טונים אחריו תקודש מקודש בקדושא רבה דעמש שיעורים : סיעו
לדיק סייונ טובד אלקים בפנוס וירחא חטא גדולים מטשיו מטשיו לפשוח רעון אביו שבשמים בתולמ"ח מפך תאד בדקדוקים ובפרעיין
ק בחקירה ודרישה גדולים חקרי . ויט שמחו לסבול כרע רבן טרע מתני"ז ולגלה כזוט לא מסיק גירסא מתפומים דעמ רבא ודינא זמרח
מביח וקורלא . לא חת עבר עליו חמות חות וכיר לילה ותיד טימנו דמי פומיה דאבה כמתני התמכבר סוב"ר הרו"יס מילי דנומתרי . הוא הרח"ש
פעל"ר ול"ת מו"ר מפ'הרב א"ח הרח"ש כמהר"ר **חיים דניאל שלמה פינסו** זלק"ל מר נריה הדבירנא דרב **אפי**
זוטרי ומשפט כתיב וס'**תולעת שני** דרב חולים ורב נובריה : רלמ

חדש הכ.י"ל הזהב כבר נודע כ"ל הרב בדרוש ד'ושע"ט של ק"ל הזלחות נקראת שם וסם הו"יז וסם סד'"ל גי' ס"ס ובודרנא ס"ל ח' כ'ספר
גי'סם : מד"ש וכ"ח גימ' ספ . סם גי'ספר חדש גת' ע"ב סם כיוו מיונא סם בכולל הם שם מלית חמה יעלו ש"ח . ליעור
גימ'ש"ח רמז הרונו לרבי' אליעור מנוזני' ע"ב ל אל פין הקורא : דברי' כהורוני אין כל
שם קדש לפורה . עד טוכחו רטיים לשמים כחתם ודבר מ' מירושלם הרדא זו תורה הא
לחנומאר את לחנומאר . כל ימי דיק דעתיי פולייס יום ליום יבע ולולה לגילה . יהה ומטלטל בלע"רו לבלכל דבריו קן בחומא
ומחפק בחומא לפי שיעורי והכסם שמור להוגיחו מחשבתינו תורת אחת ותורתו לרשיי לחמאריה : אדהכי וכהי קל מן שחיל פסיק לחל"ים
מעשרום חיים של לראות בנגנו סם מזוננים שף מדוכתיה ויעל נס ב'ם מים לחטלה בשמי מטמייס בחתרל דמחאריה : לדרכו פנס ויסו לפמיינה אל
מחנג אלקים זה מתכח סבינית סאי דישאנ לאשי פרדיסנא דקב'ה . חב בשיקרים : אתו סיום סמת רבי יום ב'ך לא'מייר ע'נושו תלי'מ תא"רי
וול'מטו יום נרס ולמחת פנס כוזה סדרים זייה . ויקרא . כל יסר'במ'רין איפקוז ומבבק . הארן לקבלה טתלי' בס"ת נסאל קינא שמת
וירם אטטו עכסם עכבס גם לרבות את השתחים וארפא. תלמשיו תלתלתא מלאכי שלום מר יבבין וכרוזא קלרי . איס טופר חיה
שוקל טורא תורתא מחבל לאמל ומשסונב לשמונב אנה פנם פנס סם ממלל לרבדבן מי כמוס מורה '. עלי לו די ויוטא אני מר תר
כי רמן מתני מנחם מטיב נפשי כבודי ומרים ראבי אבי אבי סתרי ומגיעי רמוט חדומ'עיני מי יתן ראסי מים מסי מסי אומלוה במטמאר'
חבכב נפשי רעדה אחאזני נפס חאזך מסך בעדי אבי הסבו"מני במורורי' וחול פתי נסאמת דלמ"ד"י : קלני מרחשי ת אני נשארתי לבדי אין
חדש בי'ש'רא'ל מלך '

שם כו הטוני הסבד ישראל כל טוד נשמתיו כי זכר חוזרנו סו'י מילנת כח'בער'א לגדיק לחמן ול'פ'ם ספרי דבי
רב לור יקרות טורי מאורי . ואת נחמתי בטוני לרחא בכנחתנה כי בחלה חפתמ לפשחוים רטון להוגיל לאור תהעדה בטוים
חלוי נפשלי אשר טד כה טורי ס'וגלא מזוגוא רישא אבי טרחא חיתי לי . כי בכל כחי עבדתני כל אדם חיינו חיב אלא לפום חילים ולפום
שיעורים : ברי לי לדעבדנא כ'ח ייח נפשל נפמ סיפם דימנ לב לים לטמרא רישא אנח ל'אלטי לטובה את טוניי ואת טוני ואת יטיב יחסין
אני בוטח כי זכותם דמרן אבא יטולה היא סמ'נוא הו"מ על רא למ הטפיר דכתא מבת חאיי' יטו לפן כל חורא חורה יסמ'ד
יתחרו לקום חם ס'האורב מבב כבסם מלא תרקבא דינרי . התבטניו וקראו מלא בינה אמרי חמרי בגה ברבותא הטונבו כספא והכבא ע"כ פרוטה
מתטו תולטא דעת וחבונו להבין אמרי בינה ומהינון פערי . ואלקים תמטים מלח דברי ברבות הטונבו כספא והכבא ע"כ פרוטה
פרוסות מדם גדולם גדה טודבת ימים ימים שנות פולמ' ונור מרשעוו יראל . עד כי יבא סלה חטם לישראל תטין שם חדשי בשר
חדש

הכ"ד בנ ותלמידו נטר ישראל הגטיר רחמים ישראל פינסו ס"ט

תחת ממשלת מחזנים המלך האויר החסי'שולטן עבד איל מאגיד ירום הו'ה

נדפס פה

ירושלים

תובב"א

עה"ק

עי' הרב המדפיס כבוד מו"ס **ישראל** בכהר"ר מו"ה **אברהם** ב"ק

שנת וקרא לך שם חדש לפ"ג

22. Title page of *Sefer Shem Hadash* by Hayyim Daniel Solomon Pinso (d. 1841), a commentary on the halakhic work, *Sefer Yere'im*, by Eliezer ben Samuel of Metz (twelfth century). Printed by Israel Bak, Jerusalem, 1843.

23.   Jewish woman of Istanbul, ca. 1850.

24.   Yüksek Kaldırım, a stepped street in the ethnically mixed Galata
quarter of Istanbul, ca. 1900.

25.   A Salonica rabbi, ca. 1910.

26.   An old Sephardic Jew of Salonica, ca. 1910.

27. Jewish woman of Salonica in Sabbath dress, ca. 1910.

28. Jewish youths of Salonica in Sabbath dress, ca. 1910.

29. Jewish vendor of brooms, Salonica, ca. 1910.

30. Jewish money changer (*sarraf*), Salonica, ca. 1910.

31.   Old Jewish porter (*hammal*), Salonica, ca. 1910.

32. Jewish woodcutters, Salonica, ca. 1910.

33. Jewish fruitseller, Salonica, ca. 1910.

the Jews, once again, fled in terror together with the Muslim population. The city was recaptured by the Ottomans in 1739, and many of the Jewish families returned and started again the process of reconstruction.[286] Other Jewish communities in the Balkans had similar experiences.[287]

The Jews had thrived when government was strong and orderly. Now, with the decline of effective government, as a small and weak minority, they were more exposed than others to the extortions and oppression of corrupt and rapacious officials and the violence of rebellious rulers. On the periphery, where Ottoman central authority first began to wane, the Jews appear to have suffered more than in the core provinces and the great urban centers, where the authority of the central government was still respected. However, even in these centers, including the capital, the Jews were not always safe from the violence and fury of mutinous soldiery and unruly mobs.

The Jewish community of Tripoli in Syria, which had flourished in the sixteenth century,[288] in the early decades of the seventeenth century suffered greatly from the extortions of the rebellious governor, Seyfoğlu Yusuf Pasha. Most of the Jewish population was forced to leave the town in fear, abandoning their property, and for several decades all organized community life had ceased.[289] In Safed, the Jewish community was repeatedly attacked by rebellious Druze and Bedouins in the period from 1579 to 1656.[290] Many of its residents fled to Damascus, Izmir, and other more central and safe towns (Jacob Barnai). The Jewish community of nearby Tiberias was also repeatedly attacked at that time and finally was completely dispersed in 1656. It was renewed only in 1740.[291] The Jewish community of Jerusalem also suffered greatly from the extortions of its rapacious governor, Muhammad ibn Farukh. During his short tenure of office (1625–27), the community was greatly decimated.[292]

The breakdown of public order and the rise of banditry and general lawlessness also appear to have taken a particularly heavy toll on the Jewish community. As has been noted, many Jews were engaged in internal commerce and had to travel for their business to other towns or throughout the countryside. Also, considerable numbers of Jews earned their living as itinerant salesmen, peddlers, and craftsmen. As of the end of the sixteenth century, the sources are replete with details of attacks on Jews traveling throughout the countryside in pursuit of a livelihood.[293] Jews were forced to take expensive

precautions to protect themselves, and often, in spite of these measures, the outcome was the loss of property and even life.

In September 1617, a large convoy of Jewish merchants from
Salonica, returning from a fair, was attacked near Salonica by robbers,
who plundered the convoy and massacred all its members. The Jews
of Salonica were able to recover twenty-five bodies, although the total
number of those killed was apparently greater. The massacre made
such an impact on the community that its leaders decreed the date
of the massacre (14 Elul) as an annual day of fasting and mourning
in the local Jewish calendar. It is perhaps an indication of the Jewish
community's growing sense of isolation and vulnerability that the Jews
of Salonica suspected that the attackers included Janissaries and
Sipahis, as well as local Greeks—three groups that were traditionally
hostile to each other. Rosanes expresses surprise that the incident was
hushed up in the contemporary Jewish sources, and he speculates
that persons of authority might have pressed the Jewish community
not to complain or seek redress.[294]

The ravages of war and instability resulted in a considerable
amount of Jewish internal migration within Ottoman boundaries. Jews
moved from one town to another, seeking safety and security, but
also economic opportunity. These population movements had mixed
results. The decline of some communities often resulted in the growth
in numbers, and sometimes in prosperity, of others. These migrations
also accelerated the processes of acculturation and integration within
the individual Jewish communities. The old divisions based on country
of origin in Europe had become increasingly meaningless in the course
of the seventeenth century. As has been noted, a new type of Ottoman
Jew emerged who was equally at home in Safed, Bursa, Izmir or
Istanbul. This and the necessity to face up to more difficult times,
also contributed to the growing centralization of the community's
organization and its leadership. At the same time, however, these
same processes also led to the greater impoverishment of the Jewish
population as a whole, and probably also to its numerical decline,
although there are very little data to support this assumption.

The community of Bursa was probably not typical of most other
Jewish communities. As has been noted, it was a very prosperous
community in the sixteenth century. It remained relatively prosperous
in the seventeenth and was still regarded as such in the late nineteenth
century. However, because we have some comparative data for the
Bursa community from the sixteenth, as well as the seventeenth cen-

turies, it may be used as some indication of more general change. As has been noted, in 1598/99, 48 percent of the Jewish taxpayers of Bursa were listed in the highest tax bracket, 31 percent in the middle, and 21 percent in the lowest. In 1688/89, these figures were 11, 54, and 35 percent, respectively. At the same time, the Jewish population declined from 504 households in 1583 to 141 in 1696/97, which corresponded to a similar rate of decline of the town's general population.[295] It should be immediately added, however, that these figures reflect the relative decline of Bursa as a commercial center.[296] Even so, the changes are striking. Within the span of some ninety years, the highest economic class was sharply reduced and the lowest class increased. Equally significant, however, was the increase in the size of the middle class. The tentative conclusion that could perhaps be drawn from this admittedly meager data, is that in Bursa and similar towns—which were relatively unaffected by the ravages of foreign wars and internal disorder—the Jewish upper economic class was greatly reduced by the end of the seventeenth century, but the middle class remained relatively strong. This appears to be confirmed also by other sources.

Furthermore, the central communities of Istanbul, Salonica, Edirne, Damascus, and Cairo appear to have been able to maintain a degree of affluence well into the eighteenth century. Other communities even reached new heights during this period of general decline. The community of Izmir flourished in the second half of the seventeenth century and that of Aleppo in the eighteenth century (Jacob Barnai; Thomas Philipp). The relative success of communities such as those of Istanbul, Salonica, Izmir, and Aleppo was due to the important role of these cities in the international commerce of the Mediterranean. As a result, they attracted small numbers of European Jews—mainly Portuguese Marranos who returned to Judaism, as well as Italian and French Jews, all of whom were known as Francos—who settled in these cities during the seventeenth and eighteenth centuries. The Francos played an important role in the international commerce. They were also well educated and a dynamic element. Although they remained somewhat aloof from the established Jewish communities, and their relations with them were often strained, they were not an entirely segregated caste. Their wealth, culture, and sheer presence contributed to slow down the decline and reinvigorate the established communities.[297]

However, the relative prosperity of some central communities should not obscure the overall picture. The decline and dislocation of entire communities resulted in a ripple effect felt throughout Ottoman Jewry. Jewish refugees and migrants from one town often became a burden on other Jewish communities, and the total number of the Jewish poor increased. The destruction of individual communities in various parts of the empire also reduced the overall effectiveness of the Ottoman Jewish networks with important material and cultural ramifications, for material and cultural efflorescence depended on the strength of these networks.

The Messianic Movement of Shabbetai Tzevi

During the second half of the seventeenth century, Ottoman Jewry became the center of the most widespread messianic movement in Jewish history. The movement was nurtured by the age-old longings of the Jews for spiritual and political redemption, as well as by the confluence of several immediate factors. Spiritually, the background had been prepared by the rising influence, in the 1630s and 1640s, of the Lurianic branch of Kabbalah, centered in Safed, which was permeated by messianic expectations of redemption. The movement was touched off, however, by the exceptionally brutal persecution of the Jews in Poland, beginning with the "Chmielnicki Massacres" of 1648–49, and continuing into the 1650s, through the Polish-Russian and Polish-Swedish wars. In the massacres of 1648–49 alone, about three-hundred Jewish communities were destroyed, many thousands perished, and more were displaced and scattered throughout the Jewish diaspora as refugees or captives offered for ransom. Particularly large numbers of those refugees arrived in the Ottoman Empire, whose communities were still considered the largest and wealthiest in the world, possessing a long tradition of ransoming captives.[298] The accounts of the horrors inflicted on Poland's Jewry spread throughout the Jewish diaspora, convincing many that these sufferings were the "birth pangs" of the messianic age and the redemption of the Jews.[299]

The person who became the movement's focal point was Shabbetai Tzevi (Sabbatai Sevi; 1626–76), a native of Izmir and the son of a wealthy merchant and agent for Dutch and English traders. Shabbetai Tzevi was trained in Jewish law to become a rabbi, but he also studied Kabbalah. He was recognized as a gifted student and was much liked due to his pleasant appearance, fine voice, piety, and asceticism.[300] There was, however, another aspect to his personality.

Perhaps a manic-depressive, whose mood alternated between fits of great exaltation and profound depression,[301] from time to time he was driven to commit bizarre rituals and acts, contradicting Jewish law. In 1648, when the news of the Chmielnicki Massacres first arrived in Izmir, Shabbetai Tzevi declared himself to be the Messiah. At first, his claims were largely ignored. At some point in the early 1650s, however, when the agitation around Shebbetai Tzevi increased, the rabbinic authorities had him banished from Izmir. He spent the next thirteen or fourteen years living and traveling throughout the Jewish communities of the Balkans, Egypt, and Palestine. His continued agitation caused him to be banished time and again, but in many communities he managed to establish circles of disciples and believers.

The turning point in Shabbetai Tzevi's career came in May 1665, when a young, charismatic rabbi in Gaza, known as Nathan of Gaza, proclaimed Shabbetai Tzevi to be the Messiah and redeemer. In the enthusiasm that followed, Nathan seized control of the local community and turned it into the movement's headquarters. Nathan proved to be a remarkable propagandist and organizer and from this point onward, events unfolded in rapid succession. Without leaving Gaza, through correspondence and networks of emissaries, Nathan proclaimed the news of the Messiah's arrival throughout the Jewish diaspora, where his communications produced great excitement, and swept entire communities.[302]

In spite of wide popular appeal, there were many, especially among rabbinic circles, who rejected Shabbetai Tzevi's claims. In June 1665, Shabbetai Tzevi was banished from Jerusalem by the local rabbis. Referring to the fact that he had previously been appointed to serve as an emissary to collect contributions (*shaliyah*) for the Jewish community in Jerusalem, not a very prestigious office, his critics said of him derisively the verse, *halakh shaliyah u-va mashiyah*, (he left a fund-raiser and returned a messiah).[303]

Shabbetai Tzevi's appeal with the masses was, however, overwhelming. In September 1665, he returned triumphantly to Izmir, where, by means of popular support, he deposed his opponents from the community leadership and installed his supporters (Jacob Barnai). He then declared the day of redemption to be the 5th of Sivan, 5426 (18 June 1666), and announced his intention to depose the sultan. Indeed, on 30 December 1665, Shabbetai Tzevi sailed for Istanbul.[304]

The Ottoman authorities had been apprised of Shabbetai Tzevi's activities, but up to this point did practically nothing to stop him.

However, the increased agitation caused economic disruption, and now, with an open declaration of rebellion, the government issued orders for Shabbetai Tzevi's arrest. Consequently, on 6 February 1666, the ship on which Shabbetai Tzevi had been traveling was intercepted in the Sea of Marmara. Shabbetai Tzevi was arrested, taken to Istanbul, and brought before the council (*divan*) of Grand Vezir Ahmed Köprülü. The authorities could have tried him severely as a rebel. Shabbetai Tzevi's movement was not, however, a violent one (whatever limited violence it generated was directed primarily against its opponents within the Jewish community) and did not pose any real threat to the regime. The authorities decided, therefore, to deal with Shabbetai Tzevi cautiously. He was incarcerated, first in Istanbul and later at Gallipoli, in rather comfortable quarters, and was even allowed to receive visitors.[305]

Meanwhile, Nathan of Gaza's letters continued to produce excitement in Jewish communities throughout Europe and the Ottoman Empire, and many made actual preparations to dispose of their property, rent ships, and travel to the Holy Land. Shabbetai Tzevi's place of imprisonment in Gallipoli became a center of pilgrimage for delegations of Jewish communities from near and far.[306] As the agitation appeared to increase, in September, the Ottoman authorities transferred Shabbetai Tzevi to Edirne, where he was brought again before the divan and given the choice of death or conversion to Islam. Shabbetai Tzevi chose the latter and as a Muslim he assumed the name Aziz Mehmed Efendi. The government awarded him the honorary title of chief palace gatekeeper (*kapıcı başı*) and a royal pension,[307] as was the Ottoman custom when non-Muslim dignitaries adopted Islam. Shabbetai Tzevi continued to live comfortably in Edirne and sometimes in Istanbul, leading a double life: he performed the duties of a Muslim, but also observed Jewish rituals. He maintained close relations with many of his followers and also established contacts with some Muslim mystics. In 1672, he was banished to Dulcigno (Ülgün) in Albania, where he became more isolated and his activities subsided. He died on 17 September 1676.[308]

On Shabbetai Tzevi's conversion to Islam, and even more so after his death, the great majority of his followers became disillusioned and abandoned the movement. In the Ottoman Jewish communities, where confusion, embarrassment, and fear of government retribution were rife, the rabbinical authorities and lay leaders quickly moved to suppress all public mention of Shabbetai Tzevi and pretend that nothing much had actually taken place. Their strategy was to ignore the event, at least in public, in the hope that time would heal all wounds (Jacob Barnai).

During his lifetime, Shabbetai Tzevi attracted to Islam some two hundred Jewish families, whom he exhorted to remain together as secret believers in his mission, and not intermarry with Muslims. Following his death, some three hundred additional families, mostly from Salonica, converted to Islam. They practiced and professed Islam in public, but continued to observe in secret a mixture of traditional and heretical forms of Judaism. They married only among themselves and remained a distinct religious sect until the twentieth century. They were known to Muslims as *Dönme*, meaning converts in Turkish, while the Jews referred to them as *Minim*, sectarians. Their most important center continued to be in Salonica, but Istanbul and Izmir also had significant communities.[309] However, most of those who continued to believe in Shabbetai Tzevi after his death remained within the Jewish fold and were known to other Jews as Shabbateans (*Shabbetaim*). The latter referred to themselves as Believers (*Ma'aminim*). Nathan of Gaza laid the foundation for a new mystical theory that explained the secret meaning of Shabbetai Tzevi's apostasy and his "occultation," as his death was described. The movement, which split into several offshoots, lasted in the Ottoman Empire and Europe, mostly in secret, over a century. It was gradually reabsorbed by mainstream Judaism and disappeared in the early years of the nineteenth century. In the eighteenth century, several well-known rabbis in Salonica, Edirne and Izmir—including the leading rabbi of Edirne, Samuel Primo (d. 1708), and the prolific author and revered teacher, Rabbi Meir Bikayam (d. 1769), of Izmir—were secret adherents of Shabbatean mysticism, clandestinely teaching it to small circles of devotees.[310]

The Shabbetai Tzevi affair is sometimes considered a watershed in the history of Ottoman Jewry. It is said to have had a major destructive impact on the Jewish community, accelerating its decline in two important ways: first, it is argued that it undermined the Jewish position within the Ottoman system; and second, that it contributed to the growing conservatism of the Jewish community by strengthening rabbinic authority.[311]

Actually there is little to support either assertion, although it must be admitted that the long-term impact of the Shabbetai Tzevi affair has, so far, remained little investigated.[312] It cannot be denied that this event was a traumatic and embarrassing experience for Ottoman

Jewry, especially during the years 1665–72. In many places the Jews had become the laughingstock of their non-Jewish neighbors and were humiliated and tormented by them. There are, however, no indications of any official Ottoman acts of retribution directed against the Jewish community. On the contrary, it would appear that the Ottoman authorities handled this entire affair humanely and with adroitness.[313] They seem to have regarded the movement as nothing more than a strange aberration, and their reaction was guided by caution and pragmatism. The Jewish community was discharging important functions within the Ottoman economy and administrative system. Retribution was likely to result in further agitation and negative repercussions for the Ottoman body politic. It would appear, therefore, that it was also in the interest of the government to restore tranquility and order as quickly as possible.

As for Ottoman Jewry's decline, this had been set in motion almost a century before the Shabbetai Tzevi affair, and it was destined to continue, due to the broader processes discussed in this volume. It needs to be stressed, however, that even after Shabbetai Tzevi, the Jewish position within the Ottoman body politic remained consequential for some time to come. In fact, in Izmir, the main scene of Shabbetai Tzevi's agitation, the Jewish community continued for some time to grow and prosper in the 1660s and the 1670s, until 1688, when a massive earthquake devastated the city (Jacob Barnai).

As to the supposedly increased conservatism of the Jewish community, there is little hard evidence to support this argument either. Jewish conservatism, as is discussed later, was probably due mainly to a general decline in intellectual vitality, which, in turn, was the result of the community's increasing material impoverishment and its growing isolation from European culture and from Europe's main Jewish centers. On the contrary, it may be argued that the continuing disputations between the Shabbateans and their opponents, conducted mostly in private circles and in carefully concealed allusions in the rabbinic literature, may have served to stimulate and prolong the community's intellectual vitality.[314] Salonica, where Shabbateanism was particularly entrenched, displayed the strongest degree of Jewish intellectual and cultural vitality, although other factors may have contributed to this phenomenon as well. In fact, in the eighteenth century, several rabbis bitterly complained about the decline of orthodoxy and religious observance among Jews in the important centers of the Ottoman Empire—Salonica, Istanbul, and Izmir. In a book printed in

Salonica in 1769, a leading local rabbi, Joseph Molkho, decried various indications of religious laxity. Among other things, he complained that Jewish shop owners did not perform the afternoon prayer (*minhah*) during weekdays, and Jewish merchants were lax in observing the Sabbath service and studying Torah with their sons. He went on to say: "And when one disputes with them, they answer: 'all this studying was intended only for religious scholars.'"[315]

The Shabbetai Tzevi controversy probably did contribute to strengthen rabbinic authority, which, however, was also a reflection of the community's growing integration. In the wake of the Shabbetai Tzevi affair and the fears which it generated within Ottoman Jewry, the rabbis and lay leaders were impelled to strengthen and consolidate the community's central institutions, so as to forestall the recurrence of similar incidents. The affair thus served as an additional stimulus for the emergence of stronger and more centralized community institutions. In sum, the Shabbetai Tzevi affair was a painful experience for World Jewry, and particularly for Ottoman Jews, leaving behind it a long-lasting legacy of spiritual and intellectual turmoil. From a broad historical perspective, however, its impact on Ottoman Jewry's position within the Ottoman body politic appears to have been episodic and with mixed results.

Ottoman Jewry
in the Eighteenth and Early Nineteenth Centuries

In spite of their reduced role, Jews continued to occupy a position of considerable significance in the Ottoman economy and administration well into the eighteenth century. Jews continued to serve in the administration of the customhouses and various tax farms; as contractors and purveyors for the military; and in large-scale commerce and banking. Individual Jews also continued to be employed as physicians and interpreters for the imperial court, the government, and for members of the Ottoman elite and foreign diplomats. A considerable number of central communities, such as Istanbul, Salonica, Izmir, Edirne, Bursa, Aleppo, Damascus, and Baghdad, continued to exhibit signs of material prosperity and cultural efflorescence.[316] As late as 1717, Lady Mary Wortley Montagu, the wife of the British ambassador in Istanbul, was so impressed with the position occupied by Ottoman Jews that she wrote to her sister, perhaps with some exaggeration:

I observed most of the rich tradesmen were Jews. That people are an incredible power in this country. They have many privileges . . . and have formed a very considerable commonwealth here, being judged by their own laws, and have drawn the whole trade of the empire into their hands . . . . Every pasha has his Jew, who is his *homme d'affaires*; he is let into all his secrets and does all his business. No bargain is made, no bribe received, no merchandise disposed of, but what passes through their hands. They are the physicians, the stewards, and interpreters of the great men.[317]

Other sources, from the second half of the eighteenth century, still describe Jews in prominent positions in the Ottoman economy,[318] although it is clear that by that time the community as a whole was in full retreat.

Jewish vitality in the first half of the eighteenth century was still such that the main Jewish communities of Istanbul and Salonica continued to serve as important centers of Jewish scholarship and could offer attractive opportunities for Jewish printers. In 1711, Jonah ben Jacob Ashkenazi, from Zalewicz near Lwow, and Naftali ben Azriel, from Vilnius, set up in Istanbul a new Hebrew printing press. The press operated for sixty-six years, until 1777, and printed dozens of Hebrew books. Authors from as far away as Baghdad sent their manuscripts to be printed in Istanbul. Jonah Ashkenazi is credited with having assisted Ibrahim Müteferrika to set up the first Turkish printing press, which began operating officially in 1726.[319] In 1742, an Ashkenazi Jew from Amsterdam, Betzalel Halevi, founded a printing press in Salonica, which operated until 1916.[320]

In the last third of the eighteenth century, following the disastrous Ottoman wars with Russia in 1768–74 and, again, against a Russian-Austrian coalition in 1787–92, the pace of Ottoman disintegration, and Jewish decline, appears to have considerably accelerated. During this wartime period, the Jews, as others, were required to pay oppressively high taxes to meet the needs of the war effort. Furthermore, for the first time there is mention of wholesale impressment of Jews into the military.[321] The general impoverishment of Ottoman Jewry may perhaps be gleaned from the internal budget of the Jewish community of Istanbul, one of the largest and relatively most prosperous in the empire, for 1771/72:

TABLE 2.
Annual Budget of the Jewish Community of Istanbul, 1771/72

Income	kuruş
From direct community taxes	24,000
From a community tax on kosher meat	22,000
From a community tax on cheese	3,000
Total	49,000

Expenses	kuruş
Taxes paid to the government	27,000
Interest paid on the community's debts	22,000
Payments (salaries?) to rabbis	6,000
Contribution for the Jews of Palestine	4,000
Flour for the community poor	6,000
Total	65,000

Source: Barnai, "Jewish Community of Istanbul" (Hebrew), pp. 62–63.

A note included in the budget indicates that the community's debts amounted to 325,000 *kuruş,* a very considerable sum in view of the fact that it was equal to more than six and one half times the community's annual income.[322] Servicing the debt alone amounted to about 45 percent of the total income. Since the budget reflected an additional shortfall of 16,000 kuruş, and as government taxes continued to rise in subsequent years,[323] it may be concluded that the community's debt must have increased in the coming years. On the whole, the budget tells a depressing story. Over 75 percent of the expenses were earmarked for various government taxes (in addition to direct personal taxes collected separately) and for servicing the community's debt, and less than 25 percent was earmarked for what might be considered legitimate community expenses. Furthermore, the document indicates that only a small number (1,500) of taxpayers were sufficiently well-off to pay the internal community taxes in addition to those due to the government, which appears to be a small number.[324] Of those 1,500 community taxpayers, 300 were impressed into military service and were unable to meet their tax obligations to the community.[325] Furthermore, the list of taxes paid by the community to the state suggests that the community had to pay the poll tax for 1,200 impoverished taxpayers who could not meet their tax obligations to the government.[326]

The growing impoverishment of the Ottoman Jewish communities at the end of the eighteenth century, and their increased isolation from European culture and the new Jewish centers of Europe, resulted in a general decline in scholarship and intellectual creativity. The number of yeshivot declined and the quality of their training deteriorated. In this respect, Ottoman Jewry had undergone a process similar to that which affected Muslim society, and it became increasingly more inward-oriented and conservative.[327] The intellectual and cultural decline of Ottoman Jewry may be graphically demonstrated by the following table of the number of Jewish books, in Hebrew and Judeo-Spanish, printed in the Ottoman Empire during the period 1731–1807.

TABLE 3.
Jewish Books Printed in the Ottoman Empire, 1731–1807

	1731–50	1751–70	1771–1807
Istanbul			
Hebrew books	45	23	10
Judeo-Spanish books	17	11	2
Salonica			
Hebrew books	33	39	105
Judeo-Spanish books	—	—	7
Izmir			
Hebrew books	14	13	3
Cairo			
Hebrew books	1	—	—
Total	110	86	127
Average number of books printed per year	5.5	4.3	3.43

Source: Rosanes, vol. 5, pp. 355–64.

The Hebrew printing presses, which existed in Edirne, Safed, and Damascus in the sixteenth and seventeenth centuries, had long ceased operation. One Hebrew book was published in Cairo in 1740. In Istanbul and Izmir, the printing of Jewish books sharply declined in the course of the eighteenth century, especially in the last three decades. Between 1782 and 1802, Istanbul had no Jewish printers at all. During the first decade of the nineteenth century, an Armenian printer named Araboghlu Boghos published four Hebrew books and a Judeo-Spanish translation of the Hebrew Bible.[328] Salonica, which still maintained some of its vitality, became at that time the only important center of Jewish printing, and authors and publishers had to send their works to Salonica for publication. The main printing press in Salonica at that time was the one that had been founded in 1742 by Betzalel Halevy.[329] Even so, the total number of Jewish books printed in the Ottoman Empire shows a marked decline from an annual average of 5.5 books around 1750, to 3.43 around 1800.

* * * * *

During the period of accelerated Ottoman disintegration (ca. 1770–1826), while Ottoman society as a whole was forced to bear numerous hardships, there were processes in operation that affected the Jews more adversely than others. This period was characterized by two main developments. First, military defeat weakened and discredited the central Ottoman government more than ever before. This encouraged local strongmen to break away from the central government and establish themselves as independent or semi-independent rulers known as *ayans* and *derebeys*. Some of these rulers targeted the Jews for particular oppression, because they identified them as an easy object for exploitation and despoliation, and perhaps also because some of them distrusted the Jews, regarding them as serving the interests of the central Ottoman government.

In Egypt, the rebellious Mamluk ruler, Ali Bey al-Kabir (r. 1760–73), oppressed the Jews with particular vehemence. He executed and seized the property of two of the country's most prominent and wealthy Jews—Joseph Levi, who administered the Alexandria customhouse, and Ishak al-Yahudi, who held the tax farm on the customhouse in Bulak—in 1768 and 1769, respectively. He systematically purged Egypt's financial administration of Jews, replacing them with Syrian Catholics, and he imposed on the Jewish merchants heavy fines, which ruined them financially.[330] The Jewish community of Baghdad also suffered from the predations of its rebellious Mamluk rulers in the period 1749–1831. In 1810, the Jewish banker, Baghdadli Yehezkel (Ezekiel) ben Joseph Gabbai, assisted the efforts of the central government, directed by Halet Efendi, to overthrow the rebellious Mamluk ruler, Küçük Süleyman Pasha, and restore

Baghdad to central control for a number of years.[331] The last Mamluk ruler, Davud (Dawud) Pasha (r. 1817–31), also rebeled against the Sultan and oppressed the Jewish community. As a result, many prominent Jewish families were forced to flee Baghdad.[332]

At the turn of the nineteenth century, large areas in the Ottoman Balkans were in a state of anarchy, due to the rebellions of local rulers (*ayans*), their conflicts with each other and their wars with the central government, which, from time to time, attempted to suppress them. During this time of trouble, the Jews were particularly vulnerable. The Jewish communities of the Danube districts suffered especially from the predations of the irregular forces of the rebellious governor of Vidin, Pasvanoğlu Osman Pasha. Pasvanoğlu himself was not ill-disposed toward the Jews. He employed a Jew as his personal physician and another as his banker, and he protected the Jewish community of Vidin to the best of his ability. His troops, which included many renegade Janissaries, however, were uncontrollable and they terrorized Jewish communities wherever they found them. In 1795, they attacked the Jewish quarter of Belgrade, burning down its synagogue and many homes. In 1799, the Jews of Plevna took the extraordinary measure of arming themselves, to help defend their town against Pasvanoğlu's forces. When Pasvanoğlu died in 1807, many Jews fled from Vidin in fear of the soldiers' fury.[333]

A similar fate awaited the Jews in those Ottoman areas overcome by the rise of national movements. The Jews, again, were often identified as an easy target, or as serving the interests of the Ottoman government, and Jewish communities were attacked by the local population. Thus started a movement of Jewish migration from those Balkan areas that seceded from the empire and formed new national states, to the remaining Ottoman territories, as well as to other countries.

During the Serbian wars of independence (1804–30), hundreds of Jews fled from Belgrade, some to Ottoman Bosnia and others to Austrian territories. Although Austrian Jews were among the Serbs' arms suppliers, the independence movement frequently attacked the local Jews. In 1807, the Serbs expelled the Jews from Belgrade. In 1815, when Milosh Obrenovich was recognized as Prince of Serbia, the condition of the Jews improved somewhat. In 1831, however, the Serbian government imposed economic restrictions on the Jews, limiting the crafts in which they could engage.[334] The situation of the Jewish communities in southern Greece was even worse. In the second half of the eighteenth century, as anarchy increasingly prevailed in these areas, the Jews came under the attack of Greek insurgents and bandits. At that time, several long-established Jewish communities— including those of Chalcis (Eğriboz), Thebes (Istifa), and Navpaktos (İnebahtı, Lepanto)—were either abandoned or destroyed. During the Greek war of independence (1821–30), the insurgents massacred the Jews along with the Turks. Five thousand Jews were believed to have been killed by Greek nationalists in the Morea alone, with many more fleeing to the safety of territories controlled by the Ottomans.[335]

The second important feature of this era was that, in the face of military defeat and the break-up of the empire, the state desperately sought to modernize certain sectors, particularly the military, the foreign service, and education, and to train a new bureaucracy. The government looked for people with knowledge of European languages and Western skills. The Jews had few to offer, whereas the Christians had many. Among the prominent figures who contributed to the state's modernization efforts during the reigns of the reforming sultans, Selim III (1789–1807) and Mahmud II (1808–39), were Muslims, Greeks, Armenians, as well as many Europeans.[336] The Jews were noted for their absence, except for one, Hoca Ishak Efendi (d. 1834), a Jew from Arta who converted to Islam. A mathematician, he taught at the Army Engineering School and in 1830 became its director. During his short tenure, he restructured and improved the school's curriculum and was considered a pioneer in the modernization of Ottoman education.[337] Apparently, Hoca Ishak remained on close terms with the Jewish community of Istanbul and came to its assistance. The Jews referred to him as the *hakham* of the Admiralty (*Tersane Hahamı*), the quarter where the engineering school was located.[338] On the whole, however, at this period the Jews became identified with conservatism and the old ways. As a result, when the bulwark of the old order, the Janissary corps, was crushed and suppressed in a bloody conflict in the summer of 1826, several leading Jews associated with the Janissaries and the old system, and the community as a whole, suffered the consequences (Avigdor Levy).

Ubicini, writing in the mid-nineteenth century, has succinctly described the gradual nature of the decline of the Jewish community and the reasons for it:

[The Jews] saw themselves gradually dispossessed of their positions as interpreters and other lucrative functions which they had occupied at the Sublime Porte and in the chanceries. Later even the humbler jobs which they had retained, whether in the customs or finances of the empire or in the households of the pashas, were taken from them by the Armenians. While the other communities, Christian and Muslim, familiarized themselves more and more with the languages and affairs of Europe, they continued to remain stationary, and with apparent indifference, saw their riches pass into the hands of their rivals.[339]

Indeed, the early decades of the nineteenth century witnessed the nadir of the Jewish experience in the Ottoman Empire. Rosanes characterized this period as one of great "dereliction and desolation" (*netushah va-azuvah*). Even the Jewish community of Istanbul was affected by "so much decline and degradation . . . that everyone became concerned only with his livelihood and personal affairs and not one cared enough about the community and the public welfare."[340] The impoverishment of the Jewish community of Istanbul is well reflected in the register of the Jewish court of Balat for the year 1839, in the frequent appeals to the court to enforce collections of debts, and in testimonies describing the loss of assets and income.[341]

Oscanyan, an Ottoman Armenian resident of Istanbul, has portrayed in particularly stark colors the poverty, general misery, and low social position of Ottoman Jewry in the first half of the nineteenth century, and how it appeared to others:

> The Jews of Turkey, of whom there are about 170,000, are by no means exempt from the sorrows and curses of their race. As if conscious that there is no escape from the contempt of the rest of the world, they are willing to undertake the meanest of earth's callings, literally to "eat the dirt" of their Muslim masters.
>
> Content to appear like the refuse of humanity, they strive to accumulate the miser's hoards, and receive the buffetings and cursings of their neighbors as if they were choice blessings—usury of all sorts, whether upon sequins or old clothes, peddling the meanest of wares in the streets, rag-picking, and filth-gathering in general, are their means of earning a livelihood . . . .
>
> [They live] in such places as no one else would inhabit. Their houses are like bee-hives, literally swarming with human life; even one single room serves for the only home of several families—and the streets of their quarters are almost impassable, from the collection of garbage and all sorts of refuse, which are

indiscriminately thrown from the windows of their dwellings. Their misery may partly be attributed to their practice of very early marriages, as before a man is twenty-one years of age he is burdened with the care and support of a numerous family, which reduces him to such poverty, that even the meanest economy can scarcely enable him to support his own existence and that of the helpless beings dependent on him . . . .

Yet it is most amusing to see them on a Jewish Sabbath. The filthy gabardines which they wore in the week, as they exercised their various callings, being laid aside, and bright and gaudy finery substituted, in which they strut about the streets, seeming to be other beings, and to have no relation to the wretches of yesterday. But, of course, in such a population there will be various grades of misery, and a few families of wealth are to be found among them.[342]

V
OTTOMAN JEWRY IN THE MODERN ERA (1826–1923)

Ottoman Reform and Modernization

In 1808, when Mahmud II (r. 1808–39) ascended the Ottoman throne, Sir Stratford Canning (1786–1880), the well-known British diplomat who for more than half a century was a well-informed and often first-hand observer of the political scene in Istanbul, concluded that the Ottoman Empire's political system "had worn itself out."[343] The continued survival of the state appeared to be in doubt. The latest reform efforts launched by Sultan Selim III (r. 1789–1807) had provoked a conservative armed revolt and failed miserably. The government was in disarray. In the capital, political power rested not with the legitimate institutions of government, but was exercised by a cabal of soldiers and ulema.[344] The central government wielded minimal authority over the provinces. Rebellion, uprisings, and the growing independence of self-appointed local rulers appeared to be leading the empire to its demise. The prestige of the royal family had plummeted to a low point. After two acts of regicide, the continued existence of the Ottoman dynasty hinged on the fate of its last surviving male member, the untested, twenty-three-year-old Sultan Mahmud II. A temporarily inactive state of war with Russia and Britain imposed further strains on the political fabric.

The young ruler, however, proved to be an exceptionally astute politician, who also profited from the good advice of several competent aides. Capitalizing on his very weakness, Mahmud II cautiously cemented around the throne a coalition of bureaucratic, religious, and military leaders with vested interests in the restoration of orderly government.[345] The new regime succeeded in returning the soldiers to their barracks. It concluded peace agreements with Britain (1809) and Russia (1812), and it also moved cautiously to reform the administration and the military and to restore some measure of central authority over the provinces.[346]

Mahmud II's most famous act, however, was the forceful suppression of the Janissaries and other allied military corps, in 1826, when they rose, once again, against his modest military reforms. The Janissaries had existed as a military institution for almost five centuries and had become the hallmark of Ottoman military power. Until the seventeenth century, they had been a highly disciplined and effective force and played a key role in the empire's military expansion. In subsequent years, their discipline and effectiveness eroded and they became a bulwark of conservatism, resisting any change that might jeopardize their privileged position.

It is difficult to exaggerate the impact that the suppression of the Janissaries made on contemporaries, Ottomans and Westerners alike. The European press carried detailed accounts and assessments of this event.[347] It was immediately hailed as a watershed, the end of one era and the beginning of another. The Ottoman government termed the incident "The Beneficial Event" *(Vaka-yı Hayriye)* and the court historian, Esad Efendi, was charged with recording the official version for future generations. Esad's detailed account entitled *Üss-ü Zafer* (The Foundation of Victory) was printed in 1828.

Indeed, the suppression of the Janissaries cleared the way for the government to introduce sweeping reforms, which in the period from 1839 to 1876 became known as the *Tanzimat*. The cumulative effect of these measures was to transform the Ottoman state and society, and to extend the life of the empire, although within ever more constricted boundaries, for almost another century.

The modernization of the military and the bureaucracy after Western patterns remained for some time the main focus of the state's reform efforts. Soon, however, these changes produced a ripple effect, which affected almost every sphere of life. As the government, with the help of its new disciplined army and increasingly more effective administration, was able to reassert its authority over the provinces, public order and safety increased. This, in turn, encouraged economic productivity and development. Roads were built and communications improved. Measures were taken to control epidemics and improve public health. Education was greatly expanded and modernized through the establishment of a network of state schools. Gradually these came to include institutions of all levels, from elementary schools to a university and higher professional schools for the training of physicians, surgeons, dentists, lawyers, teachers, engineers, veterinarians, agronomists, and other professionals. The state also permitted its minority communities and foreign missionary groups—American, French, British, German—to develop their own educational networks. The foreign schools included such well-respected institutions as Robert College (founded 1863), the Syrian Protestant College (1866;

later the American University of Beirut), and the Catholic Université Saint-Joseph (1875).

The modernization of education—and for that matter, the implementation of all other reform measures—had to overcome numerous difficulties. In the first place, financial resources and qualified personnel were scarce. In addition, the reformers had to overcome the strong opposition of traditionalists, whose conservative attitudes were shared in varying degrees by most segments of the society. Still, it is an indication of Ottoman society's general progress that in 1895 the empire's student population exceeded 1,358,000, or over 20 percent of the population aged from 5 to 25.[348] The vast majority of these students were concentrated at the bottom of the educational system, in primary schools, and not all the ethno-religious groups were equally represented. Overall, non-Muslims attended schools in proportionately larger numbers than Muslims; and the foreign schools and those administered by the minority communities generally offered more advanced curricula than the state schools.[349] Still, already by the 1860s, the various educational networks had produced a considerable, and growing, educated class, affected in varying degrees by Western values and representing all the major ethno-religious groups that constituted Ottoman society.

The rapid growth of literacy was reflected in the growing number of printing presses, which between 1850 and 1883 increased sixfold in Istanbul, from nine to fifty four.[350] Ottoman presses published books and periodicals in a bewildering array of languages. In Turkish alone, between 1876 and 1890, some four thousand titles were published, including numerous translations and textbooks, but also original literary, scientific, religious, and other works dealing with a wide range of subjects.[351]

The growing political diversity of the Ottoman educated class was reflected in the development of journalisn. In 1840, an English journalist, William Churchill, founded the first privately owned Turkish language newspapers, *Ceride-i Havadis* (Chronicle of Events), which remained the only newspaper for some twenty years. Beginning with 1860, however, the number of Turkish newspapers began to increase. By 1867, there were eleven newspapers, reflecting different political and cultural trends, in addition to several other periodicals.[352] The press now became the focal point for the activities of intellectuals, known as Young Ottomans, who were dissatisfied with the progress and results of the reforms introduced and directed by the government. The Young Ottomans differed greatly among themselves as to the solutions they proposed to solve the empire's problems, but they were agreed on the need for constitutional reform that would limit autocracy and the arbitrary power of the bureaucracy and would guarantee individual rights.

The criticism and outspokenness of the press prompted the government to introduce strict press controls, as of 1867. As a result, many journalists and writers went abroad where they founded dozens of newspapers and reviews, many of them short-lived, in France, England, Switzerland, Egypt, Greece, and Romania. This press served the growing communities of Ottoman expatriates, but copies of its publications were also smuggled back to the Ottoman Empire. Following the Young Turk Revolution of 1908 and the liberalization of the press laws, journalism once again flourished within the Ottoman Empire. In 1913, the number of periodicals in all Ottoman territories had reached 389, including 161 in Turkish, and others in Arabic, Greek, Armenian, Hebrew, Judeo-Spanish, and various Slavic and European languages.[353]

The Disintegration of the Ottoman Empire

In spite of considerable progress, the survival of the Ottoman Empire continued to be threatened. In the course of the nineteenth century, direct external military threat by the European powers had somewhat receded. It was replaced, however, by the greater danger of separatist nationalism from within. Following the Congress of Vienna (1815), an overall conservative international order, known as the Concert of Europe, came into existence. In the Near East, the Great Powers—Britain, Austria, Russia, Prussia, and France—generally preferred to preserve the status quo, that is the continued existence of the Ottoman Empire over the political uncertainties and possible war, which might ensue as a result of its breakup. In July 1833, the British foreign minister, Lord Palmerston, went so far as to state: "The integrity and independence of the Ottoman Empire are necessary to the maintenance of the tranquility, the liberty, and the balance of power in the rest of Europe."[354]

However, in the face of Balkan nationalist agitation and armed uprisings, the Great Powers could not remain impassive, and they were compelled, time and again, to intervene in these crises. Russia was generally more eager than the other powers to support the separatist movements and to exploit the restiveness of the Ottoman Christians to its own advantage. The other Great Powers attempted to curb Russia's adventurism, but even they, and especially Britain and France, were impelled, from time to time, by liberal public opinion to support the rising nations. Indeed, it was through European intervention that Serbia gained its autonomy in 1830 and independence in 1878; Greece became a sovereign state in 1832; the Danubian Principalities (Moldavia and Wallachia) were united in 1859, an act which paved the way for their independence in 1878 as the state of Romania; Montenegro was recognized as independent in 1878; Bulgaria first became autonomous in 1878 and, following several intermediate stages, became independent in 1908; and Albania proclaimed its independence in 1912.

The progressive breakup of the Ottoman Empire, especially as of 1875, which to a large measure was brought about through the intervention of the European powers, served as a self-fulfilling prophecy. It further undermined the confidence that the Great Powers, even those friendly to the Ottoman Empire, had in the latter's ability to survive. The Sick Man of Europe, as the Ottoman Empire became known, appeared to be approaching its demise. Consequently, in order to secure what appeared to them as their vital interests, even some of the Ottoman Empire's supporters began to seize strategically important Ottoman provinces. Britain, the country that most consistently supported the Ottoman Empire throughout most of the nineteenth century, took control of Cyprus in 1878 and of Egypt in 1882 (Egypt had been granted a special status under the hereditary rule of the house of Muhammad Ali since 1841). In 1878, Austria occupied Bosnia, Herzegovina, and Novi Bazar, and formally annexed the first two provinces in 1908. Algeria and Tunisia were occupied by France in 1830 and 1881, respectively. In 1911, Italy occupied Tripoli and the Dodecanese Islands. By the end of the Balkan Wars (1912–13), during which the Ottoman Empire was attacked by Bulgaria, Serbia, Greece, Montenegro and Albania, the Ottomans lost almost all of their remaining European possessions, including Crete, and were left only with eastern Thrace. In Asia, the Ottomans still controlled Anatolia and the Arab provinces.

The Policies of Ottomanism

The extent of the dangers inherent in the nationalities problem was recognized by successive Ottoman governments since the Serbs first rose in rebellion in the early years of the nineteenth century. The initial official Ottoman response was guided by traditional maxims of government. Acting on the assumption that the uprising was the result of external agitation, on the one hand, and internal misgovernment caused by excessive decentralization, on the other,[355] the Ottomans attempted to suppress the uprising through a combination of conciliation and force. On the one hand, they offered the Serbs extensive internal autonomy, complete amnesty, and tax relief. At the same time, however, they moved to liquidate through military force, all independent centers of power and impose a greater measure of central control throughout the affected provinces. This policy proved temporarily successful in the case of the Serbs, but it completely miscarried in the case of the Greeks.[356]

The Greek uprising (1821–30) and the eventual emergence of a small, independent Greek state (1832) through European intervention sent shockwaves throughout all echelons of the Ottoman government and the political public.[357] It was immediately apparent that Greek independence, even within limited boundaries, could become a precedent for other separatist national movements, for further European intervention, and for the eventual dismemberment of the empire. To counter this mortal threat, new and urgent measures had to be devised. The non-Muslim minorities of the empire had to be assured that their future within the Ottoman polity was preferable to what it might be in the small national successor states. Equally, or more importantly, the European Powers had to be convinced of that. Thus began an official Ottoman attempt to reshape and redefine the very nature of the Ottoman polity. This resulted in the articulation of an official theory of Ottomanism, or Ottoman patriotism. Whereas the traditional concept of the state as essentially Islamic was not discarded, two new elements, pluralism and equality before the law, were grafted onto it. The purpose of Ottomanism was to blur, and even eradicate, the traditional perception of Ottoman society as divided between a ruling people, Muslims, and non-Muslim subject peoples.

In his latter years, Sultan Mahmud II is reported to have stated: "I distinguish among my subjects, Muslims in the mosque, Christians in the church and Jews in the synagogue, but there is no difference among them in any other way. My affection and sense of justice for all of them is strong and they are all indeed my children."[358]

On November 3, 1839, in an impressive ceremony attended by the foreign diplomatic corps, the Ottoman government proclaimed the Imperial Rescript (*Hatt-ı Hümayun*; also known as Noble Rescript,

Hatt-ı Şerif) of Gülhane. This document formally introduced the new policy of Ottomanism. Among promises to reform the taxation and military conscription systems, it included a commitment for equal justice for all Ottoman subjects, regardless of religion, and the "perfect security" of their life, honor and property. The stated purpose of the rescript was to promote every subject's "devotion for state (*devlet*), *millet*, and love of country (*vatan mahabbeti*)." The meaning of the term millet in this context was left ambiguous, perhaps purposefully. Did the drafters of the document intend it to mean "nation" in the modern Western sense (i.e., the Ottoman nation), or was it intended in its traditional meaning of "religious community," more familiar to Ottomans? A French translation of the rescript, prepared by the Ottoman government and distributed at the time of the ceremony, skirted the issue altogether by not translating the term.[359] To a contemporary Ottoman, the rescript could have suggested official recognition of the religious community as an instrument to promote the loyalty of all Ottoman subjects to their state and country.

Some time in the mid-nineteenth century, and perhaps as early as 1835, a new political term, *milel-i erba'a*, entered the Ottoman political lexicon (Avigdor Levy). Literally meaning "the four communities," it came to denote the officially recognized four religious communities that constituted the Ottoman polity—"Muslims, Jews, Armenians and Greeks," as Redhouse ranged them.[360] The purpose of this term was to suggest that the Ottoman Empire, while a Muslim state, was at the same time also a plural society in which the minorities' special status was officially recognized.

As of the 1840s, the state introduced legal reforms, modeled on Western patterns, intended to implement the principle of equality before the law between Muslims and non-Muslims. Additionally, non-Muslims were appointed to newly-instituted municipal, district, provincial, and state councils. They were also encouraged to join the bureaucracy and the various branches of government, which they did in increasing numbers. However, the ideals of Ottomanism were articulated slowly and implemented hesitatingly, and they encountered opposition from many quarters. Establishing legal equality between Muslims and non-Muslims progressed fitfully. It was completed only in 1908, following the Young Turk Revolution, when to many observers it appeared that time had run out on the Ottoman experiment in pluralism.[361]

Renewed Awareness of the Overlapping Ottoman and Jewish Interests and the Office of *Haham Başı*

The need to redefine the nature of the Ottoman polity on the basis of pluralism brought the Ottoman government to reassess the status of the Jewish community, whose usefulness became immediately apparent. In contrast to the numerically strong, and in many areas densely concentrated, Orthodox (*Rum*) and Armenian communities, the Jews were practically everywhere throughout the Ottoman dominions a small minority, which could not possibly entertain separatist ambitions. Moreover, the Christians, including the small Catholic and Protestant communities, had strongly committed European patrons. The Jews did not. The Jews were, however, a universally-recognized religious community. The question of their civil liberties had become a somewhat prominent political issue in European affairs in the post-1815 era, gaining support especially among liberal circles.[362] Finally, in the collective consciousness of the Ottoman ruling elite, there might have lingered memories of Jewish past usefulness and loyalty and the coincidence of the Jews' interests with those of the Ottoman state.

Indeed, the Serbian and Greek uprisings further underscored this last point. They demonstrated that the Jews, like the Turks, had everything to fear from the rise of national states in the Balkans and much to gain from the continued survival of the Ottoman Empire. Thus, the Turkish-Jewish mutuality of interests once again came to the surface. Consequently, to promote the principle and image of a plural Ottoman society, it became a matter of state interest to advance the position of the Jewish community and grant it greater prominence. The first step in that direction was taken in 1835, with the granting of formal recognition to Ottoman Jewry as one of the "official" communities constituting the Ottoman body politic. In the spirit of the time, such formal recognition needed to be conferred on a specific representative individual, and, thus, the office of *haham başı*, or chief rabbi, came into existence.

As has been noted, in past centuries the Jews had fashioned their own unique internal leadership and administration, consisting of local lay and religious leaders. In general, the representation of the community before the Ottoman authorities was in the hands of lay leaders. Since the seventeenth century, however, the religious leadership became more or less institutionalized and vested in the office of the local chief rabbinate, which often consisted of a collective body of two or three rabbis. Each of these chief rabbis was known in Hebrew as *rav ha-kolel*. The Ottoman authorities recognized the privilege of the local Jewish communities to form their own leadership, but as a rule, they did not intervene in the process and did not grant official recognition to the individuals holding the office of chief rabbi. This situation prevailed until 1835. Now, however, in the view of the Ottoman authorities this was no longer adequate. Consequently, in January 1835, the Ottomans introduced the official position of haham başı and conferred it ceremoniously on Rabbi Abraham Levi. The new position was to be equal, in principle, to that of the Orthodox and Armenian ecclesiastical leaders. This meant that the haham başı was now regarded as the civil and religious head of the Jewish community, as well as its official representative before the authorities. This required that his appointment receive official sanction from the state through the granting of a diploma (*berat*). The new office was first introduced in Istanbul and it was accepted by the community with considerable suspicion and reluctance. The outcome was that for almost thirty years, until 1864, there were, in fact, two separate offices of "chief rabbis" in Istanbul. The rav ha-kolel continued to be regarded by the Jews as their religious and spiritual leader, while the office of haham başı was seen as an external imposition and as far as the community was concerned it was only ceremonial and representative (Avigdor Levy) . In time, however, the office of haham başı gained increased prestige and importance and came to be held by renowned scholars, such as Rabbi Jacob (Ya'akov) Avigdor (1860–63) and Rabbi Yakir Geron (Guéron; 1863–72). Consequently, by 1864, the office of haham başı appears to have completely supplanted in Istanbul the older office of rav ha-kolel.[363]

Meanwhile, however, as it gained increased importance, the office of haham başı became the focus of an intense power struggle within the Jewish community of Istanbul. The controversy involved not only personalities, but also differences between traditionalists and modernists. The Ottoman authorities in general supported the modernists. They exerted pressure on the community to reform and adopt a statute that would regulate the community's internal administration and make it more representative of the laity, as the Greek and Armenian millets had done in 1860 and 1863, respectively. Indeed, in 1865, under the leadership of Rabbi Geron, the Jewish community of Istanbul adopted an elaborate organic statute (*nizamname*), which defined different authorities within the community: religious, lay and mixed.

Due, however, to continued internal dissent, the statute remained largely a dead letter. For all these reasons, the authorities decided that it would be best to appoint in Istanbul an acting chief rabbi (*haham başı kaymakamı* or, in brief, *kaymakam*).[364] Although it was intended as a temporary measure, this arrangement lasted in the capital from 1863 to 1909. Those who held this title were Rabbis Yakir Geron (1863–72), Moshe Levi (Ha-Levi; 1872–1908), and Haim Nahum (Hayyim Nahoum; 1908–9). In spite of the seeming diminution in the title of the chief rabbi of Istanbul, his responsibilities remained the same and his powers probably increased. Since the community's statute was not implemented, and regular representative bodies did not come into existence, the acting chief rabbis and their conservative supporters effectively ruled the community until 1908. Following the Young Turk Revolution, Rabbi Haim Nahum, who had been close to Young Turk circles, was appointed Acting Chief Rabbi. In 1909, the Ottoman government conferred on him the new title, "Chief Rabbi of All the Jews of the Capital and Its Dependencies and of All the Jews Resident in the Ottoman Empire."[365] Haim Nahum was the only one to hold this title and he served in this capacity until 1920 (Esther Benbassa).

Shortly after the introduction of the office of haham başı in Istanbul, it was instituted also in other Jewish communities: in Izmir, Salonica and Bursa in September 1835; in Edirne and Sofia in July 1836.[366] In subsequent years, haham başıs were appointed also in Sarajevo (Saray Bosna; 1840), Jerusalem (1841), Baghdad (1849), and Tripoli in North Africa (1874).[367] What distinguished these cities was that they all were important Ottoman administrative centers; they were the home to significant Jewish communities; and they were also the seat of important foreign consular offices. The presence of chief rabbis, who participated in official ceremonies and served as members of local councils, contributed to the principle and appearance of pluralism. It should be pointed out, however, that both the title and office of rav ha-kolel remained in use in many Jewish communities, especially in those where a haham başı was not appointed.[368]

Although the haham başı of Istanbul was not in any sense hierarchically superior to the provincial haham başıs, he served as the representative of the Jewish millet in all important state ceremonies[369] and was regarded by the authorities as the official channel to convey the central government's wishes to all the Jewish communities throughout the empire.[370] Appointments of provincial haham başıs were technically made at the request of the haham başı of the capital. The letter granting the imperial diploma generally contained a standard formula, stating that the appointment was granted in response to "a sealed written petition" (*memhur arzuhal*) presented by the haham başı of Istanbul. In reality, the haham başı of the capital had little to do with these appointments, which were determined by the local communities.[371]

Jewish Participation in Government Service and Enrollment in State Schools

The appointment of haham başıs, however, was only the beginning. Jewish physicians began to reappear at the sultan's court. In the late 1830s, the Jewish dentist Jacob Bivaz entered the palace service where he was employed for some thirty years.[372] In 1844, Dr. Spitzer, a Moravian Jew, became a physician and political advisor to Sultan Abdülmecid (Abdul-Mejid).[373] During the reign of Abdülhamid (Abdul-Hamid) II, several Jewish physicians and dentists were employed in the palace. These included Elias Pasha Cohen, Isidore Pasha Greiwer, Leon Behar, David Hayon, and Sami Günsberg.[374]

The government, it seems, also took great care to insure that Jewish representatives were appointed to the newly instituted municipal, district, provincial, and state councils. This appears to have been a statewide policy implemented wherever significant Jewish communities were found.[375] Even in remote Tripoli in North Africa, the Ottoman authorities insured that Jewish representatives were appointed to the local councils and that they served in the newly established criminal and commercial law courts (Rachel Simon). In fact, because the Jews were primarily urban dwellers and because the government was interested in having them represented in local and state institutions, especially ones that received international notice, in some instances the Jews were overrepresented, compared to their relative share in the general population. In the latter decades of the nineteenth century, when Ottoman statistics became more reliable, it was calculated that the Jewish population of the empire constituted only a little more than one percent of the general population.[376] Jewish overrepresentation was reflected, for example, in the Council of State (*Şura-yı Devlet*), established in 1868, as a central legislative body representing statewide communities and interests. Of its thirty-eight members, all

Table 4
Estimated Numbers of Jews in the Ottoman Empire, 1904–8

Area	Year	Number of Jews	Percentage of General Population
European Turkey	1904	188,896	3.20
Palestine	1908	85,000	14.00
Asia Minor and Syria	1908	75,000	0.55
Mesopotamia	1908	40,000	?
Arabia (Yemen)	1908	40,000	?
Tripoli (Africa)	1905	18,660	1.86
Total		447,556	

Source: Ruppin, *The Jews of To-Day*, pp. 39–41.

appointed by the sultan, two were Jews, Bekhor Efendi Eskenazi and David Efendi Carmona.[377]

Jewish overrepresentation was even more pronounced in the first Ottoman parliament of 1877–78. The deputies to this body were not elected through popular suffrage, but were appointed by the provincial administrative councils, with the central government determining the number of representatives for each of the religious communities, presumably in proportion to their relative local numerical strength. In the parliament's first session, the Jews had four deputies of a total of 119, and one senator of a total of 32. In the second session, the number of Jewish deputies was increased to six, whereas the size of the Chamber declined to 113. Thus, acccording to Devereux, in the second session the Jews were represented by one deputy for every 12,500 males, whereas the Christians and Muslims had one deputy for every 110,058 and 147,953, respectively.[378] In the Ottoman parliaments in session during the period 1908–18, the Jews had a more proportionate representation of four deputies out of a total of 288. In spite of their small numbers, however, Jewish deputies were found in prominent positions in a number of parliamentary committees (Hasan Kayalı).

The Ottoman state was also interested in Jewish participation in government service and the civil bureaucracy. Since there were few Jews competent to hold such positions, in the early 1840s the authorities exerted considerable pressure on the Jewish community to send Jewish students to state educational institutions.[379] The government was particularly interested in Jewish enrollments in the Imperial School of Medicine (*Tıbhane-i Âmire*), established in 1827 for the primary purpose of training physicians for the military.[380] In 1834, the first Jewish student graduated from the school[381] and it is possible that others followed (Aron Rodrigue). Their numbers, however, must have been considerably less than what the Ottoman authorities had expected.[382] To encourage greater enrollments of Jewish students, in 1847, Sultan Abdülmecid ordered that the school employ a rabbi to supervise daily religious services; that a special kitchen be set up where Jewish dietary laws could be observed; and that Jewish students be allowed special leave every week to observe the Sabbath at their homes.[383] In that year, 15 Jewish students attended the medical school together with some 300 Turks, 40 Greeks and 29 Armenians. In the following year, 1848, there were already 24 Jewish students in the school, and their numbers continued to increase in subsequent years. The school's director at that time was the Moravian Jew, Dr. Spitzer.[384]

The results were quite remarkable. Galanté has compiled what he describes as an incomplete list of Jewish physicians who served in senior positions in the armed forces in the late Ottoman period. Of the thirty-five listed, four attained the rank of General and four others that of Admiral, which conferred on them the title Pasha. In addition, more than fifty Jewish physicians served in the civil administration and eight became instructors in the medical school itself.[385]

In the 1850s, Jews were encouraged to enroll as trainees in the Translation Bureau (*Tercüme Odası*) of the Foreign Ministry. One of those, David (Davud) Molho, attained in 1880 the position of First Translator of the Imperial Council (*Divan-i Hümayun*), an office that he held for some thirty years.[386]

Jewish students were also encouraged to enroll in the prestigious Imperial *Lycée* of Galatasaray after it was opened in 1868. In this institution, too, arrangements were made to meet the religious requirements of the Jewish students, as well as those of Muslims and Christians.[387] Thirty-four Jewish students were among the 341 students enrolled in the school in that year. The Jews thus constituted about 10 percent of the school's student population, which was approximately twice their relative share of about 5 percent of the capital's population.[388] In subsequent years, growing numbers of Jews attended

Table 5
The Population of Istanbul, 1897

Group	Number	Percentage of Total
Turks	597,000	56.36
Greeks	236,000	22.29
Armenians	162,000	15.30
Jews	47,000	4.44
Others	17,000	1.61
Total	1,059,000	100.00

Source: Karpat, *Ottoman Population,* p. 104.

state secondary and higher educational institutions.[389] Thus, it is important to note that the first organized effort to modernize and transform Ottoman Jewry through education came from the state; and its main purpose was similar to that which guided the government's efforts in creating a modern-oriented Muslim elite, namely state service.

By 1885, 99 Jewish residents of Istanbul were reported to be employed in government service. These were modest numbers. Muslims continued to constitute the overwhelming majority of state employees. Proportionately to their numbers, however, the ratio of Jews was slightly higher than that of Greeks, but somewhat lower than that of Armenians.[390] Less than two generations since the very modest

Table 6
Jews and Christians Employed in Government Service in Istanbul, 1885

Religious Group	Male Population in Istanbul (1885)	Persons Employed in Government Service	Percentage of Group's Male Population
Jews	22,394	99	0.44
Greeks	91,804	348	0.38
Armenians	83,870	494	0.58
Catholics	3,209	150	4.67

Sources: Shaw and Shaw, vol. 2, p. 244; Karpat, *Ottoman Population,* p. 105.

beginnings of the processes of modernization within the Jewish community, in relative terms, the Jews had begun to catch up with the more advanced Christian minority groups. In the coming years, the numbers of Jews in government service continued to increase. Galanté lists twenty-four Jews serving in various diplomatic, consular, and administrative positions in the Ottoman Foreign Ministry in the empire's last decades. Dozens of others served in the ministries of justice, finance, education, police, and other government branches.[391]

As the last, and smallest, ethnic group to enter government service, the Jews never quite attained the same prominent positions as did the Christians.[392] In the short period following the Young Turk Revolution (1908), however, Jews appear to have gained ground in government service. Jews active in the Committee of Union and Progress attained a number of influential and sensitive positions. Emanuel Salem was responsible for drafting new bills for presentation before the Assembly; Ezekiel Sasoon served as undersecretary in the Ministry of Agriculture and subsequently in the Ministry of Commerce; Nissim Russo held an equally important position in the Ministry of Finance; Vitali Stroumsa became a member of the Supreme Council for Financial Reform; and Samuel Israel was chief of the political section of Istanbul's police force, a most sensitive and powerful position. Jews never became cabinet ministers, as did Christians, but in Feroz Ahmad's estimate, "as undersecretaries and technocrats in key ministries . . . their role in policymaking was probably more significant than that of the minister."[393]

The Modernization of Jewish Education and the Rise of a New Leadership

While the first successful, though limited, organized drive to modernize Ottoman Jewry through education was initiated by the Ottoman state, by the end of the nineteenth century, Western Jewish philanthropical organizations assumed the leading role in this area. This, however, does not diminish the importance of the pioneering role that state institutions played in the development of a Jewish secular, educated elite, and in breaking the monopoly exercised by the conservative Jewish religious establishment over the community's educational system. The state institutions laid the groundwork for, and in many ways facilitated the work of, Western Jewish organizations.

The earliest attempt on the part of Western Jews to encourage Ottoman Jewry to introduce modern secular education was linked to the visit of Sir Moses Montefiori to Istanbul in 1840, in connection with the Damascus blood libel affair. This early attempt bore no immediate results, however, and it was only in 1854 that the first modern Jewish school was founded in Istanbul through the cooperation of Western and local Jews (Aron Rodrigue). Attempts to establish modern Jewish schools were also undertaken in Izmir, Salonica, and Edirne during the 1850s, but these efforts met with little success and they evenutally failed. In 1856, a wealthy Austrian family established in Jerusalem the Laemel School, which provided secular and religious education in German. In 1864, Ferdinand James Rothschild of Vienna established in Jerusalem the Evelina de Rothschild School for girls, in memory of his wife. The language of instruction in this institution was at first French and later English. Everywhere, however, the new schools met with strong opposition by conservatives led by influential figures from within the religious establishment.[394]

A new era in modern Jewish education in the Ottoman Empire began in the 1860s, with the establishment of modern schools sponsored by the Alliance Israélite Universelle. Founded in Paris in 1860, the aims of the Alliance were "to work everywhere for the emancipation and moral progress of the Jews,"[395] and for their integration within the societies of their respective countries. One of the principal means adopted by the Alliance to achieve its objectives was through educational work and the foundation of modern schools. The educational activities of the Alliance in the Ottoman Empire unfolded slowly and hesitatingly. Of the first three schools founded in Baghdad, Damascus, and Volos in 1864, the last two closed within a few years.[396] The activities of the Alliance began to take hold only in the 1870s, with the successful establishment of schools in Edirne (1867), Izmir (1873), Salonica (1873), and Istanbul (1875).[397]

The Alliance's mode of operation varied from place to place and over time. In general, however, the Alliance provided part of the funds necessary to establish and operate its schools; it also provided curricula, teachers, principals, a plan of action, and leadership. Its success depended, however, on the material and moral cooperation of the local communities, or, at the very least, on the support of some leading elements within them. Also crucial to the successful operations of the Alliance was the attitude of the Ottoman authorities. In spite of their strong French orientation, the Alliance schools were set up as local community institutions, and, unlike other European schools, they did not request the protection of foreign powers. Their curricula stressed modernity and Ottoman patriotism and they were seen, therefore, by the Ottoman authorities as complementing the work of the state schools. The modernizing, and often French-speaking, Ottoman bureaucratic elite appears to have been particularly supportive of the Alliance activities. The well-known reformer, Midhat Pasha, for example, while governor of Baghdad (1869–71) was instrumental in expanding and developing the local Alliance school. In 1880, when he served as governor of Damascus, Midhat played an important role in the reopening of the Alliance school of Damascus after it had remained closed for more than a decade.[398] The supportive attitude of the Ottoman authorities insured, in effect, the success of the Alliance's educational work within the Jewish community.

The Alliance's activities were intensified after 1890, when it expanded its network in the large urban centers, and also extended it to smaller communities, in places such as Bursa, Aydın, Kasaba, Tire, Bergama, Manisa, Tekirdağ, Jaffa, Haifa, Safed, Tiberias, Basra, Mosul, Hilla, Amara, and Kirkuk.[399] By 1912, the Alliance operated 115 schools in the Ottoman Empire of which 71 were for boys and 44 for girls. Geographically, 52 of the schools were located in European provinces and 63 in the Asiatic provinces.[400] As of 1890, the number of students enrolled in the Alliance schools sharply increased, as can be seen from the following figures pertaining to schools located within the borders of present-day Turkey: in 1875, 773 students were enrolled; in 1900, 7,267; in 1910, 11,101; and in 1913, 11,687.[401] On the eve of the First World War, the Alliance schools throughout the Ottoman Empire had a total enrollment of approximately 19,000 students,[402] which constituted almost 5 percent of the total Jewish population. In Istanbul, about 35 percent of the Jewish school-age population attended Alliance schools, and this appears to have been the average for all these communities located within the borders of present-day Turkey.[403]

In addition to a major school system, the Alliance established in the Ottoman Empire a network of related and ancillary organizations, which included alumni associations, mutual-aid societies, and reading clubs. The Alliance became, thereby, a major factor in shaping the world-view of Ottoman Jewry. Its activities also contributed to the strengthening of ties among the Jewish communities throughout the Ottoman Empire, and between them and the world Jewish diaspora.

These had important ramifications for the advancement of the Jews' socioeconomic and cultural condition.

Within the major Jewish communities of the Ottoman Empire, the graduates of the Alliance schools and all those who subscribed to the Alliance's vision of "regeneration" were known as Alliancists. By the late nineteenth century, they had emerged as a major opinion group, challenging rabbinical authorities and their conservative supporters who controlled the community's institutions. In several important areas, the Alliance's ideology coincided with that of the Young Turks, and many of the Alliancists became active in the ranks of the Young Turks, or were close to them. Following the Young Turk Revolution, three of the four Jews serving in the new Ottoman Chamber of Deputies, Carasso, Farraggi and Masliah, were both Alliance graduates and members of the Committee of Union and Progress.[404] Indeed, from 1908 and until 1920, Alliancist notables came to dominate the Jewish community's institutions. Their point man was Haim Nahum, who at the age of thirty-six became the Chief Rabbi of the Ottoman Empire (Esther Benbassa).

In addition to the Alliance schools, considerable numbers of Jewish students attended a variety of other European institutions, a few of them Jewish, but mostly not. French and British schools, including missionary institutions, appear to have been particularly popular.[405] In 1906, for example, 490 Jewish students were attending English Protestant schools in the Hasköy quarter of Istanbul. A similar number were enrolled in French schools in Istanbul, supported by the French government.[406]

Jewish Upward Mobility and the Resurgence of Christian Anti-Semitism

The modernization of Ottoman Jewry through the various networks of state schools, the Alliance, and other Western organizations, resulted in considerable upward economic and social mobility. Although the Jews continued to lag behind the Greeks and the Armenians, by the end of the nineteenth century a new, and growing, Jewish middle class had emerged. Equipped with modern education and skills, increasing numbers of Jews were steadily able to make their way into the liberal professions, new sectors of commerce and finance, government service, and the trades.[407]

For their economic advancement, however, the Jews had to pay a price. The Greek and Armenian communities were particularly resentful of Jewish penetration into areas of economic activity, which had been dominated by them for a long time. This appears to have been a major factor contributing to the resurgence of anti-Semitic attitudes among the Ottoman Christians after 1860, resulting in acts of violence directed against Jews. As far as the Jews were concerned, these circumstances further underscored the commonality of interests that they felt they shared with the Muslim element and the state, which protected them against violence (Jacob M. Landau).[408]

Ottoman Jewry's Cultural Diversity and Growing Politicization: Young Turks and Zionists

The processes of modernization greatly affected also the internal structure of Ottoman Jewry by further increasing its cultural diversity and contributing to its growing politicization. The Jews, like other segments of the society, were caught up between the conflicting forces of traditionalism and modernity, and between Ottoman patriotism and separatist nationalism. For most of the nineteenth century, a plural Ottomanism had clearly been the preferred option for most politically minded Jews, and important segments of the Jewish political public continued to adhere to these ideals to the very end of the empire. It was for this reason that Jews played a disproportionately important role in the Young Turk movement (a later extension of the Young Ottoman movement), in general, and in the affairs of the Committee of Union and Progress (CUP or Unionists, in brief), in particular. They were far, however, from dominating the CUP, as claimed by the latter's critics and detractors (Şükrü Hanioğlu).[409]

Before the 1908 Young Turk Revolution, the CUP, together with other political groups, strove to end Abdülhamid's despotism and reestablish a constitutional regime, in order to save the empire from a predictable collapse. Following the revolution, however, as external challenges and internal difficulties combined to further break up the empire and frustrate the hopes of Ottomanism, the CUP increasingly espoused elements of Turkish nationalism. Even at this stage, Jews continued to hold prominent positions within the movement. Of all the Ottoman minorities, the Jewish community was the only one to provide the CUP with a front-line leader, Emanuel Carasso (Karasu), and an important ideologue, Moise Cohen Tekinalp.[410] The Jewish representatives who served in the Ottoman parliaments during the years 1908–18 were all CUP members (Hasan Kayalı). It is arguable, however, to what extent these individuals represented wide currents within the Jewish community (Jacob M. Landau).[411]

Another outcome of modernization was the increased familiarity of growing numbers of Ottoman Jews with the ideas of political Zionism. Zionism appeared to offer a range of ideals and solutions similar to those espoused by important segments of the political elites of most of the empire's ethnic groups. Additionally,. Zionism had the advantage that it appealed to a sentiment deeply rooted within the Jewish psyche, and many—traditionalists, as well as modernists—embraced it.[412] In fact, Zionism was the only mass movement that could bridge the chasm between tradition and modernity. Since there were currents within Zionism that stressed a cultural revival, rather than a political one, and since the establishment of a Jewish state was not an imminent possibility, to many Ottoman Jews, as well as to some Young Turk spokesmen, the contradictions between Zionism and Ottomanism did not appear unbridgeable (İlber Oratylı).

No doubt, many Ottoman Jews shared the views of Lucien Sciuto, author of "The Outcasts," and later editor of the pro-Zionist Jewish paper *L'Aurore*, who saw Zionism and Ottomanism as complementing each other and who advocated an Ottoman-Zionist alliance. In February 1913, he wrote: "Our dearest dream—the dream of the whole of Jewry—is to see a great and strong Turkey marching resolutely towards its future, parallel with a powerful Jewry also going freely to its destiny."[413] World Jewry, continued Sciuto, could not support the Ottoman Empire with armed forces, but with assets even more powerful: "By its speakers, by its thinkers, by its politicians and . . . financiers . . . it is a great force of a different kind to be reckoned with, because it can lead all the others."[414] Sciuto called on the Ottoman government to abolish all restrictions on Jewish immigration to Palestine. Nothing concrete ever came out of this and other similar proposals, and Ottoman policy continued to be basically opposed to Zionist aims. Nevertheless, the CUP appears to have regarded Zionism in a category by itself, different from that of other nationalist movements, and its leaders were prepared to engage in a dialogue with Zionist spokesmen (Şükrü Hanioğlu; İlber Ortaylı).[415]

Within the Jewish community, support for Zionism appears to have sharply increased following the Young Turk Revolution. The greater freedom of expression and association contributed to this process. With the coming to power of the Alliancist notables, the Zionists sought to play the role of a party in opposition to the ruling establishment. This, too, contributed to their growing popularity even among Alliance graduates. The objective of the local Zionists appears to have been to gain enough popular support so as to be in a position to influence the community's leadership and through them the Ottoman authorities. For the most part, however, the local Zionists limited their activities to the Jewish community and conducted them in a semicovert fashion. For this reason, and in spite of the spirited debate in the local Jewish press, the degree of Zionism's popularity among Ottoman Jewry appears to have escaped the notice of most outside observers (Esther Benbassa).

Jewish Immigration and Emigration

Many Jews responded to the political turmoil and economic hardships that marked the last years of the empire with their feet, namely, by emigration. In this respect, it is possible to say that the Western education provided by the Alliance and the other Western organizations, facilitated Jewish mobility not only upward, but also outward. The demographic picture of Ottoman Jewry in the last decades of the empire is that of a community in a high state of flux, experiencing both considerable in- and outmigration.

Throughout the nineteenth century, and especially after 1875, as the Ottoman Empire continued to withdraw, giving rise to new nation-states in the Balkans, a pattern of a population movement set in, whereby considerable numbers of Jews, together with even larger numbers of Muslims, migrated from the newly independent states to the remaining Ottoman territories. The Balkan Jews were joined by considerable numbers of Russian Jews also seeking refuge in the Ottoman Empire. These immigrants were generally well received, and even assisted, by the Ottoman authorities and the local Jewish communities (Kemal H. Karpat). In 1893, Sultan Abdülhamid II even entertained the idea, never actually realized, of a mass settlement of Jewish refugees from Russia and other countries in eastern Anatolia.[416] Although Jews could settle almost anywhere in the Ottoman Empire, the Ottoman government vigorously, but unsuccessfully, resisted Zionist settlement in Palestine.[417]

Many of the Jewish immigrants remained, however, in the Ottoman Empire only temporarily, although sometimes for extended periods. Once uprooted from their ancestral homes, and finding it difficult to strike new roots in the impoverished Ottoman Empire, many of these immigrants moved again, mainly to Western Europe, the Americas, and several African countries. This outward movement also swept with it established Ottoman Jews, who were attracted by economic opportunity in the West. The modern education and Western languages that many of them had recently acquired further facilitated this movement.[418] Between 1899 to 1912, close to 8,000 Ottoman Jews immigrated to the United States alone.[419] In France, several thousand Ottoman Jews were found stranded in 1914, when the First World War had placed France and the Ottoman Empire in opposing camps.[420] The Jews of the Ottoman Empire had thus joined their brothers from Eastern Europe in the great migratory movement to the West.

Jewish Settlement in Palestine

The increased mobility of Ottoman Jews had also significant ramifications for the modern Jewish settlement in Palestine. The relation of Ottoman Jewry to Palestine had been unique throughout the centuries. Considerable amounts of money were regularly collected in Jewish communities for the support of scholarly and charitable institutions in Palestine, particularly in Jerusalem, Safed, Tiberias, and Hebron. Many Jews considered it an act of piety to spend their last years in the Holy Land, or at least to have their remains interred in its soil. Younger persons, including some prominent rabbis, were also attracted by the sanctity of the land and chose to settle there. The Jewish communities generally helped those of their members, who were desirous of living in Palestine.[421]

"Modern" Jewish immigration to Palestine began in the late eighteenth century, with the arrival of groups of Jewish immigrants from Poland and North Africa. In the 1820s, considerable numbers of Jews arrived in Palestine from the Balkans and especially from those areas affected by the Greek uprising and the Ottoman-Russian War of 1828–29.[422] In the 1830s and 1840s, with improved communications and public order, Jewish travel to, and settlement in, Palestine appreciably increased. The sources are replete with information regarding leading Ottoman Jewish figures, who went to Palestine for purposes of pilgrimage, study, or settlement.[423] For example, the haham başı of Izmir, Rabbi Joshua Raphael Pinhas de Ciégura (Segura; also known as Moreno), on his retirement in 1847, moved to Jerusalem, where he died in 1851.[424] The acting chief rabbi of Istanbul, Yakir Geron, settled in Jerusalem in 1872 after resigning from his office.[425] Rabbi Abraham Rosanes of Rusçuk, the father of the historian Solomon Rosanes, attempted, in 1867, to settle in Palestine, but returned after some time to his native town. In 1874, the twelve-year-old Solomon went with his uncle Mordekhai Rosanes, a wealthy merchant and contractor for the Ottoman army, on an extended pilgrimage to Palestine. In the course of the visit in Jerusalem, Mordekhai had the prayer plaza facing the Western (Wailing) Wall repaved.[426] In the 1870s, the family of Haim Nahum, the future chief rabbi of the Ottoman Empire, moved from Manisa to Tiberias, where the young Haim obtained his elementary education.[427] In addition to these well-known figures and additional individuals whose settlement in Palestine was documented, there were also many others.

Indeed, in the years 1916–18, the Zionist Organization conducted a thorough and detailed census of the Jewish population in Palestine. The census revealed that of 472 Jewish immigrants, who had come to Palestine in the period 1842–81 (before the beginning of Zionist immigration), and who survived until 1916–18, 37 percent came from Asia and North Africa, reflecting essentially an internal Jewish migration within the Ottoman Empire, exclusive of its European provinces; 29.4 percent came from Russia; and 33.6 percent came from various other European countries.[428] In the period 1882–1903 (the First *Aliyah*), for which detailed statistics are available, 63.6 percent of the Jewish immigrants came from Russia; 18.9 percent came from Asia, Africa, and the Balkans, reflecting, again, largely an internal Ottoman migration; and smaller numbers came from other countries. For the period 1904–14 (the Second Aliyah), the figures are 67.1 percent from Russia and 24.8 percent from Asia, Africa, and the Balkans.[429] These numbers suggest that Ottoman Jewry was the most important single source of Jewish immigration to Palestine from 1842 to 1881, when Palestinian Jewry increased from about 7,000 or 8,000 to an estimated 25,000 persons. From 1882 to 1914, when Palestinian Jewry rose from 25,000 to an estimated 94,000 persons,[430] Ottoman Jews constituted the second most important source, after Russia's Jewry, contributing about 20 percent of all the immigrants, in spite of the fact that Ottoman Jewry represented only about four percent of the world's total Jewish population (Kemal H. Karpat).

Jewish Losses, 1912–23

The decade encompassing the Balkan Wars (1912–13), the First World War (1914–18), and the Turkish War of Independence (1918–

23) witnessed particularly heavy losses of life and property throughout the Ottoman Empire. The Jews, like other groups, were also affected by the carnage and destruction. However, for a variety of reasons, the full account of their losses has remained largely untold (Justin McCarthy).

The "Best Years" of Ottoman Jewry in Modern Times

In modern times, perhaps the best years for Ottoman Jewry were the 1890s—the period immediately preceding the violent unrest, intense political agitation, revolution, war and the eventual demise of the empire, which occurred in the early decades of the twentieth century. At the end of the nineteenth century, Ottoman Jewry, approximately 400,000 strong, constituted the fifth largest Jewish community in the world, after those of Russia, Austria-Hungary, the United States, and Germany (see Table 7).[431] The great majority of the Jewish population was poor and little educated. As a group, their condition was perhaps somewhat better than that of the Muslims, but they lagged behind the Greeks and the Armenians and they still occupied the bottom of the social ladder. Within the community, there were deep cleavages: old ones, based on different traditions, religious rituals and native languages; and new ones, caused by the processes of modernization. There was a chasm between the traditionalists and modernists and the latter were divided by educational background, cultural and political orientation, and socioeconomic status. Yet, there was also a sense of progress, hope, and confidence. In the preceding decades, Ottoman society had greatly changed: new opportunities had become available and considerable segments of the Jewish population had advanced economically. They also gained greater social respectability. Literacy and cultural creativity were on the rise. The contacts between Ottoman Jewry and Western Jewish communities had proliferated and become stronger. And, as always, the Jews continued to enjoy the freedom to live wherever they wanted, to engage in any occupation for which they were qualified, to practice their religion, to maintain their educational, cultural, and social institutions and to administer their own community affairs. Although, overall, the Jews remained a small minority, most of them lived in cities and towns, where they usually constituted a significant segment of the population. Ottoman society had always been plural, and now, at least among the upper strata, social acceptability and integration were on the rise.

Table 7
The World's Ten Largest Jewish Population Groups by Country, ca. 1900

Country	Year and Source	Jewish Population
1. The Russian Empire		
in Europe	1897 census	5,110,548
in Asia	1897 census	105,257
Total		5,215,805
2. Austria-Hungary	1900 census	2,076,277
3. The United States	1907 estimate	1,777,185
4. Germany	1905 census	607,862
5. The Ottoman Empire		
in Europe	1904 estimate	188,896
in Asia	1908 estimate	240,000
in Africa (Tripoli)	1905 estimate	18,660
Total		447,556
6. Romania	1899 census	266,652
7. Great Britain (excl. Ireland)	1905 estimate	250,000
8. Morocco	1908 estimate	150,000
9. The Netherlands	1899 census	103,988
10. France	1905 estimate	100,000

Source: Ruppin, *The Jews of To-Day*, pp. 38–42.

Moreover, in the nineteenth-century Ottoman Empire, the Jews sometimes had the feeling, not common in the Jewish experience in the diaspora, that they were a somewhat favored minority; that their interests overlapped with those of the Muslim majority and that the government was supportive of their needs. These feelings were reflected in the 1893 annual report of the Alliance on the status of Ottoman Jewry, which included the following passage:

> There are but few countries, *even among those which are considered the most enlightened and the most civilized,* where Jews enjoy a more complete equality than in Turkey. H.M. the Sultan and the gov-

ernment of the Porte display towards Jews a spirit of largest toleration and liberalism. In every respect, Abdul-Hamid proves to be a generous sovereign and a protector of his Israelite subjects. . . . The unflinching attachment of Jews to His Person and to the Empire is the only way in which they can express their gratitude. Thus, the Sultan, as well as his officials know that Jews are among the most obedient, faithful and devoted subjects of Turkey [italics added].[432]

Indeed, Ottoman Jewry's sense of relative well-being was further strengthened, when informed Ottoman Jews could compare their condition to that of their brothers in other countries. In the Russian Empire, where close to half of the world's Jewish population lived, the Jews were regarded as enemies of the regime, or at the very least, as dangerous aliens. They suffered from government-sponsored pogroms and numerous disabilities. The latter included limitations on their places of residence, occupations, and educational opportunities. The condition of the Jews in the neighboring Balkan countries was not much better. Significant numbers of Jewish refugees, arriving in the Ottoman Empire from both Russia and the Balkan countries, served as a constant reminder of the contrast between the lot of the Jews in those countries and in the Ottoman Empire. Even in the "civilized" West, most notably in France, Germany, and Austria-Hungary, new forms of anti-Semitism were on the rise in the 1880s and 1890s, leading to such phenomena as the Dreyfus Affair (1894) and the repeated reelection in the 1890s of the blatantly anti-Semitic Karl Lueger as mayor of Vienna. Faced with these realities, and before the United States gained world-wide recognition as the greatest Jewish haven in modern times, Ottoman Jewry could consider itself, and with good reason, among the most fortunate Jewish communities in the world. Such sentiments were best expressed by the director of the Alliance school in Izmir, Gabriel Arié, who was himself a Bulgarian Jew. Writing in 1893, he stated:

> What strikes a Bulgarian when he enters Turkey is, before everything else, the air of freedom that one breathes. Under a theoretically despotic government, one definitely enjoys more freedom than in a constitutional state. . . . The Jews, in particular, can, quite justifiably, consider themselves in this country as the happiest among all their coreligionists in the world . . . ."[433]

* * * * *

The celebration, in 1892, of the fourth centennial of the Sephardic Jews' settlement in the Ottoman Empire was a deliberate political act supported by international Jewish organizations. It was meant to remind "enlightened" Western governments and publics that in its treatment of the Jews, the record of the Ottoman Empire, considered "uncivilized" by most Europeans, was better than most. Equally important, it was also intended to please the Ottoman government. In this respect, and from the perspective of a century later, it might have reflected a lingering sense of Jewish insecurity and feeling of "apartness." Whatever the motives, the sentiments of gratitude were sincere. For on balance, the record of the Jewish experience in the Ottoman Empire was exceptionally good and long-lasting.

Notes

1. Avram Galante [Abraham Galanté], *Histoire des Juifs de Turquie* (9 vols., Istanbul: Editions Isis, n.d. [1985]. This is a reprint of Abraham Galanté's collected works. It is cited henceforth as Galante (Isis)), vol. 8, p. 8.

2. The Hebrew text of the prayer is reproduced in ibid., pp. 10–12.

3. For examples, see ibid., vol. 6, pp. 241–45 and vol. 8, pp. 10–15.

4. Ibid., vol. 9, p. 221.

5. The text of the poem has been reprinted in ibid., vol. 8, pp. 13–15. Lucien Sciuto, a native of Salonica, was a graduate of the Salonica Alliance Israélite Universelle (Alliance) school. Following the Young Turk Revolution (1908), he became the publisher of the pro-Zionist newspaper, *L'Aurore*, which appeared in Istanbul. See ibid., vol. 2, p. 97; Neville J. Mandel, *The Arabs and Zionism before World War I* (Berkeley: University of California Press, 1976), p. 146; Aron Rodrigue, *French Jews, Turkish Jews. The Alliance Israélite Universelle and the Politics of Jewish Schooling in Turkey, 1860–1925* (Bloomington: Indiana University Press, 1990), p. 127.

6. Cf. Yitzhak Baer, *A History of the Jews in Christian Spain*, vol. 2 (Philadelphia: The Jewish Publication Society, 1966), p. 443, who assesses this event as a tragic milestone in Jewish history, comparable to the destruction of the Second Jewish Commonwealth, in antiquity, and the Holocaust, in modern times.

7. For the views of Rabbi Samuel de Medina (1506–89), for example, see: Morris S. Goodblatt, *Jewish Life in Turkey in the XVIth Century* (New York: The Jewish Theological Seminary of America, 1952), p. 118; Also see: Solomon [Shelomoh] A. Rosanes, *Divrei Yemei Yisrael be-Togarmah* [History of the Jews in the Ottoman Empire], vol. 1 (2nd rev. ed., Tel Aviv: Devir, 1930), p. 1. The first three volumes of Rosanes' six-volume history were published in two editions. The first volume was first published in Husijatin in 1907; only the second edition is cited in this work. The second volume was published in Husijatin in 1911 and in Sofia in 1937; the first edition of this volume is cited here. The third volume was published in Husijatin in 1911 and in Sofia in 1938; the second edition is cited in this work; the title of this and the last three volumes was changed to *Korot ha-Yehudim be-Turkiyah ve-Artzot ha-Kedem* [History of the Jews in Turkey and the Lands of the East]. Volumes 4 and 5 were published in Sofia in 1934 and 1937, respectively. Volume 6 was published in Jerusalem by the Rabbi Kook Institute in 1945. Cf. Salvator Israel, "Solomon Avraam Rozanes—Originator of the Historiography of the Bulgarian Jews (1862–1938)," in Social, Cultural and Educational Association of the Jews in the People's Republic of Bulgaria, Central Board, *Annual*, vol. 19 (Sofia, 1984), pp. 363–64.

8. Galante (Isis), vol. 8, p. 10.

9. Ibid., vol. 6, pp. 244–45.

10. Similarly, Muslims referred to these territories as *Rum*. Rosanes, vol. 1^2, p. 11.

11. Goodblatt, p. 11; Yaakov Geller, "Ha-Yahasim ha-Bein-Adatiyim ba-Imperyah ha-Otmanit" [Inter-Community Relations in the Ottoman Empire], *Mi-Kedem U-mi-Yam*, vol. 2 (1986), pp. 29–54.

12. Rosanes, vol. 1², pp. 11–12. Among those were also Jews of French origin, including the renowned Rabbi Yitzhak Tzarfati. Cf. Goodblatt, p. 11.

13. Rosanes, vol. 1², p. 36; Galante (Isis), vol. 2, p. 120.

14. Goodblatt, pp. 10–12.

15. Rosanes, vol. 1², pp. 11–12. They included Rabbi Gedaliah ibn Yahya of Lisbon and Rabbi Hanokh Saporta of Catalonia. The latter moved to Edirne at a later date.

16. Rosanes, vol. 1², p. 62 and n. 55 (pp. 62–63) estimates that in 1492 no more than 7,000 or 8,000 refugees settled in the Ottoman Empire and that even this figure needs to be considered as a high estimate.

17. There are widely different estimates as to the numbers of Jews expelled from Spain. It is generally accepted that the expulsion decree affected approximately 300,000 Jews. Of those, many adopted Christianity to avoid expulsion. Baer's authoritative study (op. cit., vol. 2, p. 438) appears to accept the estimate that the total numbers of those who left ranged between 150,000 and 170,000. Of those, 100,000 to 120,000 found temporary shelter in Portugal.

18. In the years 1496–97, Portugal issued decrees intended to force the conversion of the Jews. This set in motion another major wave of migration. In 1498, Navarre expelled its Jews. The Jews were expelled from Provence and other French regions during various dates in the 1490s. In 1492, they were expelled from Sicily and, in 1510–11, from the Kingdom of Naples. Cf. Salo Wittmayer Baron, *A Social and Religious History of the Jews*, vol. 18 (2nd ed., New York: Columbia University Press, 1983), pp. 36–37; Raymond Renard, *Sephard: Le monde et la langue judéo-espagnole des Séphardim* (Mons, Belgium: Annales Universitaires de Mons, n.d. [1966?]), pp. 51–53.

19. See preceeding note.

20. Rosanes, vol. 1², p. 84.

21. Rosanes, vol. 1², pp. 88–90; Aryeh Shmuelevitz, *The Jews of the Ottoman Empire in the Late Fifteenth and Sixteenth Centuries* (Leiden: E.J. Brill, 1984), p. 193.

22. Rosanes, vol. 1², pp. 61–62.

23. Mark Alan Epstein, *The Ottoman Jewish Communities and their Role in the Fifteenth and Sixteenth Centuries* (Freiburg: Klaus Schwarz Verlag, 1980), pp. 190–286; Bernard Lewis, *The Jews of Islam* (Princeton: Princeton University Press, 1984), p. 118.

24. Cf. Uriel Heyd, "The Jewish Communities of Istanbul in the Seventeenth Century," *Oriens*, vol. 6 (1953), pp. 299–307. Epstein, *Ottoman Jewish Communities*, pp. 178–80, contains a list, dated 1540, of forty-five congregations (including three Karaite) whose names suggest their resettlement from other Ottoman towns.

25. The problems of interpreting the data contained in the Ottoman registers into concrete population numbers are many, and they have been the subject of a considerable literature. Until the nineteenth century, the

Ottomans counted their population primarily for purposes of taxation. It was, therefore, in the interest of the individual taxpayers, as well as the various groups to which they belonged, to avoid full and complete registration. Consequently, the accuracy of the data in the Ottoman registers depended, in the first place, on the efficiency, and honesty, of the officials conducting the counts. (On this subject, with special reference to the Jews, see Shmuelevitz, pp. 86–92, 122–25.) A second set of problems arises from the fact that Ottoman methods of enumeration apparently differed from one place to another and over time (Heath Lowry). Finally, there is uncertainty as to what the terms employed in the registers exactly meant. Of critical importance is the term "household" (*hane*). Scholars can only conjecture how many persons constituted an "average" household. In general, it is assumed that a household consisted of a married man and his family, although cases are known where several families were grouped together and considered as one household. Evidence from the late nineteenth century indicates that in Ottoman Jewish society, where early marriages had been the norm for centuries, households could include married children and their families. Thus, households numbering ten to fifteen individuals were not uncommon. See Paul Dumont, "Jewish Communities in Turkey during the Last Decades of the Nineteenth Century in the Light of the Archives of the Alliance Israélite Universelle," in Benjamin Braude and Bernard Lewis (eds.), *Christians and Jews in the Ottoman Empire. The Functioning of a Plural Society* (2 vols., New York: Holmes & Meier, 1982), vol. 1, pp. 211–12. Scholars have used different methods to estimate the size of a household, with most using a coefficient of between five and seven. A succinct discussion of the various aspects of this subject is in Amnon Cohen and Bernard Lewis, *Population and Revenue in the Towns of Palestine in the Sixteenth Century* (Princeton: Princeton University Press, 1978), pp. 3–18. In the last study, Cohen and Lewis chose to use a "conjectural coefficient" of six per household. Having said all this, it is important to note that the information contained in the Ottoman registers has the advantage of being grounded in reality. It is, therefore, superior by far to any other sources, such as travellers' accounts, whose numbers are generally based on hearsay. Although fragmentary and deficient, the Ottoman records allow us, nevertheless, to form an approximate idea, within certain parameters, of the population size; they give us a sense of the relative strength of each group in a given location and its relative economic position; and they allow us to follow long-range demographic and economic trends.

26. Cf. Rosanes, vol. 1^2, p. 119; Lewis, *Jews of Islam*, p. 122. One source, dated 1594, estimated the number of Jewish males in Istanbul at 150,000!

27. Lewis, ibid., p. 118.

28. Epstein, *Ottoman Jewish Communities*, pp. 178–80.

29. Ibid., pp. 186–87.

30. Four of the new names refer to small groups, which may have been listed separately only because of their tax-exempt status, and it is possible that they were not actual congregations. Ibid., pp. 183–85; Heyd, "Jewish Communities of Istanbul," p. 300 and ff.

31. Epstein, ibid., pp. 187–88; Heyd, ibid., pp. 299–305.

32. Epstein, ibid., p. 260.

33. Cf. Huri İslamoğlu and Çağlar Keyder, "Agenda for Ottoman History," in Huri İslamoğlu-İnan (ed.), *The Ottoman Empire and the World-Economy* (Cambridge: Cambridge University Press, 1987), pp. 56–57.

34. Epstein, op. cit., pp. 186–88.

35. Rosanes, vol. 4, pp. 107–8. The immigrants included the two brothers, David and Meir Rosanes, the founders of the Ottoman branch of the Rosanes family. Also see Galante (Isis), vol. 2, p. 120.

36. Heyd, "Jewish Communities of Istanbul," p. 313.

37. Halil Inalcik, "The Ottoman Economic Mind and Aspects of the Ottoman Economy," in M.A. Cook (ed.), *Studies in the Economic History of the Middle East* (London: Oxford University Press, 1970, pp. 207–18), p. 207; Epstein, *Ottoman Jewish Communities*, pp. 122–23.

38. Epstein, ibid., pp. 153–54.

39. Epstein, ibid., pp. 198–287; Lewis, *Jews of Islam*, p. 118.

40. Epstein, ibid.; Lewis, ibid.

41. Sephardic immigration to Palestine and Egypt had preceded the Ottoman conquest. By the 1460s and 1470s, Sephardic Jews had assumed leadership positions within the community in Jerusalem. However, the Ottoman conquest resulted in new waves of immigration to both countries. Cf. Joseph R. Hacker, "Links between Spanish Jewry and Palestine, 1391–1492," in Richard I. Cohen (ed.), *Vision and Conflict in the Holy Land* (Jerusalem: Yad Izhak Ben-Zvi, 1985), pp. 111–39; Abraham David, "Yishuvei ha-Yehudim ba-Me'ot ha-16—ha-18" [Jewish Settlements from the Sixteenth Century to the Eighteenth Century], in Jacob M. Landau (ed.), *Toledot Yehudei Mitzrayim ba-Tekufah ha-Othmanit (1517–1914)* [The Jews in Ottoman Egypt (1517–1914)] (Jerusalem: Misgav Yerushalayim, 1988), pp. 13–26.

42. Unless otherwise indicated, all the data here are based on Epstein, op. cit., pp. 198–287.

43. Cengiz Orhonlu, "Trablus," *Islam Ansiklopedisi* [Encyclopedia of Islam] (Istanbul and Ankara: Maarif Vekaleti, 1940 to date; henceforth IA), vol. 12 (1), pp. 452–55.

44. Cohen and Lewis, *Population and Revenue*, p. 128.

45. Rosanes, vol. 1², p. 182.

46. Abraham Ben-Ya'akov, *Yehudei Bavel mi-Sof Tekufat ha-Ge'onim ad Yameinu (1038–1965)* [The Jews of Iraq from the End of the Gaonic Period to Our Times (1038–1960)] (Jerusalem: The Ben-Zvi Institute, 1965), pp. 83–84.

47. David, "Jewish Settlements in Egypt" (Hebrew), pp. 16, 22–24, 26.

48. Cf. Baron, *Social and Religious History*, vol. 18², pp. 119–21.

49. C. J. Heywood, "Sir Paul Rycault, A Seventeenth-Century Observer of the Ottoman State: Notes for a Study," in Ezel Kural Shaw and C. J. Heywood, *English and Continental Views of the Ottoman Empire, 1500–1800* (Los Angeles: University of California, Los Angeles, 1972), p. 34.

50. Cited in ibid., p. 40,

51. Baer, *Jews in Spain*, vol. 2, p. 438.

52. An abridged, and somewhat loose, English translation of the letter, variably dated around the mid-fifteenth century, is found in Franz Kobler (ed.), *Letters of Jews through the Ages* (London: Ararat Publishing Society, 1953), vol. 1, pp. 283–85. Lewis, *Jews of Islam*, pp. 135–36, cites several central passages. A copy of the Hebrew text has been located in the Bibliothéque Nationale in Paris and was published in Adolph Jellinek (ed.), *Zur Geschichte der Kreuzzüge* (Leipzig, 1854), pp. 14–25.

53. Niccolo Machiavelli, *The Prince*, tr. and ed. by Robert M. Adams (New York: Norton, 1977), pp. 12–13, 39.

54. Charles Thornton Foster and F.H. Blackburne Daniell, *The Life and Letters of Ogier Ghiselin de Busbecq* (2 vols., London, 1881), vol. 1, pp. 153–54.

55. The subject of Islam's attitudes to religious minorities, in general, and to Jews, in particular, has been discussed in a large number of studies. For succinct recent discussions and further bibliography, see C.E. Bosworth, "The Concept of *Dhimma* in Early Islam," in Braude and Lewis (eds.), *Christians and Jews*, vol. 1, pp. 37–51; Lewis, *Jews of Islam*, especially pp. 3–66.

56. H.A.R. Gibb and Harold Bowen, *Islamic Society and the West*, vol. I, pt. II (London: Oxford University Press, 1957), p. 123; Halil Inalcik, *The Ottoman Empire. The Classical Age 1300–1600*, trs. Norman Itzkowitz and Colin Imber (London: Weidenfeld and Nicolson, 1973), p. 181. Inalcik theorizes that the Turkish states preferred the Hanafi rite, because it allowed their rulers "to retain as much freedom as possible in their political and executive authority."

57. Antoine Fattal, *Le Statut Légal des Non-Musulmans en Pays d'Islam* (Beirut: Imprimerie Catholique, 1958), pp. 114–18.

58. Cf. A.D. Alderson, *The Structure of the Ottoman Dynasty* (Oxford: Clarendon Press, 1956), pp. 83–100.

59. Cf. I. Metin Kunt, "Transformation of *Zimmi* into Askeri," in Braude and Lewis (eds.), *Christians and Jews*, vol. 1, pp. 63–65.

60. Cf. Gibb and Bowen, vol. I, pt. II, pp. 114–38; Inalcik, *The Ottoman Empire*, pp. 70–75.

61. Kunt, "Transformation," pp. 55–67.

62. Kunt, ibid.

63. Epstein, *Ottoman Jewish Communities*, pp. 183–85; Shmuelevitz, pp. 121–27. Occasional references to Jews in the Ottoman military service are extant from different periods. Kunt, "Transformation," p. 65, note 2 (citing Halil Inalcik, ed., *Suret-i Defter-i Sancak-ı Arnavud*, Ankara, 1954), mentions a Jewish *timar*-holder (member of the feudal cavalry) in the 1430s. Alexandar Matkovski, *A History of the Jews in Macedonia*, tr. David Arney (Skopje: Macedonian Review Editions, 1982), p. 46, mentions a Jewish *subaşı* (an officer in the feudal cavalry) in 1636. Rosanes maintains that Jews served in the Ottoman military during the reigns of Murad II (1421–51), Süleyman the Magnificent (1520–66) and at later times. Rosanes, vol. 1^2, pp. 10–11 and note 18; p. 14, note 25. In 1772, three hundred Jews from Istanbul were mobilized to serve in the army, perhaps in labor battalions, in the war with Russia. Jacob Barnai, "Kavim le-Toledot Kehillat Kushta ba-Me'ah ha-18" [Notes on the Jewish

Community of Istanbul in the Eighteenth Century], *Mi-Kedem U-mi-Yam* (1981), p. 56.

64. Michael Winter, "Yahasei ha-Yehudim 'im ha-Shiltonot ve-ha-Hevrah ha-lo-Yehudit" [The Relations of Egyptian Jews with the Authorities and with the Non-Jewish Society], in Landau (ed.), *The Jews in Ottoman Egypt*, pp. 377–78.

65. Uriel Heyd, *Ottoman Documents on Palestine, 1552–1615* (London: Oxford University Press, 1960), pp. 164–66.

66. Translated and cited by Baron, *Social and Religious History*, vol. 18², p. 58.

67. Translated and cited by Goodblatt, p. 187.

68. Samuel Usque, *Consolation for the Tribulations of Israel*, tr. Martin A. Cohen (Philadelphia: The Jewish Publication Society, 1965), p. 231. This work was first published in Portuguese in Ferrara in 1553.

69. Cf. Shlomo Zalman Havlin, "Ha-Yetzirah ha-Ruhanit" [Intellectual Creativity], in Landau (ed.), *The Jews in Ottoman Egypt*, pp. 245–310.

70. R.J.Z. Werblowsky, *Joseph Karo, Lawyer and Mystic* (London: Oxford University Press, 1962), pp. 84–94 and ff.

71. For similar motives for the settlement of Jews in Egypt, see Michael Littman, "Ha-Mishpahah ha-Yehudit be-Mitzrayim" [The Jewish Family in Egypt], in Landau (ed.), *The Jews in Ottoman Egypt*, pp. 217–18.

72. Kobler, *Letters*, vol. 1, p. 284.

73. Hacker, "Spanish Jewry and Palestine," pp. 111–39.

74. *Sefer Divrei ha-Yamim le-Malkhei Tzarefat u-Malkhei Beit Ottoman ha-Toger* [A History of the Kings of France and the Kings of the Ottoman Dynasty] (Sabionetta, 1554), pp. 261b–262a.

75. Goodblatt, p. 175.

76. My translation of the Hebrew text in Goodblatt, p. 214, note 2.

77. By the end of the fourteenth century, Bursa had become the most important Ottoman commercial center and a major entrepôt in international trade, and the Jews played an important role in its development. Cf. Inalcik, *The Ottoman Empire*, pp. 121–22; idem, "Jews in the Ottoman Economy and Finances, 1450–1500," in C.E. Bosworth, Charles Issawi et al. (eds.), *The Islamic World from Classical to Modern Times: Essays in Honor of Bernard Lewis.* (Princeton: The Darwin Press, 1989), pp. 523–24.

78. Although Edirne served as a major Ottoman administrative and military center since its occupation in 1361 and until the end of the empire, it is not clear when exactly it replaced Bursa as the official Ottoman capital (cf. M. Tayyib Gökbilgin, "Edirne," IA, vol. 4, pp. 107–27). Whereas most historians give the date as 1361, or 1362, others suggest 1402. See Inalcik, *The Ottoman Empire*, p. 76.

79. Mark A. Epstein, "The Leadership of the Ottoman Jews in the Fifteenth and Sixteenth Centuries," in Braude and Lewis (eds.), *Christians and Jews*, vol. 1, p. 102.

80. Inalcik, *The Ottoman Empire*, p. 141; Heath Lowry, "'From Lesser Wars to the Mightiest War': The Ottoman Conqest and Transformation of Byzantine Urban Centers in the Fifteenth Century," in Anthony Bryer and

Heath Lowry (eds.), *Continuity and Change in Late Byzantine and Early Ottoman Society* (Birmingham, England, and Washington, D.C., 1986), pp. 323–35.
  81. Rosanes, vol. 1², pp. 21–22, 132–37; Epstein, *Ottoman Jewish Communities*, pp. 28–30.
  82. Epstein, ibid., p. 101.
  83. Ibid., p. 112,
  84. Ibid., pp. 102–20.
  85. Halil Inalcik, "The Turkish Impact on the Development of Modern Europe," in Kemal H. Karpat (ed.), *The Ottoman State and Its Place in World History* (Leiden: E.J. Brill, 1974), pp. 51–58.
  86. Cited in Inalcik, ibid., p. 55, from Sinan's *Ma'arifname*, an Ottoman Mirror for Princes. On the career and works of Sinan, see Hasibe Mazioğlu, "Sinan Paşa," IA, vol. 10, pp. 666–70.
  87. Baer, *Jews in Spain*, vol. 2, pp. 249–50.
  88. Fernand Braudel, *Civilization and Capitalism: 15th–18th Century, Volume II: The Wheels of Commerce*, tr. Siân Reynolds (New York: Harper and Row, 1982), pp. 157–59, 165–67.
  89. Rosanes, vol. 1², p. 68; Renard, *Sepharad*, pp. 66–67.
  90. Inalcik, *The Ottoman Empire*, pp. 126–27.
  91. Nikolai Todorov, *The Balkan City, 1400–1900* (Seattle: University of Washington Press, 1983), p. 68; Shmuelevitz, pp. 129–32.
  92. Nicholas de Nicolay visited the Ottoman Empire in 1551. He attributed the ascendancy of Jewish physicians to "the knowledge which they have in the language and letters, Greek, Arabian, Chaldee and Hebrewe." *The Nauigations, Peregrinatians and Voyages, made into Turkie by Nicholas Nicholay etc.*, tr. T. Washington (London, 1585), p. 93a. Pierre Belon de Mans visited the Ottoman Empire at about 1547. His statement that "all those who practice medicine in Turkey, Egypt, Syria, Anatolia and other cities in the lands of the Turks are for the most part Jews" (cited in Renard, *Sepharad*, p. 69) is an exaggeration, but it underscores general impressions.
  93. Joseph Nehama, *Histoire des Israélites de Salonique* (vols. 1–5, Salonique: Librairie Molho, 1935–36; vols. 6–7, Thessalonique: Communauté Israélite de Thessalonique, 1978), vol. 4, p. 57.
  94. Shmuel Avitsur, "Tzefat—Merkaz le-Ta'asiyat Arigei Tzemer ba-Me'ah ha-15," [Safed—Center of the Manufacture of Woven Woolens in the Fifteenth Century], *Sefunot*, vol. 6 (1962), pp. 41–69. In spite of its title, this article deals mainly with the sixteenth century.
  95. Nicholas de Nicolay, *op. cit.*, p. 130b.
  96. Inalcik, *The Ottoman Empire*, p. 160; idem, "Jews in the Ottoman Economy," pp. 521–23.
  97. Nehama, vol. 4, pp. 56–57 and ff.
  98. Marc D. Angel, *The Jews of Rhodes. The History of a Sephardic Community* (New York: Sepher-Hermon Press, 1978), p. 46.
  99. Epstein, *Ottoman Jewish Communities*, p. 141.
  100. Epstein, ibid., pp. 123–41.
  101. Eliezer Bashan, "Hayyei ha-Kalkalah ba-Me'ot ha-16—ha-18," [Economic Life from the Sixteenth to the Eighteenth Century], in Landau

(ed.), *The Jews in Ottoman Egypt*, pp. 63–112; H.Z. [J.W.] Hirschberg, *Toledot ha-Yehudim be-Afrikah Ha-Tzefonit* [A History of the Jews in North Africa] (2 vols., Jerusalem: Bialik Institute, 1965), vol. 2, pp. 48, 121 and ff.; Andrew C. Hess, *The Forgotten Frontier. A History of the Sixteenth Century Ibero-African Frontier* (Chicago: The University of Chicago Press, 1978), pp. 174–75; Ben Ya'akov, *The Jews of Iraq* (Hebrew), pp. 85–86.

102. Bashan, "Economic Life" (Hebrew), p. 97. Castro also served for many years as the lay leader of Egypt's Jewry. He supported Jewish scholarship and is also believed to have contributed to the costs of reconstructing the city walls of Jerusalem executed by Süleyman the Magnificent. He leased or purchased real estate in Jerusalem and is believed to have owned a place of residence in the city.

103. Winter, "Relations of Egyptian Jews" (Hebrew), pp. 381–88. By the seventeenth century, many of the tax farmers in Egypt, as well as in other Ottoman provinces, were military officers.

104. Cited in Baron, *Social* and *Religious History*, vol. 18², p. 89.

105. Lewis, *Jews of Islam*, pp. 123–24.

106. Epstein, *Ottoman Jewish Communities*, pp. 42–43

107. Heyd, *Ottoman Documents*, pp. 167–68.

108. Epstein *Ottoman Jewish Communities*, pp. 26–27, 127; Lewis, *Jews of Islam*, pp. 124–25; Winter, "Relations of Egyptian Jews" (Hebrew), p. 409.

109. Galante (Isis), vol. 9, p. 87.

110. In Egypt, the Ottoman governor's private banker was known by the title *çelebi*. He often combined in his hands several official positions in the financial administration of Egypt. These included the office of *sarraf başı* (chief banker and money changer) who was in charge of all the accredited *sarraf*s. In addition, he often controlled also the Egyptian mint and various tax farms. See: Winter, "Relations of Egyptian Jews" (Hebrew), pp. 388–89; Minna Rozen, "Tzarefat vi-Yhudei Mitzrayim—Anatomiah shel Yahasim, 1683–1801" [France and the Jews of Egypt: An Anatomy of Relations, 1683–1801] in Landau (ed.), *The Jews in Ottoman Egypt*, pp. 431–33.

111. Rosanes, vol. 3², pp. 65–66, 280–84; J.H. Mordtmann, "Die jüdischen kira im Serai der Sultane," in *Mitteilungen des Seminars für orientalischen Sprachen*, Berlin, vol. 32/2 (1929), pp. 1–38.

112. S.A. Skilliter, "Three Letters from the Ottoman 'Sultana' Safiye to Queen Elizabeth I," in S.M. Stern (ed.), *Oriental Studies III. Documents from Islamic Chanceries. First Series* (Cambridge, Massachusetts: Harvard University Press, 1965), pp. 119–57.

113. Baron, *Social and Religious History*, vol. 18², pp. 145–46.

114. Rosanes, vol. 4, pp. 188–89.

115. M. Franco, *Essai sur l'Histoire des Israélites de l'Empire Ottoman* (Paris, 1897), p. 30. According to Galante (Isis), vol. 9, pp. 81–82, the first physicians in the service of the Ottoman court were Romaniot Jews.

116. Steven Runciman, *The Fall of Constantinople, 1453* (London: Cambridge University Press, 1965), p. 77.

117. Galante (Isis), vol. 5, p. 157; vol. 9, pp. 82–85; Inalcik, "Jews in the Ottoman Economy," p. 526. According to Galante (Isis), vol. 9, p. 85, another

Jewish physician, Ephraim son of Sandji, was employed in the service of Mehmed the Conqueror.

118. The fascinating career of Hekim Yakub has been the subject of several studies. See: Bernard Lewis, "The Privilege Granted by Mehmed II to his Physician," *Bulletin of the School of Oriental and African Studies*, vol. 14 (1952), pp. 550–63; Eleazar Birnbaum, "Hekim Ya'qub, Physician to Sultan Mehmed the Conqueror," *The Hebrew Medical Journal*, vol. 1 (1961), pp. 222–50; Epstein, *Ottoman Jewish Communities*, pp. 79–84.

119. Nicholas de Nicolay, op. cit., p. 93a.

120. Uriel Heyd, "Moses Hamon, Chief Jewish Physician to Sultan Süleyman the Magnificent," *Oriens*, vol. 16 (1963), pp. 152–70; Epstein, *Ottoman Jewish Communities*, pp. 84–88; Galante (Isis), vol. 9, pp. 85–87. According to Galante (vol. 9, pp. 88–89), a list of Jewish doctors employed in the court, dating from 1618, includes the name Yahuda son of Hamon. It is possible, therefore, that descendants of the Hamon family continued to serve as physicians in the Ottoman court well into the seventeenth century.

121. The careers of Joseph Nasi and his paternal aunt, Gracia Nasi Mendes, have received considerable attention in the writings of their contemporaries. They also have been the subject of several modern biographical studies, some of them romanticized. The best known are Cecil Roth, *The House of Nasi* (2 vols., Philadelphia: Jewish Publication Society, 1947–48); P. Grunebaum-Ballin, *Joseph Naci, duc de Naxos* (Paris: Mouton, 1968). A shorter comprehensive account is included in Baron, *Social and Religious History*, vol. 18², pp. 77–118. Epstein, *Ottoman Jewish Communities*, pp. 88–93 and ff., contains new information, culled from the Ottoman archives, on some of the Nasis' financial activities in the Ottoman Empire.

122. Inalcik has suggested that in view of the fact that the Nasi-Mendes family was heavily engaged in the spice trade, and considering that the Ottoman Empire was at that time the world center of that trade, the settlement of the Nasis in Istanbul could have been "not solely on religious grounds." Inalcik, "Turkish Impact on . . . Modern Europe," p. 56.

123. Epstein, *Ottoman Jewish Communities*, pp. 89–90.

124. Izhak Ben-Zvi, *Eretz Yisrael ve-Yishuvah bi-Ymei ha-Shilton ha-Otmani* [Eretz-Israel under Ottoman Rule] (Jerusalem: Bialik Institute, 1962), pp. 196–214.

125. Rosanes, vol. 1², p. 62.

126. Ibid., p. 63

127. Goodblatt, p. 58. Angel's impression of the condition of the community in Rhodes, also based on responsa, is somewhat more sanguine: ". . . although there were no doubt some needy individuals, the overall situation was good. The Jews . . . clearly benefited from the city's prosperity." *Jews of Rhodes*, pp. 41–42.

128. Heyd, "Jewish Communities of Istanbul," p. 308.

129. Inalcik, "Jews in the Ottoman Economy," pp. 523–24,

130. Haim Gerber, "Yehudim be-Hayyei ha-Kalkalah shel ha-'Ir ha-Anatolit Bursah ba-Me'ah ha-17: He'arot u-Mismakhim" [Jews in the Economic Life of the Anatolian City Bursa in the Seventeenth Century: Notes

and Documents], *Sefunot*, New Series, vol. 1 (16) (1980), p. 254. In subsequent decades, the community appears to have declined in both numbers and wealth. Gerber found that in 1688/89, only 11 percent were in the highest tax bracket, 54 percent in the middle, and 35 percent in the lowest. In spite of the apparent decline, the condition of the Bursa community, compared with others, appears to have remained strong. Records of the Alliance Israélite Universelle indicate that even in the late nineteenth century, the Bursa community was considered relatively prosperous. Cf. Paul Dumont, "Jewish Communities in Turkey during the Last Decades of the Nineteenth Century in the Light of the Archives of the Alliance Israélite Universelle," in Braude and Lewis (eds.), *Christians and Jews*, vol. 1, p. 217.

131. Amnon Cohen, *Jewish Life under Islam. Jerusalem in the Sixteenth Century* (Cambridge, Massachusetts: Harvard University Press, 1984), p. 34.

132. Ibid., pp. 213–19.

133. Nehama, vol. 4, pp. 52–54; Cohen, *Jewish Life*, pp. 147–60, 187–92; Ben-Zvi, *Eretz-Israel* (Hebrew), pp, 170–72; Angel, *Jews of Rhodes*, pp. 43–44; Bashan, "Economic Life" (Hebrew), pp. 107–9; Gerber, "Jews in Bursa" (Hebrew), pp. 251–52.

134. For Salonica, see: Nehama, vol. 4, pp. 37–51; Goodblatt, pp. 54–55; Shmuel Avitsur, "Le-Toledot Ta'asiyat Arigei ha-Tzemer be-Saloniki" [The Woolen industry in Salonica], *Sefunot*, vol. 12 (1971–78), pp. 145–68; for Safed: Ben-Zvi, *Eretz-Israel* (Hebrew), pp. 172–73; Avitsur, "Safed" (Hebrew), pp. 41–60; Heyd, *Ottoman Documents*, p. 163; for Rhodes: Angel, *Jews of Rhodes*, pp. 42–43; for Bursa: Gerber, "Jews in Bursa" (Hebrew), pp. 248–51; for Egypt: Bashan, "Economic Life" (Hebrew), p. 109. See also: Inalcik, "Jews in the Ottoman Economy," pp. 521–23.

135. Nehama, vol. 4, pp. 54–55; Cohen, *Jewish Life*, pp. 162–70; Bashan, "Economic Life" (Hebrew), p. 109; Gerber, "Jews in Bursa" (Hebrew), pp. 245–47.

136. Nehama, vol. 4, pp. 54–55; Angel, *Jews of Rhodes*, pp. 44–45; Cohen, *Jewish Life*, pp. 170–75; Bashan, "Economic Life" (Hebrew), p. 111.

137. Nehama, vol. 4, p. 54; Cohen, *Jewish Life*, pp. 160–62, 179–82; Epstein, *Ottoman Jewish Communities*, p. 106; Bashan, "Economic Life" (Hebrew), pp. 109–11; Gerber, "Jews in Bursa" (Hebrew), pp. 246–47.

138. Nehama, vol. 4, pp. 56–57.

139. Rosanes, vol. 3², p. 45; vol. 4, p. 108; Ben-Zvi, *Eretz-Israel* (Hebrew), p. 196; David Benvenisti, *Yehudei Saloniki ba-Dorot ha-Aharonim* [The Jews of Salonica in the Last Generations] (Jerusalem: Kiryat Sefer, 1973), pp. 149–60.

140. Benvenisti, pp. 156–57.

141. Nehama, vol. 4, p. 52; Angel, *Jews of Rhodes*, pp. 42, 48; Cohen, *Jewish Life*, pp. 209–10; Ben-Zvi, *Eretz-Israel* (Hebrew), p. 189; Bashan, "Economic Life" (Hebrew), p. 111.

142. Itzhak [Izhak] Ben-Zvi, *The Exiled and the Redeemed* (Philadelphia: The Jewish Publication Society, New Edition, 1961), pp. 30–53; Abraham L. Udovitch and Lucette Valensi, *The Last Arab Jews: The Communities of Jerba, Tunisia* (Chur: Harwood Academic Publishers, 1984), pp. 13–14; Hirschberg, *Jews in North Africa* (Hebrew), vol. 2, p. 45 and ff.

143. Bernard Lewis, *Notes and Documents from the Turkish Archives* (Jerusalem: Israel Oriental Society, 1952), p. 9; Ben-Zvi, *Eretz-Israel* (Hebrew), pp. 189–92.

144. Matkovski, *The Jews of Macedonia*, p. 46

145. Cf . Rosanes, vol. 3^2, p. 31; Cohen, *Jewish Life*, pp. 195–98; Inalcik, "Jews in the Ottoman Economy," pp. 515–24. The following studies contain comprehensive and detailed accounts of the Jews' place in Ottoman commerce: Shmuelevitz, pp. 128–78; Bashan, "Economic Life" (Hebrew), pp. 69–96; Haim Gerber, "Yozmah u-Mishar Bein-Le'umi ba-Pe'ilut ha-Kalkalit shel Yehudei ha-Imperiah ha-Othmanit ba-Me'ot 16-17" [Entrepreneurship and International Commerce in the Economic Activity of the Jews of the Ottoman Empire in the Sixteenth–Seventeenth Centuries], *Zion*, vol. 43 (1978), pp. 38–67.

146. Cf. James W. Redhouse, *A Turkish and English Lexicon* (New Impression; Constantinople, 1921), p. 322; Ferit Devellioğlu, *Osmanlıca-Türkçe Ansiklopedik Lûgat* [Ottoman-Turkish Encyclopedic Dictionary] (Ankara: Doğuş Matbaası, 1962), p. 92; *Türkçe-Ingilizce Büyük Lûgat. Comprehensive Turkish-English Dictionary*, compiled by Tarhan Kitabevi (Ankara: Tarhan Kitabevi, 1959), p. 121.

147. Rosanes, vol. 3^2, p. 31; Angel, *Jews of Rhodes*, pp. 98–100

148. Bashan, "Economic Life" (Hebrew), p. 109; Fernand Braudel, *The Mediterranean and the Mediterranean World in the Age of Phillip II*, tr. Siân Reynolds (2 vols., New York: Harper and Row, 1973), vol. 2, p. 814.

149. Rosanes, vol. 3^2, pp. 31–32

150. Cf. Rosanes, vol. 1^2, pp. 69–70, 77–78; Joseph Hacker, "The Intellectual Activity of the Jews of the Ottoman Empire during the Sixteenth and Seventeenth Centuries," in Isadore Twersky and Bernard Septimus (eds.), *Jewish Thought in the Seventeenth Century* (Cambridge, Massachusetts: Harvard University Press, 1987), pp. 95–135.

151. Goodblatt, p. 8; I. S. Emmanuel, *Histoire des Israélites de Salonique* (Paris: Librairie Lipschutz, 1936), p. 13.

152. Rosanes, vol. 1^2, P. 90.

153. Rosanes, vol. 1^2, pp. 81–82, 90; Nehama, vol. 4, pp. 5–22, 154–221; Goodblatt, pp. 8–12, 15–21, 105–107; Israel M. Goldman, *The Life and Times of Rabbi David Ibn Abi Zimra* (New York: The Jewish Theological Seminary, 1970), pp. 191–94; Hacker, "Intellectual Activity," pp. 104–105, 116–19.

154. Nehama, vol. 2, pp. 135–66; vol. 4, pp. 154–59; Harry Friedenwald, *The Jews and Medicine: Essays* (2 vols., Baltimore: Johns Hopkins Press, 1944), vol. 1, pp. 332–46 and ff.

155. This work is also known as *Sefer ha-Turim* (The Book of Columns). Cf. Rosanes, vol. 1^2, pp. 63, 316; Baron, *Social and Religious History*, vol. 18^2, p. 42. According to the testimony of Medina, the book was very popular and was found in most homes. Goodblatt, pp. 107 and 212, note 52.

156. Rosanes, vol. 1^2, pp. 63–65, 69–81, 95–101; vol. 2, pp. 10–25 and ff.; Jacob Barnai, "Ha-Yehudim ba-Imperiah ha-Othmanit" [The Jews in the Ottoman Empire], in Yosef Tobi, Jacob Barnai et al., *Toledot ha-Yehudim be-Artzot ha-Islam. Ha-Et ha-Hadashah—ad Emtza ha-Me'ah ha-19* [History of the

Jews in the Islamic Countries. Modern Times—until the Middle of the Nineteenth Century], vol. 1 (Jerusalem: Zalman Shazar Center, 1981), pp. 102–104; Hacker, "Intellectual Activity," pp. 106–109, 116–17 and passim.

157. Rosanes, vol. 1², p. 182; vol. 2, pp. 34–38, 124–25 and ff; Hacker, "Intellectual Activity," passim.

158. Ben-Zvi, *Eretz-Israel* (Hebrew), pp. 176–87; Werblowsky, *Karo*, pp. 38–83 and ff.

159. Ben-Zvi, *Eretz-Israel* (Hebrew), pp. 161–64, 215–16; Goldman, *David ibn Abi Zimra*, pp. 160–68.

160. Ben-Zvi, *Eretz-Israel* (Hebrew), pp. 196–202.

161. Goldman, *David ibn Abi Zimra*, pp. 4–21, 183–85; Shlomo Zalman Havlin, "Ha-Yetzirah ha-Ruhanit" [Intellectual Creativity], in Landau (ed.), *The Jews in Ottoman Egypt*, pp. 245–66 and ff.

162. Mehmet Zeki Pakalın, *Osmanlı Tarih Deyimleri ve Terimleri Sözlüğü* [A Dictionary of Ottoman Historical Expressions and Terms] (3 vols., Istanbul: Milli Eğitim Basımevi, 1946), vol. 2, p. 712; Ismail Hakkı Uzunçarşılı, *Osmanlı Devleti Teşkilatından Kapukulu Ocakları* [The Kapukulu Corps in the Organization of the Ottoman State] (2 vols., Ankara: Türk Tarih Kurumu Basımevi, 1943–44), vol. 1, pp. 407–10; Lewis, *Jews of Islam*, p. 133. Jews may also have served as physicians to the Janissaries. Uzunçarşılı, ibid., p. 406, found two documents dated 1811 and 1813 that describe a Jew named Daviçon as Chief Physician of the Janissary Corps (*Ser tabib-i ocağ-ı yeniçeriyan*). On the relations of Jews with the military in Egypt, see Winter, "Relations of Egyptian Jews" (Hebrew), pp. 381–88.

163. See, for example, Rosanes, vol. 1², pp. 43–44; Epstein, *Ottoman Jewish Communities*, p. 40; Winter, "Relations of Egyptian Jews" (Hebrew), p. 390.

164. Emmanuel, *Histoire*, p. 243.

165. Uriel Heyd, "Alilot Dam be-Turkiyah ba-Me'ot ha-15 ve-ha-16" [Ritual Murder Accusations in Fifteenth and Sixteenth Century Turkey], *Sefunot*, vol. 5 (1961), pp. 135–49.

166. Rosanes, vol. 1², p. 5; Haim Gerber, "Le-Toledot ha-Yehudim be-Kushta ba-Me'ot ha-17-18" [On the History of the Jews in Istanbul in the Seventeenth and Eighteenth Centuries], *Pe'amim*, no. 12 (1982), pp. 27–30.

167. Rosanes, vol. 1², p. 5 and note 11. The term was also known in Egypt. See Winter, "Relations of Egyptian Jews" (Hebrew), pp. 382, 412.

168. Winter, ibid., p. 412.

169. Cf. Joseph Hacker, "'Ha-Rabbanut ha-Roshit' ba-Imperiah ha-Othmanit ba-Me'ot ha-15 ve-ha-16" [The "Chief Rabbinate" in the Ottoman Empire in the 15th and 16th Centuries], *Zion*, vol. 49 (1984), pp. 225–63; and the following contributions in Braude and Lewis (eds.), *Christians and Jews*, vol. 1: Braude and Lewis, "Introduction," pp. 12–13; Braude, "Foundation Myths of the Millet System," pp. 69–88; Kevork B. Bardakjian, "The Rise of the Armenian Patriarchate of Constantinople," pp. 89–100.

170. Cf. S. D. Goitein, *A Mediterranean Society: The Jewish Communities of the Arab World as Portrayed in the Documents of the Cairo Geniza. Volume II: The Community* (Berkeley and Los Angeles: University of California Press, 1971), pp. 5–40; Mark R. Cohen, *Jewish Self-Government in Medieval Egypt*, Princeton: Princeton University Press, 1980.

171. Ignaz Maybaum, *The Office of a Chief Rabbi*, booklet no. 1 in the series *Judaism Today*, ed. Ignaz Maybaum (London: The Reform Synagogues of Great Britain, 1964), p. 5.

172. Ottoman tax records from the early decades of the sixteenth century show twenty-one congregations in Salonica. The largest of these, Congregation Aragon, listed 315 households; four other congregations had over 200 households; seven had between 100 and 200; nine had less than 100. Of the latter, the smallest listed only 4 households. During this period, the congregations in Istanbul tended to be considerably smaller than those of Salonica. Ottoman records from 1540, showing only congregations established before 1492, list a total of 50 (including three Karaite). Only three congregations had over 100 households (the largest had 116); seven had 51–100 households; twenty-five 11–50, and fifteen congregations had 10 households or less; of the latter, the smallest had only two households. In Istanbul, the trend for the older congregations was to merge into larger units. Records for the first decade of the seventeenth century show twenty-five "old" congregations and seventeen "new" (post–1492) ones. The congregations were now larger. Of a total of forty-two congregations, four had over 100 households (the largest 125); nineteen, 51–100; fourteen, 11–50; and five had 10 households or less. Epstein, *Ottoman Jewish Communities*, pp. 178–80, 186–88, 263–64.

173. Cf. Geller, "Inter-Community Relations" (Hebrew), p. 36.

174. There were also private primary schools supported by tuition fees paid by the parents. These served primarily the wealthier classes. The employment of private tutors was also common among the well-to-do. Goodblatt, p. 105; Hacker, "Intellectual Activity," p. 107.

175. For a detailed description of the organization of the Jewish community in Cairo in the sixteenth and seventeenth centuries, reflecting similar patterns, see Leah Bornstein-Makovetzky, "Ha-Kehillah u-Mosdoteihah" [The Community and its Institutions], in Landau (ed.), *The Jews in Ottoman Egypt*, pp. 129–216.

176. The Ottomans usually identified these independent groups as *taife*, literally meaning sect. The more accurate Hebrew term is *edah*, meaning a group of Jews hailing from one country and following distinctive customs and ritual (Heath Lowry, Amnon Cohen).

177. Leah Bornstein, "Ha-Hanhagah shel ha-Kehillah ha-Yehudit ba-Mizrah ha-Karov mi-Shilhei ha-Me'ah ha-15 ve-ad Sof ha-Me'ah ha-18" [The Jewish Communal Leadership in the Near East from the End of the Fifteenth Century through the Eighteenth Century] (Ph.D. diss., Bar-Ilan University, 1978), pp. 69–72.

178. Cf. Rosanes, vol. 1^2, p. 78.

179. Ibid., vol. 3^2, p. 30.

180. Ibid., vol. 1^2, pp. 78–80; Goodblatt, pp. 112–13; Baron, *Social and Religious History*, vol. 18^2, pp. 61–63.

181. See Bornstein, "Jewish Communal Leadership" (Hebrew), pp. 107–108, 111–14.

182. M. Almosnino, *Extremos y Grandezas de Constantinopla* (Madrid, 1638), p. 90, cited in Epstein, "Leadership," p. 109.

183. Bornstein, "Jewish Communal Leadership" (Hebrew), pp. 124–26.

184. Emmanuel, *Histoire*, p. 151 and ff.

185. Angel, *Jews of Rhodes*, pp. 24–25.

186. Bornstein, "Jewish Communal Leadership" (Hebrew), pp. 127–28.

187. Epstein, "Leadership," p. 110 and p. 114, n. 34. For the Arab provinces, see Amnon Cohen and Daniel Schroeter.

188. Rosanes, vol. 1², pp. 132, 137.

189. He was the father of Joseph Taitatzak (ca. 1487–ca. 1545) and was also a native of Castile, but had settled in Portugal. Rosanes, vol. 1², p. 133.

190. Rosanes, vol. 1², pp. 132–33; Emmanuel, *Histoire*, pp. 85–87.

191. Rosanes, vol. 1², pp. 81, 138–39.

192. Emmanuel, *Histoire*, pp. 167–91; Goodblatt, pp. 24–46 and ff.

193. *Social and Religious History*, vol.18², p. 42.

194. Rosanes, vol. 1², p. 12; vol. 5, pp. 389–93.

195. Cf. Epstein, "Leadership," p. 102; Bornstein, "Jewish Communal Leadership" (Hebrew), p. 151.

196. Primarily Elijah Capsali, *Seder Eliyahu Zuta*, written in 1523 by a relative of Moses Capsali, and numerous references in the rabbinic literature. For bibliographic details, see Hacker, "The Chief Rabbinate" (Hebrew).

197. Epstein, "Leadership," p. 104.

198. Hacker, "The Chief Rabbinate" (Hebrew), pp. 246–49.

199. Braude, "Foundation Myths," pp. 79–80.

200. Rosanes, vol. 6, p. 27.

201. Cf. Geller, "Inter-Community Relations" (Hebrew), p. 36.

202. Epstein, "Leadership," p. 105.

203. Hacker, "The Chief Rabbinate" (Hebrew), p. 255.

204. Hacker suggests that one such official might have been Yeshaya Messini. See Joseph R. Hacker, "Ottoman Policy toward the Jews and Jewish Attitudes toward the Ottomans during the Fifteenth Century," in Braude and Lewis (eds.), *Christians and Jews*, vol. 1, pp. 122 and 126, note 31.

205. See, for example, Rosanes, vol. 1², pp. 23–24; Gibb and Bowen, Part II, p. 217; Baron, *Social and Religious History*, vol. 18², pp. 28–29.

206. Hacker, "The Chief Rabbinate" (Hebrew), pp. 246–49.

207. Epstein, "Leadership," pp. 107–108.

208. Cf. Braude, "Foundation Myths," pp. 79–81; Hacker, "The Chief Rabbinate" (Hebrew), pp. 241, 245–46; Bornstein, "Jewish Communal Leadership" (Hebrew), p. 150.

209. Epstein, "Leadership," pp. 104–105.

210. Hacker, "The Chief Rabbinate" (Hebrew), pp. 247–48.

211. Rosanes, vol. 1², pp. 73–77. His numerous responsa were collected in two published works: *She'elot u-Teshuvot* and *Mayyim Amukim*. Additional information on his scholarly activities is included in the responsa of his contemporaries and disciples. Cf. Shmuelevitz, p. 192.

212. Epstein, "Leadership," pp. 106–107.

213. Elijah Mizrahi, *She'elot u-Teshuvot* (Responsa) (Jerusalem: Darom Publishers, 1938) no. 66, p. 214.

214. Rosanes, vol. 1², p. 74.

215. Hacker, "The Chief Rabbinate" (Hebrew), pp. 251–52.

216. Ibid., pp. 252–53.

217. Ibid., pp. 241–42. This appears to be the explanation given by Rabbi Samuel de Medina. See his responsum, dated approximately 1573–74, cited in ibid., p. 237.

218. On the *imâret* institution and its role in the development of Istanbul, see Inalcik, *The Ottoman Empire*, pp. 140–44.

219. Epstein, *Ottoman Jewish Communities*, pp. 178–80.

220. Heyd, "Jewish Communities of Istanbul," pp. 299–304 and ff.

221. Ibid., pp. 308–309, cites several examples of the Ottoman usage of these terms of which the earliest appear to be from the 1580s. This terminology remained in use until the nineteenth century.

222. See, for example, Rosanes, vol. 3², p. 30.

223. Rosanes, vol. 1², p. 182; David, "Jewish Settlements" (Hebrew), p. 24; Bornstein-Makovetzky, "The Community and its Institutions" (Hebrew), pp. 200–203.

224. Heyd, "Jewish Communities of Istanbul," pp. 307–8.

225. Rosanes, vol. 3², p. 30.

226. Ibid., vol. 3² p. 28.

227. Ibid.

228. Ibid., vol. 3² pp. 28–30

229. Ibid., vol. 3², p. 30. The text of the *haskamah* is on pp. 339–46. It contains the formula: "We attest with our signatures on behalf of all the Holy Congregations of Romania and Sepharad."

230. Ibid., vol. 3², p. 30.

231. Ibid., vol. 3², p. 32; Bornstein, "Jewish Communal Leadership" (Hebrew), states, without citing her sources, that he was the spiritual leader of the Romaniots. Shmuelevitz, p. 190, states simply that he "became chief rabbi of the capital in about 1575." According to Rosanes, vol. 1², p. 215, the spiritual leader of the Romaniots towards the end of the sixteenth century was Rabbi Gabriel ben Elijah.

232. Rosanes, vol. 3², p. 32.

233. Ibid., p. 30.

234. Ibid.

235. Ibid.

236. Franco, *Essai*, pp. 88–89.

237. Cf. Rosanes, vol. 3², p. 30.

238. Ibid., vol. 1², p. 215.

239. Barnai, "The Jewish Community of Istanbul" (Hebrew), pp. 60–62.

240. Leah Bornstein-Makovetzky, "Seridim mi-Pinkas Beit-Din Balat be-Kushta, Shenat 1839" [Remnants of the Register of the Court of Balat in Istanbul, 1839], *Sefunot* (New Series), vol. 4 (19) (1989), pp. 57–58, 61–62.

241. Rosanes, vol. 1², pp. 213, 216.

242. Ibid., vol. 1², pp., 206, 215.

243. Ibid., vol. 1², p. 78; Goodblatt, pp. 10, 139–43.

244. Rosanes, vol. 1², pp. 216–17.

245. Yitzhak [Izhak] Ben-Zvi, *Mehkarim u-Mekorot* [Studies and Documents] (Jerusalem: Ben-Zvi Institute, 1966), pp. 15–20; Ben-Ya'akov, *The*

Jews of Iraq (Hebrew), pp. 83–86, 93–99; Bornstein-Makovetzky, "The Community and its Institutions" (Hebrew), pp. 200–204; Barnai, "The Jews in the Ottoman Empire" (Hebrew), in Tobi, Barnai et al., vol. 1, p. 79.

246. Cf. İslamoğlu and Keyder, "Agenda," pp. 55–58.

247. Cf. Bornstein, "Jewish Communal Leadership" (Hebrew), p. 99.

248. Epstein, *Ottoman Jewish Communities*, p. 210.

249. Bornstein, "Jewish Communal Leadership" (Hebrew), pp. 112–13, 153–55; Geller, "Intercommunity Relations" (Hebrew), pp. 35–36.

250. Ottoman records dated 1544 show that Bitola had a total of 60 Jewish households and 27 tax-paying bachelors. In 1597, 250 tax-paying individuals were listed. Epstein, *Ottoman Jewish Communities*, p. 244.

251. Bornstein, "Jewish Communal Leadership" (Hebrew), p. 105.

252. Angel, *Jews of Rhodes*, pp. 62–64.

253. Ibid., pp. 64–66.

254. Cf. Jacob Barnai, "Reshit ha-Kehillah ha-Yehudit be-Izmir ba-Tekufah ha-Othmanit" [The Origins of the Jewish Community in Izmir in the Ottoman Period] , *Pe'amim*, no. 12 (1982), pp. 47–58; idem, "Rav Yosef Eskapa ve-Rabbanut Izmir" [Rabbi Joseph Eskapa and the Rabbinate of Izmir], *Sefunot*, New Series, vol. 3 (18) (1985), pp. 53–82; idem, "Kavim le-Toledot ha-Hevrah ha-Yehudit be-Izmir be-Shilhei ha-Me'ah ha-18 u-ve-Reshit ha-Me'ah ha-19" [On the Jewish Community of Izmir in the Late Eighteenth and Early Nineteenth Centuries], *Zion*, vol. 47 (1982), pp. 56–76; Haim Gerber and Jacob Barnai, *Yehudei Izmir ba-Me'ah ha-19* [The Jews in Izmir in the Nineteenth Century] (Jerusalem: Misgav Yerushalayim, 1984), pp. 1–17.

255. Bornstein, "Jewish Communal Leadership" (Hebrew), p. 153.

256. And also *kelalut, kolel* and by other terms. See ibid., pp. 107–110.

257. Ibid., p. 153.

258. Nehama, vol. 6, pp. 93–106; Bornstein, "Jewish Communal Leadership" (Hebrew), p. 153.

259. Ibid., pp. 151–52.

260. Ibid., p. 114.

261. Jacob Barnai, *Yehudei Eretz-Yisrael ba-Me'ah ha-18 ba-Hasut "Pekidei Kushta"* [The Jews in Eretz-Israel in the Eighteenth Century under the Patronage of the Constantinople Committee Officials of Eretz-Israel] (Jerusalem: Ben-Zvi Institute, 1982), pp. 177–88; Bornstein, "Jewish Communal Leadership" (Hebrew), p. 113.

262. Bornstein, ibid., pp. 113–14.

263. Ibid., pp. 107–108.

264. Barnai, *Jews in Eretz-Israel* (Hebrew), pp. 131–32.

265. Barnai, "The Jewish Community of Istanbul," p. 62.

266. Cf. Zeynep Çelik, *The Remaking of Istanbul. Portrait of an Ottoman City in the Nineteenth Century* (Seattle and London: University of Washington Press, 1986), pp. 7–9, 22–30.

267. Barnai, "The Jewish Community of Istanbul" (Hebrew), pp. 62–63.

268. The number of studies dealing with Ottoman decline, or various aspects of it, is legion. For some pertinent recent contributions, see: Ömer

Lütfi Barkan, "The Price Revolution of the Sixteenth Century: A Turning Point in the Economic History of the Near East," *International Journal of Middle East Studies*, vol. 6 (1975), pp. 3–28; Halil Inalcik, *The Ottoman Empire: The Classical Age, 1300–1600* (London: Weidenfeld and Nicolson, 1973), pp. 41–52, 179–85; idem, "Military and Fiscal Transformation in the Ottoman Empire, 1600–1700," *Archivum Ottomanicum*, vol. 6 (1980), pp. 283–337; Kemal H. Karpat (ed.), *The Ottoman State and Its Place in World History* (Leiden: E. J. Brill, 1974) [contributions by William H. McNeill, Andrew C. Hess, Halil Inalcik, C. Max Kortepeter, Kemal H. Karpat, and Charles Issawi]; I. Metin Kunt, *The Sultan's Servants: The Transformation of Ottoman Provincial Government, 1550–1650*, New York: Columbia University Press, 1983; Avigdor Levy, "Military Reform and the Problem of Centralization in the Ottoman Empire in the Eighteenth Century," *Middle Eastern Studies*, vol. 18 (1982), pp. 227–49; Huri İslamoğlu-İnan (ed.), *The Ottoman Empire and the World Economy* (Cambridge: Cambridge University Press, 1987) [contributions by Huri İslamoğlu-İnan, Peter Gran, Huri İslamoğlu and Çağlar Keyder, İlkay Sunar, Murat Çizakça, Suraiya Faroqhi, Mehmet Genç and Halil Inalcik.]

269. Cf. Inalcik, *The Ottoman Empire*, pp. 41–52; Charles Issawi, "The Ottoman Empire in the European Economy, 1600–1914. Some Observations and Many Questions," in Karpat (ed.), *The Ottoman State and Its Place in World History*, pp. 111–15.

270. Cf. Inalcik, "Military and Fiscal Transformation," pp. 311–33; İlkay Sunar, "State and Economy in the Ottoman Empire," in İslamoğlu-İnan (ed.), *The Ottoman Empire and the World Economy*, pp. 65–74.

271. Inalcik, *The Ottoman Empire*, p. 162; İslamoğlu and Keyder, "Agenda," pp. 55–58.

272. Gerber, "Jews in Bursa" (Hebrew), pp. 243–45.

273. Epstein, *Ottoman Jewish Communities*, pp. 85–86.

274. Galante (Isis), vol. 5, p. 156; Lewis, *Jews of Islam*, p. 214, n. 29.

275. Galante (Isis), vol. 5, p. 158; vol. 9, pp. 86–94; Nil Akdeniz, *Osmanlılarda Hekim ve Hekimlik Ahlâkı* [Physicians and Medical Ethics in Ottoman Times] (Istanbul University Ph.D. Dissertation, 1977), pp. 156–57. Uzunçarşılı, *Kapukulu*, vol. 1, p. 406, mentions a Jew named Daviçon who served as Chief Physician of the Janissary Corps (*ser tabib-i ocağ-ı yeniçeriyan*) in the years 1811 and 1813.

276. Rosanes, vol. 3^2, pp. 349–54; Galante (Isis), vol. 9, pp. 86–87; Baron, *Social and Religious History*, vol. 18^2, pp. 130–31.

277. Galante (Isis), vol. 9, p. 92.

278. Rosanes, vol. 4, pp. 187–88; Galante (Isis), vol. 9 p. 92; Harry Friedenwald, *The Jews and Medicine: Essays* (2 vols., Baltimore: The Johns Hopkins Press, 1944), vol. 1, pp. 168, 236; vol. 2, p. 604.

279. Rosanes, vol. 4, pp. 188–89; Galante (Isis), vol. 9, pp. 92–93.

280. Rosanes, vol. 5, p. 6; Galante (Isis), vol. 9, p. 94.

281. Cf. Jacob Barnai, "Zikah ve-Nittuk bein Hakhmei Turkiyah le-Hakhmei Polin u-Merkaz Eiropah ba-Me'ah ha-17" [Relation and Disengagement between the Scholars of Turkey and the Scholars of Poland and Central Europe in the Seventeenth Century], *Gal'ed*, vol. 9 (1986), pp. 13–26.

282. Carter V. Findley, *Bureaucratic Reform in the Ottoman Empire. The Sublime Porte, 1789–1922* (Princeton: Princeton University Press, 1980), pp. 91–93.

283. Nehama, vol. 5, pp. 84–86; Isaac Samuel Emmanuel, *Histoire de l'Industrie des Tissus des Israélites de Salonique* (Paris: Librairie Lipschutz, 1935), pp. 55–57; Angel, *Jews of Rhodes*, p. 43; Ben-Zvi, *Eretz-Israel* (Hebrew), pp. 205–13.

284. Rosanes, vol. 3^2, pp. 376–79.

285. Between 1642 and 1688, the Belgrade *yeshivah* became an important center of scholarship under the leadership of Rabbis Judah Lerma, Simhah ben Gershon Cohen, and Joseph Almosnino. Cf. Daniel Furman, "Belgrade," *Encyclopedia Judaica* (Jerusalem: Keter, 1972; henceforth EJ), vol. 4, pp. 426–27.

286. Rosanes, vol. 5, p. 45; M. Cavid Baysun, "Belgrad," IA, vol. 2, p. 479.

287. See Rosanes, vol. 5, p. 44, on the tribulations of the community of Nish.

288. According to an Ottoman population count, dated 1594/95, the town had 139 Jewish households of a total population of 1594 households, including Muslims and Christians. Cengiz Orhonlu, "Trablus," IA, vol. 12 (1), pp. 452–55.

289. Rosanes, vol. 3^2, pp. 414–17; Orhonlu, ibid.

290. Rosanes, vol. 3^2, pp. 422–27; Ben-Zvi, *Eretz-Israel* (Hebrew), pp. 205–13; Baron, *Social and Religious History*, vol. 18^2, pp. 154–55

291. Rosanes, vol. 3^2, pp. 422–23; Ben-Zvi, *Eretz-Israel* (Hebrew), pp. 213–14.

292. Rosanes, vol. 3^2, pp. 417–22; Ben-Zvi, *Eretz-Israel* (Hebrew), pp. 220–25; Minna Rozen, *Ha-Kehillah ha-Yehudit bi-Yrushalayim ba-Me'ah ha-17* [The Jewish Community of Jerusalem in the Seventeenth Century] (Tel Aviv: Tel Aviv University, 1984), pp. 38–49.

293. Cf. Rosanes, vol. 3^2, pp. 415–16; vol. 5, p. 44 and ff.

294. Rosanes, vol. 3^2, pp. 433–40; Emmanuel, *Histoire*, pp. 257–60.

295. Gerber, "Jews in Bursa" (Hebrew), pp. 237, 254.

296. Ibid., p. 236,

297. Rosanes, vol. 5, pp. 33–34.

298. On the strong ties between the Ottoman and Polish Jewish communities, the flow of Polish refugees to the Ottoman Empire and its impact on Ottoman Jewry, see Barnai, "Relation and Disengagement" (Hebrew), especially pp. 16–18.

299. Gershom Scholem, *Sabbatai Ṣevi: The Mystical Messiah, 1626–1676*, tr. R. J. Zwi Werblowsky (Princeton, N. J.: Princeton University Press, 1973), pp. 77–93. This is the most exhaustive study of the careers of Shabbetai Tzevi and his "prophet," Nathan of Gaza. An excellent shorter account, which goes beyond the lifetimes of Shabbetai Tzevi and Nathan of Gaza and which traces the evolution of the Shabbatean movement until the nineteenth century, was written by Scholem and published in EJ, vol. 14, pp. 1219–54.

300. Cf. Rosanes, vol. 4, pp. 49–50; Franco, *Essai*, pp. 94–95.

301. On this theory, see Scholem, pp. 125–38.
302. Cf. Rosanes, vol. 4, pp. 57–59.
303. Ibid., p. 57.
304. Cf. ibid., pp. 59–67.
305. Scholem, pp. 446–60; Galante (Isis), vol. 3, pp. 199–200.
306. Cf. Franco, *Essai*, pp. 110–12.
307. Scholem, pp. 668–86; Galante (Isis), vol. 3, pp. 200–202.
308. Scholem, pp. 882–918; Rosanes, vol. 4, pp. 77–89.
309. Galante (Isis), vol. 8, pp. 224–47; Gershom Scholem, "Doenmeh," EJ, vol. 6, pp. 148–52; A recent Turkish study of the Dönme movement is Abdurrahman Küçük, *Dönmeler ve Dönmelik Tarihi* [A History of the Dönmes and the Dönme Movement] (Istanbul: Ötüken Neşriyat, n. d. ca. 1980).
310. Franco, *Essai*, pp. 113–14; Gershom Scholem, "Doenmeh," EJ, vol. 6, pp. 148–52; idem, "Shabbetai Zevi," EJ, vol. 14, pp. 1241–54; Barnai, "The Jews in the Ottoman Empire" (Hebrew), in Tobi, Barnai et al., vol. 1, pp. 105–108.
311. See, for example, Rosanes, vol. 4, p. 93; Lewis, *Jews of Islam*, pp. 146–47.
312. On the adverse impact that "rabbinic censorship" had on the study of the Shabbetai Tzevi affair, even in modern times, see Scholem, *Sabbatai Sevi*, "Preface," pp. IX–XIII.
313. Cf. Rosanes, vol. 4, p. 93,
314. Cf. Barnai, "The Jews in the Ottoman Empire" (Hebrew), in Tobi, Barnai et. al., vol. 1, pp. 107–108.
315. From *Orhot Yosher*, cited in Barnai, ibid., pp. 108–109.
316. Cf. Barnai, "Jewish Community of Istanbul" (Hebrew), pp. 64–65; Gerber, "Entrepreneurship" (Hebrew), pp. 44–67; Thomas Philipp, "Beit Farhi ve-ha-Temurot be-Ma'amadam shel Yehudei Suryah ve-Eretz-Yisrael, 1750–1860" [The Farhi Family and the Changing Position of the Jews in Syria and Palestine], *Cathedra*, no. 34 (1985), pp. 98–99; Ben Ya'akov, *The Jews of Iraq* (Hebrew), pp. 93–99.
317. *The Letters and Works of Lady Mary Wortley Montagu* (London, 1893), vol. 1, p. 283.
318. Barnai, "Jewish Community of Istanbul" (Hebrew), pp. 55–56.
319, Rosanes, vol. 5, pp. 346–49; Ben-Ya'akov, *The Jews of Iraq* (Hebrew), pp. 95–98.
320. Rosanes, vol. 5, p. 351.
321. Barnai, "Jewish Community of Istanbul" (Hebrew), pp. 56–57.
322. This amount was then equivalent to about 32,500 British pounds. By way of comparison, Eton, reporting "from the most authentic documents," states that in 1776 the government's annual income from the Istanbul customhouse, a major source of income, amounted to 936,000 kuruş and the total revenue of the Ottoman government was 44,942,500 kuruş, or about 4,494,250 British pounds. See William Eton, *A Survey of the Turkish Empire* (2nd. ed., London, 1799), pp. 39–47, where a detailed list of government revenue sources is given.

323. Eton, ibid., p. 41.

324. We do not know the total number of taxpayers at that time, but in 1690–91, over 5,000 Jews paid the poll tax to the government. Cf. Heyd, "Jewish Communities of Istanbul," p. 310.

325. Barnai, "Jewish Community of Istanbul" (Hebrew), p. 56.

326. Ibid., p. 59.

327. Barnai, "Relation and Disengagement" (Hebrew), pp. 23–25.

328, Rosanes, vol. 5, p. 350.

329. Ibid., pp. 350–54.

330. Winter, "Relations of Egyptian Jews" (Hebrew), pp. 389–90.

331. Ben-Ya'akov, *Jews of Iraq* (Hebrew), pp. 100–101; Franco, *Essai*, pp. 132–33; Ahmed Cevdet, *Tarih* [History] (12 vols., Istanbul, 1854–1883), vol. 9, pp. 246–63, 265–66; Foreign Office Archives, London (henceforth FO), 196/1, Stratford Canning's no. 17 of 14 October, 1810, and no. 28 of 24 December, 1810.

332. Ben-Ya'akov, *Jews of Iraq* (Hebrew), pp. 103–104,

333. Rosanes, vol. 5, pp. 180–84; Daniel Furman, "Belgrade," EJ, vol. 4, p. 427; Simon Marcus, "Pleven," EJ, vol. 13, p. 645; idem, "Vidin," EJ, vol. 16, pp. 120–21; A. Cevat Eren, "Pazvand-Oğlu, Osman," IA, vol. 9, pp. 532–35.

334. Furman, "Belgrade," EJ, vol. 4, p. 427; Simon Marcus, "Yugoslavia," EJ. vol. 16, pp. 868–69.

335. Franco, *Essai*, p. 137; Ben-Zvi, *Eretz-Israel* (Hebrew), p. 362; Simon Marcus, "Greece," EJ, vol. 7, pp. 876–77.

336. Stanford J. Shaw, *Between Old and New. The Ottoman Empire under Sultan Selim III, 1789–1807* (Cambridge, Mass.: Harvard University Press, 1971), pp. 86–111, 138–66 and ff.; Avigdor Levy, "The Officer Corps in Sultan Mahmud II's New Ottoman Army, 1826–1839," *International Journal of Middle East Studies*, vol. 2 (1971), pp. 21–39; Findley, *Bureaucratic Reform*, pp. 205–209.

337. He is credited with having authored and translated numerous scientific works and with having command of Turkish, Arabic, Hebrew, Persian, Greek, Latin, and French. Archives de la Guerre, Paris (Henceforth AG), MR 1619, 39, memorandum by Lieutenant Foltz of 1 May, 1831; Ahmed Lutfi, *Tarih* [History] (8 vols., Istanbul, 1873–1910), vol. 2, p. 143. For detailed information on Hoca Ishak and his works, see Faik Reşit Unat, "Başhoca Ishak Efendi," *Belleten*, vol. 28 (1964), pp. 89–116; Niyazi Berkes, The *Development of Secularism in Turkey* (Montreal: McGill University Press, 1964), pp. 118–19.

338. Galante (Isis), vol. 8, pp. 74–75.

339. A. Ubicini, *Lettres sur la Turquie*, vol. II (Paris, 1854), p. 377, cited in Lewis, *Jews of Islam*, p. 140.

340. Rosanes, vol. 5, p. 350.

341. Leah Bornstein-Makovetzky, "Seridim mi-Pinkas Beit-Din Balat be-Kushta, Shenat 1839" [Remnants of the Register of the Court of Balat in Istanbul of 1839], *Sefunot*, New Series, vol. 4 (19) (1989), pp. 58–59, 86–89 and ff.

342. C. Oscanyan, *The Sultan and his People* (New York, 1857), pp. 376–79.

343. Stanley Lane-Poole, *The Life of the Right Honourable Stratford Canning* (2 vols., London, 1888), vol. 1, p. 49
344. Cevdet, *Tarih*, vol. 9, p. 16.
345. Ibid., pp. 59–61.
346. Avigdor Levy, "Merkezde İktidar Politikaları, 1808–1812: Osmanlı Padişahlığının Silkinişi" [Power Politics at the Center, 1808–1812: The Resurgence of the Ottoman Sultanate], *Tarih ve Toplum*, no. 41 (1987), pp. 52–56.
347. See, for example, *The Times* (London), July 15, 18 and August 21, 22, 23 (1826); *Journal des Débats* (Paris), August 21, 22, 23 (1826).
348. Stanford J. Shaw and Ezel Kural Shaw, *History of the Ottoman Empire and Modern Turkey. Volume II: Reform, Revolution, and Republic: The Rise of Modern Turkey* (Cambridge: Cambridge University Press, 1977), p. 113.
349. Among the Muslims, about 18.6 percent of the 5–25 age group attended school, compared with 25.5 percent among non-Muslims. Non-Muslims were represented to an even greater degree in the more advanced educational institutions. Ibid., pp. 106–13 and ff.
350. Kemal H. Karpat, "The Mass Media: Turkey," in Robert E. Ward and Dankwart A. Rustow (eds.), *Political Modernization in Japan and Turkey* (Princeton: Princeton University Press, 1964), p. 259.
351. Ibid., p. 265.
352. Shaw and Shaw, vol. 2, pp. 128–29.
353. Karpat, "The Mass Media," pp. 257–68; Galante (Isis), vol. 2, pp. 91–98; Avner Levi, "Ha-Itonut ha-Yehudit be-Izmir" [The Jewish Press in Izmir], *Pe'amim*, no. 12 (1982), pp. 87–104.
354. Harold Temperley, *England and the Near East: The Crimea* (London: Longmans, Green and Co., 1956), p. 73.
355. See the text of an Imperial Order *(Hatt-ı Hümayun)* dated 12 Rebiyülahır, 1224/27 May, 1809, cited in Cevdet, *Tarih*, vol. 9, pp. 349–51.
356. Avigdor Levy, "Ottoman Attitudes to the Rise of Balkan Nationalism," in Béla K. Király and Gunther E. Rothenberg (eds.), *War and Society in East Central Europe*, vol. 1 (New York: Columbia University Press, 1979), pp. 325–45.
357. Cevdet, *Tarih*, vol. 9, p. 190.
358. Cited in Enver Ziya Karal, "Non-Muslim Representatives in the First Constitutional Assembly, 1876–1877," in Braude and Lewis (eds.), *Christians and Jews*, vol. 1, p. 388. Karal gives the date of this statement as 1830. See also Ed. Engelhardt, *La Turqie et le Tanzimat* (2 vols., Paris, 1882–1884), vol. 1, p. 33; Reşat Kaynar, *Mustafa Reşit Paşa ve Tanzimat* [Mustafa Reşit Paşa and the Tanzimat] (Ankara: Türk Tarih Kurumu Basımevi, 1954), pp. 99–100. The last source suggests that this statement was made in the late 1830s to a group of European ambassadors.
359. The phrase cited in the text was officially translated as *"l'amour du Prince et de la patrie [et] le dévouement [au] pays."* The Turkish text of the rescript was published in *Takvim-i Vakayı* (the official Ottoman government newspaper, henceforth TV), no. 187 (15 Ramazan, 1255/22 November, 1839). Facsimiles of the TV text and the French translation distributed at the ceremony have been reproduced in T. C. Maarif Vekâleti, *Tanzimat*, vol. 1 (Istanbul, 1940), following p. 48. Partial English translations are found in Shaw and Shaw, vol.

2, pp. 60–61; J. C. Hurewitz (ed.), *The Middle East and North Africa in World Politics*, vol. 1 (2nd rev. ed., New Haven: Yale University Press, 1975), pp. 269–71. For a comprehensive discussion of this document, see Şerif Mardin, *The Genesis of Young Ottoman Thought: A Study in the Modernization of Turkish Political Ideas* (Princeton: Princeton University Press, 1962), pp. 155–68 and ff.

360. Redhouse, *Lexicon*, p. 1972.

361. Cf. Karal, "Non-Muslim Representatives," pp. 388–400; Carter V. Findley, "The Acid Test of Ottomanism: The Acceptance of Non-Muslims in the Late Ottoman Bureaucracy," in Braude and Lewis (eds.), *Christians and Jews*, vol. 1, pp. 339–68.

362. Cf. Howard Morley Sachar, *The Course of Modern Jewish History* (New York: Dell Publishing Co., 1963), pp. 100–107.

363. Franco, *Essai*, pp. 152, 168–69.

364. Ibid., pp. 166, 182–86.

365. Cf. Galante (Isis), vol. 5, p. 39; Esther Benbassa, *Un Grand Rabin Sepharade en Politique 1892–1923* (Paris: Presses du CNRS, 1990), pp. 26–32.

366. Başbakanlık Arşivi (Office of the Prime Minister's Archives; henceforth BA); Istanbul, *Gayr-ı Müslim Cemaatlere Ait Defterler* [Registers pertaining to non-Muslim communities; henceforth GMC], vol. 17, pp. 95–97.

367. See Ben Ya'akov, *Jews of Iraq* (Hebrew), p. 156; Mordekhai (Mordecai) Ha-Cohen, *Higgid Mordekhai: Korot Luv vi-Yhudeihah, Yishuveihem u-Minhageihem* [History of Libya and its Jews and their Settlements and Customs], ed. Harvey Goldberg (Jerusalem: Ben-Zvi Institute, 1978), p. 147; Haim Z. Hirschberg, "Hakham Bashi," EJ, vol. 7, pp. 1146–48; Zvi Loker, "Sarajevo," EJ, vol. 14, pp. 869–70.

368. Cf. Rosanes, vol. 5, p. 410.

369. *Takvim-i Vakayı*, no. 187, dated 15 Ramazan, 1255/22 November, 1839, for example, reports that at the ceremony at Gülhane proclaiming the *Hatt-ı Hümayan*, the *Haham Başı* was present together with Muslim religious dignitaries and the Orthodox, Armenian and Catholic patriarchs.

370. See, for example, the circular letter in Turkish, Hebrew, and Judeo-Spanish, sent in 1840 by the *Haham Başı*, Hayyim Moshe Fresco, to all the Jewish communities in the empire, urging the introduction of the study of the Turkish language in Jewish schools. Archives of the American Jewish Historical Society, Waltham, Mass., no. I-238.

371. BA, GMC, vol. 17, pp. 95–97; Rosanes, vol. 5, pp. 406–10.

372. Franco, *Essai*, p. 239; Galante (Isis), vol. 9, p. 109.

373. Galante (Isis), vol. 9, pp. 109–10.

374. Ibid., vol. 9, pp. 97, 99, 106, 109. Sami Günsberg went on to serve as the dentist of Mustafa Kemal Atatürk, the first President of the Turkish Republic. Ibid., vol. 9, p. 109.

375. Franco, *Essai*, p. 150; Ben Ya'akov, *Jews of Iraq* (Hebrew), pp. 142–48; Roderic H. Davison, *Reform in the Ottoman Empire, 1856–1876* (Princeton: Princeton University Press, 1963), pp. 140–42, 147–48 and ff.; Steven Rosenthal, "Minorities and Municipal Reform in Istanbul, 1850–1870," in Braude and Lewis (eds.), *Christians and Jews*, vol. 1, pp. 369–85; Benjamin Braude, "Councils and Community: Minorities and the *Majlis* in *Tanzimat* Jerusalem," in *The Islamic World From Classical to Modern Times: Essays in Honor of Bernard Lewis* (Princeton: Darwin Press, Inc., 1989), pp. 651–60.

376. An exact determination of the size of the Ottoman general population and its Jewish component is complicated by the following factors: a) The
incompleteness of Ottoman censuses; b) Significant numbers of Jews resident
in the Ottoman Empire were foreign nationals and were, therefore, listed as
foreigners and not as Jews. In 1899, for example, the total number of foreign
nationals resident in the Ottoman Empire was recorded as 236,547, of which
over 90 percent were found in Istanbul, Izmir, Baghdad, and Jerusalem, all
of which had large Jewish communities. Cf. Kemal H. Karpat, *Ottoman Population, 1830–1914: Demographic and Social Characteristics* (Madison: University
of Wisconsin Press, 1985), p. 161. There is no question that a significant
number of these foreign nationals were Jews, although it is impossible to
determine how many; c) In the three decades prior to World War I, significant
numbers of Jews living in the Ottoman Empire were either recent arrivals or
temporary residents, staying sometimes for extended periods of time. This
was particularly true for Palestine and the *vilayet* of Aydın, which included
the city of Izmir. For one reason or another, these people were not recorded
by the Ottoman census takers (Kemal H. Karpat). For all these factors, the
numbers of Jews given below and their percentage as part of the general
Ottoman population should be corrected upwards. Considering, however,
the large size of the general Ottoman population, these corrections could not
be very significant as far as the relative share of the Jewish population within
the general population. In the Ottoman general census of 1881–1893, about
184,000 Jews were counted among a total population count of some
17,400,000. Thus, the Jews constituted about 1.06 percent of the total popu-
latian counted. However, the actual numbers of both the general population
and the Jews were higher, because the census was not completed in some
provinces, and in others it was not conducted at all. The total Ottoman population for that period was estimated to have been close to 28 million and the
total number of Jews was probably well over 300,000. See Karpat, *Ottoman
Population*, pp. 30–34, 122–51. In 1897, the Jews numbered about 215,000
(1.13 percent) of an incomplete population count of some 19 million. Shaw
and Shaw, vol. 2, p. 240; Karpat, *Ottoman Population*, pp. 160–61. Justin
McCarthy has concluded that in 1911–12, the Jewish population comprised
about 357,000 Ottoman subjects, which constituted 1.14 percent of the total
population. McCarthy's figures, however, do not include the Jews of Ottoman
Arabia (especially Yemen, estimated by him at 35,000–40,000), and non-Ot-
toman subjects, especially significant in Istanbul, Izmir, and Palestine. If the
latter groups are added, then the total number of Jews in the Ottoman Empire
in 1911–12 was more than 400,000 (Justin McCarthy). These figures are more
or less in agreement with the totals, although not all the particulars, of the
numbers provided by Ruppin (see Table 4). In comparing Ruppin's figures
with those by McCarthy, Ottoman territorial losses in Europe and Africa
(Tripoli) need to be considered. See Arthur Ruppin, *The Jews of To-Day* (tr.
Margery Bentwich, introd., Joseph Jacobs; London: G. Bell and Sons, 1913),
pp. 39–41.

377. Franco, *Essai*, p. 239; Davison, *Reform*, pp. 239–44.

378. Robert Devereux, *The First Ottoman Constitutional Period: A Study of
the Midhat Constitution and Parliament* (Baltimore: The Johns Hopkins Press,
1963), p. 144. The accuracy of Devereux's statistical sources, especially with

respect to the numbers of the Jewish population, is questionable, but it does not change the basic fact of a considerable Jewish overrepresentation, compared with the other groups.

379. Galante (Isis), vol. 9, p. 95. The Ottoman provincial authorities in Libya exhibited similar attitudes as of the 1860s (Rachel Simon).

380. Osman Ergin, *Türkiye Maarif Tarihi* [History of Turkey's Education] (5 vols., Istanbul: Osmanbey Matbaası, 1939–43), vol. 2, pp. 285–86.

381. Hayyim J. Cohen, *The Jews of the Middle East, 1860–1972* (Jerusalem: Israel Universities Press, 1973), p. 131.

382. Apparently, in 1842, the government had asked the Jewish Community of Istanbul to provide 38 students for the medical school, or about 10 percent of the student body. John Mason, *Three Years in Turkey: The Journal of a Medical Mission to the Jews* (London, 1860), p. 178, cited in Berkes, *Secularism*, pp. 114–15.

383. Franco, *Essai*, p. 156; Galante (Isis), vol. 9, p. 95.

384. Berkes, *Secularism*, pp. 114–15, citing Charles McFarlane, *Turkey and its Destiny* (Philadelphia, 1850), vol. 2, pp. 163, 165 and John Mason, op. cit., p. 178. See also H. Cohen, *Jews of the Middle East*, p. 131. Dr. Spitzer (1813–1895) was first appointed to the medical school in 1839 as professor of anatomy. At about 1844, he became a physician to the imperial palace and also served as a political advisor to Sultan Abdülmecid. As of 1850, he served in the Ottoman diplomatic corps. Galante (Isis), vol. 9, pp. 109–10.

385. Galante (Isis), vol. 8, pp. 76–78; vol. 9, pp. 96–115.

386. Ibid., vol. 6, pp. 55–56.

387. Berkes, *Secularism*, pp. 188–90; Shaw and Shaw, vol. 2, pp. 108–109.

388. In the eighteenth and nineteenth centuries, the relative proportion of the Jewish population of Istanbul steadily declined due to a large influx of other groups, mainly Muslims and Armenians. From the mid-fifteenth century through the seventeenth, the Jews comprised approximately 10 percent of the capital's population, and they formed the third largest group after the Muslims and Greeks. In the course of the eighteenth century, the Armenians began to outnumber the Jews, who declined to the fourth place. In 1856, the Jewish population of Istanbul was estimated to comprise about six percent of the total population, or some 26,000 souls of a total population of approximately 430,000. Shaw and Shaw, vol. 2, pp. 241–42. In subsequent years the Jewish population increased appreciably, but due to the larger growth of other groups, mainly Muslim, its relative share of the total population continued to decline. In 1897, the Jews constituted less than 5 percent of the total population (see Table 5). Karpat, *Ottoman Population*, p. 104.

389. H. Cohen, *Jews of the Middle East*, p. 131.

390. Of the minority groups, only the very small Catholic community had a significant number of state employees proportionate to its size (see Table 6). Shaw and Shaw, vol. 2, p. 244; Karpat, *Ottoman Population*, p. 105.

391. Galante (Isis), vol. 8, pp. 78–87.

392. Findley, "Acid Test of Ottomanism," pp. 346–47, 360–61.

393. Feroz Ahmad, "Unionist Relations with the Greek, Armenian, and Jewish Communities of the Ottoman Empire, 1908–1914," in Braude and Lewis (eds.), *Christians and Jews*, vol. 1, p. 428.

394. Ben-Zvi, *Eretz-Israel* (Hebrew), pp. 366–68; Kurt Grunwald, "Jewish Schools under Foreign Flags in Ottoman Palestine," in Moshe Maoz (ed.), *Studies on Palestine during the Ottoman Period* (Jerusalem: The Magnes Press, 1975), pp. 171–73; Yehoshua Ben-Arieh, *Jerusalem in the Nineteenth Century. Volume I: The Old City* (New York: St. Martin's Press, 1984), pp. 340–43; Rodrigue, *French Jews*, pp. 44–46.

395. N. Leven, *Cinquante Ans d'Histoire: L'Alliance Israélite Universelle (1860–1910)* (2 vols., Paris: Librairie Felix Alcan, 1911–1920), vol. 1, p. 69.

396. Leven, vol. 2, pp. 53–63; Rodrigue, *French Jews*, pp. 47–49.

397. Leven, vol. 2, pp. 65–71, 159–71, 177–79; Rodrigue, *French Jews*, pp. 50–57.

398. Ben Ya'akov, *The Jews of Iraq* (Hebrew), p. 145; André Chouraqui, *Cent Ans d'Histoire: L'Alliance Israélite Universelle et la Renaissance Juive Contemporaine (1860–1960)* (Paris: Presses Universitaires de France, 1965), p. 166; H. Cohen, *Jews of the Middle East*, p. 139; Rodrigue, *French Jews*, pp. 140–41.

399. H. Cohen, *Jews of the Middle East*, pp. 117, 130.

400. Chouraqui, *Cent Ans*, pp. 161–66.

401. H. Cohen, *Jews of the Middle East*, p. 130.

402. This estimate is based on the calculations of H. Cohen for schools located within the boundaries of present-day Turkey (11,687 in 1913), Iraq (3,920 in 1913), Syria (2,173 in 1910), and Lebanon (516 in 1910). Ibid., pp. 117, 130, 139–40, 193 n. 89. Figures for the seven Alliance institutions in Palestine are not provided. In 1914, the Alliance in North Africa, the Middle East, and the Balkans operated a total of 188 schools with 48,000 students. Chouraqui, *Cent Ans*, p. 161.

403. Rodrigue, *French Jews*, p. 92. There were considerable differences among the various Jewish communities. In Izmir, only 14 percent of the Jewish children attended the Alliance schools, compared to 50 percent in Edirne. Ibid.

404. Rodrigue, *French Jews*, p. 125.

405. H. Cohen, *Jews of the Middle East*, pp. 116, 128–29, 136, 139.

406. Rodrigue, *French Jews*, p. 93.

407. Chouraqui, *Cent Ans*, p. 166; Dumont, "Jewish Communities," pp. 209–23; Rodrigue, *French Jews*, pp. 115–18.

408. Also see Dumont, "Jewish Communities," especially pp. 222–25; Haim Gerber and Jacob Barnai, *Yehudei Izmir ba-Me'ah ha-19. Te'udot Turkiyot mi-Beit ha-Din ha-Shar'i* [The Jews in Izmir in the Nineteenth Century. Ottoman Documents from the Shar'i Court] (Jerusalem: Misgav Yerushalayim, 1984), p. 10.

409. The role that Jews played in the Young Turk movement has been the subject of a considerable, and controversial, literature. For a recent contribution, and further bibliography, see Robert W. Olson, "The Young Turks and the Jews: A Historiographical Revision," *Turcica*, vol. 18, (1986), pp. 219–35.

410. Cf. Ahmad, "Unionist Relations," pp. 425–28.

411. Also see Jacob M. Landau, *Tekinalp, Turkish Patriot 1883–1961*. Leiden: Publications de l'Institut historique et archéologique néerlandais de Stanboul, vol. 53, 1984, especially pp. 1–43.

412. Esther Benbassa, "Ha-Tenu'ah ha-Tziyonit be-Turkiyah be-Shilhei ha-Me'ah ha-19 u-ve-Hathalat ha-Me'ah ha-20" [The Zionist Movement in Turkey at the End of the Nineteenth Century and the Beginning of the Twentieth Century], *Pe'amim*, no. 40 (1989), pp. 54–75.

413. Cited in Mandel, *Arabs and Zionism*, p. 146.

414. Ibid.

415. Also see ibid., pp. 146–48.

416. Galante (Isis), vol. 1, pp. 260–61.

417. Mandel, *Arabs and Zionism*, pp. 2–18; Isaiah Friedman, "The System of Capitulations and its Effects on Turco-Jewish Relations in Palestine, 1856–1897," in David Kushner (ed.), *Palestine in the Late Ottoman Period: Political, Social and Economic Transformation* (Jerusalem: Yad Izhak Ben-Zvi, 1986), pp. 285–89.

418. Angel, *Jews of Rhodes*, pp. 145–49; Dumont, "Jewish Communities," pp. 212–14.

419. Dumont, ibid., p. 214.

420. Rodrigue, *French Jews*, p. 156.

421. Goodblatt, pp. 108–110; Barnai, *Jews in Eretz-Israel* (Hebrew), pp. 129–58 and passim; idem, "Le-Toledot ha-Kesharim she-Bein Yehudei Izmir li-Yhudei Eretz-Yisrael ba-Me'ot ha-17 ve-ha-18" [On the History of the Relations between the Jews of Izmir and the Jews of Palestine in the Seventeenth and Eighteenth Centuries], *Shalem*, vol. 5 (1987), pp. 95–114.

422. Ben-Zvi, *Eretz-Israel* (Hebrew), p. 362; Sherman Lieber, "Hitpathutah shel ha-Okhlosiyah ha-Yehudit bi-Tzfat, 1800–1839" [The Development of the Jewish Population in Safed, 1800–1839], *Cathedra*, no. 45 (1987), pp. 13–44.

423. Cf. Bornstein-Makovetzky, "Register of the Court of Balat" (Hebrew), pp. 58, 88, 105–107; Ha-Cohen, *Higgid Mordekhai*, pp. 168–69.

424. Galante (Isis), vol. 3, pp. 13–14; Gerber and Barnai, *Jews in Izmir* (Hebrew), pp. 21–23.

425. Franco, *Essai*, pp. 182, 185.

426. Salvator Israel, "Rozanes," pp. 348–49; Abraham David, "Rosanes," EJ, vol. 14, pp. 261–62.

427. Galante (Isis), vol. 4, pp. 57–58; Hayyim J. Cohen, "Haim Nahoum," EJ, vol. 12, p. 791; Benbassa, *Un Grand Rabbin*, p. 17.

428. Roberto Bachi, *The Population of Israel* (Jerusalem: The Institute of Contemporary Jewry, 1974), pp. 32–33, 74.

429. Ibid., p. 94.

430. Ibid., p. 32.

431. Ruppin, *The Jews of To-Day*, pp. 38–42, estimates the world's total Jewish population ca. 1900 at about 11,500,000.

432. *Bulletin de l'Alliance Israélite Universelle*, no. 18 (1893), pp. 38–39, cited in Dumont, "Jewish Communities," p. 221.

433. Cited in Rodrigue, *French Jews*, pp. 169–70.

Chronology

Ca. 1280	The Turkish warrior Osman Gazi founded the Ottoman (*Osmanlı*) principality at Söğüt, in the northwest corner of Anatolia.
Ca. 1280–1326	The Ottoman Turks gradually expanded toward the Black Sea and the Sea of Marmara.
1290	The Jews were expelled from England, then from France (1306 and 1322).
1326	The Ottomans conquered Prousa (Bursa) and established it as their capital. Jews were encouraged to settle in Bursa.
1326–61	The Ottomans continued to expand in western Anatolia, crossed into Europe (1352), and began the conquest of Thrace.
1361	The Ottomans conquered Adrianople (Edirne) and subsequently established it as their new capital. Jews were encouraged to settle in Edirne. Within several decades, the Jewish population became a prosperous community, comprising local Romaniots, as well as immigrants from Hungary, France, Italy, and Sicily (the Jews were expelled from Hungary in 1376 and from France, again, in 1394).
1361–1400	The Ottomans continued to expand in the Balkans and Anatolia, conquering Bulgaria, Macedonia, Thessaly, and Karaman. By 1400, most of the territories between the Danube and eastern Anatolia were under the rule of Bayezid I.
1385	Jews were forbidden to live in Christian quarters in Spain.
1391	Jewish massacres in Spain led to the emigration of Sephardim to Palestine and other lands of the eastern Mediterranean.
1400	Timur the Lame (Tamerlane, Timurlenk) invaded Anatolia from the east.
1402	Battle of Ankara: Timur defeated Bayezid and divided the Ottoman state into several principalities.

1403	A civil war erupted between Bayezid's sons, lasting until 1413, when Mehmed I succeeded in reuniting the much reduced Ottoman territories.
1411	Forced conversions of Jews in Spain.
1413–51	Mehmed I (1413–21) and Murad II (1421–51) restored and consolidated Ottoman power in Anatolia and the Balkans.
1421	Jews were burned in Vienna and expelled from Austria, then from Cologne (1426), Augsburg (1439), Bavaria (1452), Franconia (1453), and other German lands, leading to the settlement of Ashkenazim in the Ottoman Empire.
Ca. 1450	Isaac Tzarfati issued a letter, calling on European Jews to immigrate to the Ottoman Empire.
1453	Mehmed II (1451–1481) conquered Constantinople (Istanbul) and established it as the new Ottoman capital. He rebuilt the city and repopulated it with large numbers of Muslims, Christians and Jews. Most of the empire's Jewish population was transferred to Istanbul, where they constituted over 10 percent of the city's total population.
Ca. 1453 –Ca. 1496	Moses Capsali Chief Rabbi of Istanbul.
1453–1503	Mehmed II and Bayezid II (1481–1512) expanded Ottoman rule in Anatolia, Greece, Serbia, Bosnia, Albania, and the Crimea. Wallachia, Moldavia, and the Crimean Khanate became Ottoman tributary states.
1467–74	Intermittent massacres and attacks against Jews and Marranos in Spain.
1480	The Inquisition was established in Spain, leading to the emigration of Sephardim to the Ottoman Empire, Palestine and Egypt.
Ca. 1483	Death of Hekim Yakub (Jacopo of Gaeta), Chief Physician of Mehmed II.
1484–86	Jews were attacked in Provence.
1492–1511	The Jews were expelled from Spain, Sicily and Savoy (1492), then from Navarre, Provence (1498), Marseilles (1507), and the Kingdom of Naples (1510–1511). The Jews of Portugal were forced to convert

	(1496–1497). Mass immigration of Jews to the Ottoman Empire, as well as to Palestine, Egypt, and North Africa.
1493	A Hebrew printing press was founded in Istanbul, then in Salonica (1515).
Ca. 1496–1526	Elijah Mizrahi was the leading rabbinical authority in Istanbul.
Ca. 1497	Joseph Caro's family settled in Istanbul.
1512–18	Joseph Hamon served as physician to Selim I and established a dynasty of court physicians.
1514–16	Selim I defeated the Safavids and annexed eastern Anatolia.
1516–17	Selim conquered Syria, Palestine, and Egypt, opening these lands to further Jewish settlement.
1520–66	Reign of Süleyman the Magnificent, considered the apogee of Ottoman power and cultural efflorescence. Süleyman conquered Hungary and laid siege to Vienna (1529). He annexed Iraq and Yemen and extended Ottoman control of North Africa from Egypt to the borders of Morocco.
Ca. 1520	Abraham Castro was appointed to administer the Egyptian mint.
1534	Solomon Alkabetz settled in Safed.
1536	The Inquisition was established in Portugal, leading to the flight of Marranos.
1536–42	Süleyman rebuilt the city walls of Jerusalem.
Ca. 1536–75	Joseph Caro in Safed.
1542	The Jews were expelled from Prague.
Ca. 1545	Death of Joseph Taitatzak in Salonica.
1546	Death of Jacob Berab (Beirav) in Safed. Restoration of the Jewish community in Hebron.
1553	David ibn Abi Zimra settled in Jerusalem. A Hebrew printing press was founded in Edirne, then in Cairo (1557).
1553–54	The Nasi family settled in Istanbul.
Ca. 1554	Death of Moses Hamon, physician to Selim I and Süleyman the Magnificent.
1555	Joseph Caro completed the *Shulhan Arukh*.
1558	Amatus Lusitanus settled in Salonica.
Ca. 1560	Tiberias was granted to Gracia and Joseph Nasi.

1564	Solomon Ashkenazi settled in Istanbul.
1569	An Ottoman expedition against Muscovy and an attempt to build a Don-Volga canal failed.
	Death of Gracia Nasi in Istanbul.
1570–71	The Ottomans conquered Cyprus, but the Ottoman navy was destroyed in the Battle of Lepanto (1571).
1572	Death of Isaac Luria Ashkenazi in Safed.
1574–81	The Ottomans consolidated their control of North Africa.
1576–90	Ottoman war with Iran. The Ottomans occupied Georgia, Azerbaijan, and Shirvan.
1577–87	A Hebrew printing press operated in Safed.
1579	Death of Joseph Nasi in Istanbul.
	The first of many attacks by rebellious Druze and Bedouin on the Jewish communities of Safed and Tiberias.
1579–86	The Jewish community of Jerusalem was oppressed.
1587	Betzalel Ashkenazi settled in Jerusalem.
1589	Outbreak of intermittent military revolts in Istanbul and the provinces.
	Death of Samuel de Medina in Salonica.
1593–1606	An Ottoman war with Austria resulted in a stalemate. Prince Michael of Wallachia's rebellion against the sultan (1594) resulted in massacres of Turks and Jews in Bucharest. The Jewish communities of Nikopol and Plevna were destroyed.
1596	Outbreak of widespread popular rebellions, known in Anatolia as the Celali (Jelali) revolts.
1598–99	Forty-eight percent of the Jewish taxpayers at Bursa were listed in the highest tax category.
Ca. 1600	Forty-one Jews and twenty-one Muslims were employed as physicians in the imperial court.
1602–18	Ottoman war with Iran. The Ottomans lost Azerbaijan and Georgia.
Ca. 1612	Sephardim and Marranos immigrated to the Ottoman Empire from the Low Countries.
1618–22	Reign of Osman II. The sultan's attempts to reform the military and administration were cut short by a military uprising, culminating in his assassination.

1620	Death of Hayyim Vital in Damascus.
1623–40	Reign of Murad IV. The first half of his reign (until 1632) witnessed rebellion and unrest in Istanbul and many provinces. The central government's authority was challenged in Anatolia, Syria, Egypt, and Yemen.
1624	The Iranians seized Baghdad and much of Iraq.
1625–27	The Jewish community of Jerusalem was persecuted.
Ca. 1630	A joint chief rabbinate (*kolelut, rav ha-kolel*) was established in Izmir.
1631–32	Anarchy in Istanbul.
1632	Murad launched extensive purges throughout the administration, and the military and was able to re-establish orderly government.
1638	Murad reconquered Baghdad and Iraq from the Iranians.
1645	An Ottoman expedition to Crete set off a long conflict with Venice, which lasted until 1669.
1648	The Venetian fleet blockaded the Dardanelles, causing food shortages in Istanbul, the fall of Sultan Ibrahim (1640–48), and the accession of Mehmed IV (1648–87), a child of six years.
1648–56	Anarchy in Istanbul and many provinces, coupled with severe inflation and food shortages.
1648–49	Chmielnicki Massacres in Poland.
	Shabbetai Tzevi (born ca. 1626) declared himself the Messiah in Izmir.
Ca. 1650	Shabbetai Tzevi was banished from Izmir by the rabbinic authorities.
Ca. 1650	Fourteen Muslims and four Jews were employed as physicians in the sultan's court.
1656	The Venetians destroyed a large Ottoman fleet off the Dardanelles, leading to the appointment of Mehmed Köprülü as Grand Vezir.
	The Jewish community of Tiberias was dispersed.
1656–61	Grand vezirate of Mehmed Köprülü. Having been granted absolute powers, he ruthlessly purged the administration and the military, restored order, and vigorously pressed on the war with Venice.
1658	A Hebrew printing press was founded in Izmir.

1661–76	Grand vezirate of Fazıl Ahmed Köprülü, who succeeded his father, Mehmed, and was able to maintain orderly government.
1663–64	An Ottoman war with Austria ended inconclusively, in spite of an Austrian victory at the Battle of St. Gotthard (1664).
1665	Nathan of Gaza proclaimed Shabbetai Tzevi to be the Messiah (May). Having been banished from Jerusalem (June), Shabbetai Tzevi returned to Izmir (September) and then sailed for Istanbul to depose the sultan (December).
1666	Shabbetai Tzevi was arrested (February), then forced to convert to Islam (September).
1669	The Ottomans completed the conquest of Crete.
1672	Shabbetai Tzevi was banished to Albania, where he died (1676).
1672–76	Ottoman-Polish war. The Ottomans captured most of Podolia and the Polish Ukraine, representing the high watermark of Ottoman expansion in eastern Europe.
1675	Israel Conegliano (Conian) settled in Istanbul.
1676	On the death of Fazıl Ahmed Köprülü, his foster brother, Kara Mustafa, was appointed Grand Vezir.
1677–81	Unsuccessful campaigns against Russia forced the Ottomans to abandon their claims to most of the Ukraine.
Ca. 1680	A joint chief rabbinate was established in Salonica.
1682–99	Ottoman war with Austria, which was allied with Poland.
1683	The Ottoman siege of Vienna was broken and ended in a rout.
1684	Venice joined the war against the Ottomans in a Holy League sponsored by the Pope.
1686	The Austrians captured Buda and pillaged the Jewish quarter. Jews were prohibited from residing in Buda until 1689.
	The Venetians took the Morea and Athens (1687). Jewish communities in Greece were attacked, and the Jews abandoned Patras and the islands of the Aegean Sea.

1687	The Russians laid siege to Azov, which finally fell in 1696.
1688	The Austrians captured Belgrade, then Vidin (1689), leading to anti-Ottoman rebellions in Serbia and Bulgaria.
	The Jewish community of Belgrade was dispersed.
1690	The Ottomans counterattacked and recaptured Belgrade and the Jews returned.
1697	Eugene of Savoy decisively defeated the Ottomans at the Battle of Zenta.
1699	The Treaty of Karlowitz. Considered a watershed in Ottoman history, it signaled the beginning of the Ottoman retreat from Europe. The Ottomans lost to Austria most of Hungary, as well as Transylvania, Croatia, and Slavonia. Venice acquired the Morea and most of Dalmatia. Poland regained Podolia. Russia signed a separate peace in 1700, which confirmed its occupation of Azov.
1699–1702	Grand vezirate of Amcazade Hüseyin Pasha, who introduced reforms in the administration, the military, and the economy.
1700	Judah Hasid and his followers settled in Jerusalem.
1702	Daniel de Fonseca settled in Istanbul.
Ca. 1703– ca. 1714	Tobias Cohn served as physician to Ahmed III.
1710–11	The Ottomans waged war against Russia to help Sweden and Poland. A large Ottoman army surrounded Peter the Great on the Pruth River and forced him to sign the Treaty of the Pruth (1711), which required Russia to relinquish Azov.
1711	A new Hebrew printing press was established in Istanbul by the Polish Jews Jonah Ashkenazi and Naftali ben Azriel.
1714–18	Ottoman war with Venice and Austria (beginning in 1716). The Ottomans were successful against Venice in the Morea, but lost to the Austrians on the Danube. The Treaty of Passarowitz (1718) confirmed the Ottoman reconquest of the Morea and their losses to Austria of the Banat of Temesvar, Little Wallachia, and northern Serbia, including Belgrade, which the Jews had abandoned again in 1717.

1714–30	Daniel de Fonseca served as physician to Ahmed III.
1717	Lady Mary Wortley Montagu reported from Istanbul on the "incredible power" of the Jews.
1718–30	Grand vezirate of Damad Ibrahim Pasha. He preferred diplomacy to war and improved relations with the European Powers. He sent embassies to European capitals to learn modern ways and introduced elements of a Western life-style. Interest in the cultivation of tulips became widespread and the period became known as the Tulip Era (*Lâle Devri*). However, debasement of the currency and other fiscal measures resulted in inflation, increased poverty, and widespread unrest.
Ca. 1720	A Turkish printing press was founded in Istanbul by Ibrahim Müteferrika, a Hungarian convert, reportedly with the assistance of Jonah Ashkenazi.
Ca. 1722	A joint chief rabbinate was established in Edirne.
1723–30	Ottoman attempts to expand in Iran ended in a military defeat and an uprising in Istanbul (the Patrona Revolt, 1730), which overthrew the regime and ended the Tulip Era.
1730–54	The reign of Mahmud I witnessed some modest European-style military reforms directed by Claude-Alexandre Comte de Bonneval (Humbaracı Ahmed Pasha), a French nobleman who converted to Islam.
1733	Jews from Istanbul and Salonica settled in Jerusalem.
1733–35	The Ottomans were again defeated by Iran.
1736–39	Ottoman war with Austria and Russia. The Russians recaptured Azov, raided the Crimea, and advanced to Jassy, but the Ottomans were successful on the Austrian front. By the Treaty of Belgrade (1739), Austria surrendered northern Serbia and Belgrade, and the Russians were forced to give up Azov. The war, however, necessitated raising oppressive taxes, which created unrest. Local leaders were able to recruit private armies and control entire regions as semi-independent rulers, known as *ayan*s (notables) and *derebey*s (lords of the valley). In Egypt, Syria, Iraq, and North Africa the local military seized power and became increasingly independent.

1739	Jews rebuilt the community of Belgrade.
1740	Jews from Izmir renewed the Jewish community of Tiberias.
1742	Betzalel Halevi from Amsterdam founded a new Hebrew printing press in Salonica, which operated until 1916.
1743–46	An Ottoman war with Iran ended inconclusively, marking the establishment of a balance of power between the two states.
1756–63	Grand vezirate of Mehmed Ragıb Pasha. A man of letters and able administrator, he strove to keep the empire at peace and to improve the condition of the common people. He introduced administrative and fiscal reforms and improved the justice system.
1760–73	Ali Bey al-Kabir of Egypt rebelled against the sultan. He executed prominent Jews, confiscated their property, and oppressed the Jewish community.
1761–66	The Jewish community of Jerusalem was persecuted.
1768–74	Ottoman war with Russia. Russian armies swept through Moldavia, Wallachia, and the Crimea. A Russian fleet destroyed the Ottoman navy at Cheshme (1770), and went on to raise a rebellion in Greece. In the course of the Greek uprising, the Jewish communities were decimated and several, including those of Thebes, Navpaktos, and Chalcis, were destroyed. The war ended with the Treaty of Kuchuk Kaynarja (Küçük Kaynarca; 1774), a momentous document that registered a new phase in Ottoman decline. Moldavia and Wallachia were returned to the sultan, although the Russians reserved the right to intervene in their administration. Russia received the territory between the Dnieper and the Bug, as well as the ports of Azov and Kinburun. The Crimean Tatars were recognized as independent of the sultan's sovereignty, but they were to continue to recognize him as their spiritual leader, or Caliph. Russia was given the right to build and protect an Orthodox church in Istanbul, which the czars later interpreted as giving them the right to intercede on behalf of all the Orthodox Christians in the empire.

1774–89   Reign of Abdülhamid I. Although a relatively stable period, the government had to contend with the rising power of local rulers, whose independence increased as a result of the last war. The sultan introduced reforms in the administration and the economy and modernized the military. He brought large numbers of European military advisors, predominantly French.

1776   The Jewish community of Jaffa was dispersed.

1777–81   Immigration of East European Hasidim to Jerusalem.

1779   Russia annexed the Crimea after years of intervention in its internal affairs. The sultan was forced to acknowledge the occupation by the Agreement of Aynalı Kavak (1784).

1787–92   An Ottoman war with Russia and Austria (beginning in 1788) witnessed further Ottoman military defeats. The war ended with the Treaty of Jassy (1792), which confirmed Russia's occupation of the port of Oczakov and the territories between the Bug and the Dniester.

1789–1807   Reign of Selim III. The sultan introduced administrative, fiscal, and military reforms, including the establishment of a modern infantry corps (*Nizam-i Cedid*) modeled on European lines. In spite of the reforms, however, the central government remained weak and anarchy throughout the empire increased, adversely affecting numerous Jewish communities.

1795   The Jewish quarter of Belgrade was attacked by rebellious Janissaries.

1798   Napoleon's expedition to Egypt ended in failure and the surrender of the French forces (1801). Among the campaign's other results was the decimation of the Jewish community of Gaza (1799).

1804   Beginning of the Serb uprising, which led to Serbian autonomy (1830). The Serbs expelled the Jews from Belgrade (1807).

1806–12   Ottoman war with Russia.

1807   Selim III was deposed by the opponents of his reforms, led by the Janissaries.
The Jews fled from Vidin.

1808–39   Reign of Mahmud II.

1809	Mahmud disciplined the Janissaries in Istanbul.
1812	The Treaty of Bucharest ended the war with Russia. The Ottoman Empire ceded to Russia the province of Bessarabia.
1812–22	Mahmud suppressed the Balkan and Anatolian notables and introduced reforms in the tax-collection system.
1817–31	Baghdad came under the rule of the rebellious Mamluk governor Davud (Dawud) Pasha, who oppressed the Jewish community and forced many Jews to flee.
1820	The Jewish community of Jaffa was restored through the efforts of Isaiah Adjiman (Acıman) of Istanbul.
1821	Beginning of the Greek uprising, which led to the establishment of an independent Greek state (1832). The Jewish communities of Greece, and especially those in the Morea, were greatly decimated.
1826	Mahmud suppressed the Janissaries and began to introduce wide-scale modernizing reforms. Execution of Isaiah Adjiman, Çelebi Bekhor Carmona, and Yehezkel Gabbai, who were reputed to have had links with the Janissaries. Their property was confiscated.
1828	Sir Moses Montefiore's first journey to Palestine.
1828–29	Ottoman-Russian war. The Russian armies advanced as far as Edirne and occupied the city. By the Treaty of Edirne (Adrianople; 1829), Russia abandoned most of her conquests.
Ca. 1830	Jewish immigration to Palestine from the Balkans, mainly from areas affected by the Greek uprising and the Ottoman-Russian war.
1831	Israel Bak from Berdichev established a Hebrew printing press in Safed (destroyed in 1837).
1832–33	Muhammad Ali, the governor of Egypt, rebelled against the sultan, occupied Palestine and Syria, and advanced into Anatolia.
1833	The defensive Treaty of Hünkâr Iskelesi between the Ottoman Empire and Russia against Muhammad Ali caused grave concerns in Britain and led to a major shift in British policy in support of Ottoman territorial integrity.

1834	The Jewish communities of Jerusalem, Hebron, and Safed were sacked.
1835	The office of an officially appointed *haham başı* (chief rabbi) was introduced, and Abraham Levi became its first incumbent in Istanbul (he died in 1836).
1836–37	Shemuel Hayyim served as haham başı of Istanbul.
1839	Proclamation of the Imperial Rescript of Gülhane, which promised reform and equal justice to all Ottoman subjects, regardless of religion.
1839–41	Moshe Fresco served as haham başı of Istanbul.
1840	Blood libel accusations against the Jews in Damascus and Rhodes.
	Sir Moses Montefiore was granted an audience with Sultan Abdülmecid (Abdul-Mejid).
	The European Powers, led by Britain, forced Muhammad Ali to withdraw from Syria and Palestine. A British "plan" was proposed to "protect" Jewish interests in Palestine and, ultimately, throughout the Ottoman Empire.
	Jewish immigration to Palestine increased.
1841	Israel Bak established a printing house in Jerusalem.
1841–54	Jacob Behar David served as haham başı of Istanbul.
1842	The Ottoman government instructed the Jewish community to recruit students for the Imperial Medical School.
1844	Dr. Spitzer was appointed as physician to Abdülmecid.
1853–56	The Crimean War
1854	The first modern Jewish school was opened in Istanbul.
1854–60	Hayyim Hacohen served as haham başı of Istanbul.
1856	Proclamation of the Reform Decree (*Islahat Fermanı, Hatt-ı Hümayun*), intended to strengthen legal equality among all Ottoman subjects and to reform the internal administration of the non-Muslim *millet*s.
	The Laemel School was opened in Jerusalem.
1860	Foundation of the Alliance Israélite Universelle in Paris (henceforth: Alliance).
1860–63	Jacob Avigdor served as haham başı of Istanbul.
1862	Moldavia and Wallachia were united under the new name of Romania. Anti-Semitism became rampant in the new state.

1863–72	Yakir Geron served as acting haham başı of Istanbul.
1864	The first Alliance schools in the Ottoman Empire were opened in Baghdad, Damascus, and Volos.
1865	The Jewish community of Istanbul adopted an organic statute (*nizamname*).
1867	An Alliance school was opened in Edirne, then in Izmir (1873), Salonica (1873), and Istanbul (1875).
1870	The Alliance established in Palestine the agricultural school Mikveh Yisrael.
1871–72	Attacks on Jews in Romania.
1872–1908	Moshe Levi (Halevi) served as acting haham başı of Istanbul.
1875–76	Insurrections in Herzegovina, Bosnia, and Bulgaria. Ottoman war with Serbia and Montenegro.
1876–1909	Reign of Abdülhamid II.
1876	Proclamation of the Ottoman Constitution by Midhat Pasha.
1877	The first Ottoman parliament was convened, then prorogued.
1877–78	The Ottoman war with Russia led to the Treaty of Berlin (1878), which sharply reduced the Ottoman Empire in Europe: Serbia, Romania, and Montenegro became fully independent states; Bulgaria became autonomous; Austria occupied Bosnia, Herzegovina, and Novi Bazar. In Asia, Russia received Batum, Kars, and Ardahan, and the British occupied Cyprus. The wars and the Ottoman territorial losses in the Balkans set in motion a considerable migration of Muslims and Jews to the remaining Ottoman territories.
1881	The French occupied Tunis.
1881–84	Pogroms in Russia.
1882	Beginning of modern Zionist immigration to Palestine (The First Aliyah). The Ottoman authorities imposed restrictions intended to limit Jewish immigration to Palestine. The British occupied Egypt.
1890	Great expansion of the Alliance's educational activities in the Ottoman Empire.
1891	Jews were expelled from Moscow.
1892	Ottoman Jewry and international Jewish organizations commemorated the "fourth centennial" of the settlement of the Sephardim in the Ottoman Empire.

	The Ottoman authorities imposed restrictions intended to limit Jewish land acquisitions in Palestine.
1893	Abdülhamid's "plan" for the mass settlement of Jewish refugees from Russia and other countries in east Anatolia.
1896–1908	Development of the Young Turk Movement.
1897	The first Zionist Congress met at Basel and founded the Zionist Organization.
1903–06	Pogroms in Russia.
1908	The Young Turk Revolution restored the 1876 constitution.
	The Ottoman parliament was reconvened.
	Bulgaria declared its full independence.
	Austria annexed Bosnia and Herzegovina.
	Haim Nahum was appointed acting haham başı of Istanbul.
	A Zionist representation was established in Istanbul.
1909	Abdülhamid was deposed and the constitution revised to limit the powers of the sultan.
	Tel Aviv was founded.
1909–18	Reign of Mehmed V.
1909—20	Haim Nahum served as haham başı of all the Jews of the Ottoman Empire.
1911	B'nai B'rith lodges were established in Istanbul.
1911–12	Italy occupied Libya and the Dodecanese Islands, including Rhodes.
1912	The Alliance operated in the Ottoman Empire 115 schools with a total enrollment of some 19,000 students.
1912–13	The Balkan Wars resulted in the loss of most of the remaining Ottoman territories in Europe. Salonica was occupied by the Greek army (1912). Mass emigration of Muslims and Jews from the lost territories.
1914–23	The Ottoman government entered the First World War on the side of the Central Powers (1914), resulting in the empire's collapse (1918) and the establishment of the Turkish Republic (1923).

Selected Bibliography

Adler, Elkan Nathan. *Jews in Many Lands.* Philadelphia: The Jewish Publication Society, 1905.

——. *Jewish Travellers.* London: G. Routledge and Sons, 1930.

Ahmad, Feroz. *The Young Turks: The Committee of Union and Progress in Turkish Politics, 1908–1914.* Oxford: The Clarendon Press, 1969.

Alderson, A.D. *The Structure of the Ottoman Dynasty.* Oxford: The Clarendon Press, 1956.

Anderson, M.S. *The Eastern Question, 1774–1923.* London: Macmillan, 1966.

Angel, Marc D. *The Jews of Rhodes: The History of a Sephardic Community.* New York: Sepher-Hermon Press, 1978.

Armistead, Samuel G. and Joseph H. Silverman. *The Judeo-Spanish Ballad Chapbooks of Yacob Abraham Yona (Folk Literature of the Sephardic Jews I).* Berkeley: University of California Press, 1971.

——. *Judeo-Spanish Ballads from Bosnia* (University of Pennsylvania Publications in Folklore and Folklife 4). Philadelphia: University of Pennsylvania Press, 1971.

Ashtor, Eliyahu. *The Jews of Moslem Spain.* Philadelphia: The Jewish Publication Society, 1973.

——. *The Levant Trade in the Later Middle Ages.* Princeton: Princeton University Press, 1983.

——. *The Jews and the Mediterranean Economy, 10th–15th Centuries.* London: Variorum Reprints, 1983.

Avitsur, Shmuel. "Tzefat — Merkaz le-Ta'asiyat Arigei Tzemer ba-Me'ah ha-15" [Safed—Center of the Manufacture of Woven Woolens in the Fifteenth Century]. *Sefunot* 6 (1962): 41–69.

——. "Le-Toledot Ta'asiyat Arigei ha-Tzemer be-Saloniki" [The Woolen Industry in Salonica]. *Sefunot* 12 (1971–78): 145–68.

Baer, Gabriel. "The Administrative, Economic and Social Functions of Turkish Guilds." *International Journal of Middle East Studies* 1 (1970): 28–50.

Baer, Yitzhak. *A History of the Jews in Christian Spain.* 2 vols. Philadelphia: The Jewish Publication Society, 1961–1966.

Barkan, Ömer Lütfi. "The Price Revolution of the Sixteenth Century: A Turning Point in the Economic History of the Near East." *International Journal of Middle East Studies* 6 (1975): 3–28.

Barnai, Jacob. *Yehudei Eretz-Yisrael ba-Me'ah ha-18 ba-Hasut "Pekidei Kushta"* [The Jews in Eretz-Israel in the Eighteenth Century under the Patronage of the Istanbul Committee Officials of Eretz-Israel]. Jerusalem: Ben-Zvi Institute, 1982.

——. "Kavim le-Toledot Kehillat Kushta ba-Me'ah ha-18" [Notes on the Jewish Community of Istanbul in the Eighteenth Century]. *Mi-Kedem U-mi-Yam* 1 (1981): 53–66.

——. "Reshit ha-Kehillah ha-Yehudit be-Izmir ba-Tekufah ha-Othmanit" [The Origins of the Jewish Community in Izmir in the Ottoman Period]. *Pe'amim*, no. 12 (1982): 47–58.

——. "Kavim le-Toledot ha-Hevrah ha-Yehudit be-Izmir be-Shilhei ha-Me'ah ha-18 u-ve-Reshit ha-Me'ah ha-19" [On the Jewish Community of Izmir in the Late Eighteenth and Early Nineteenth Centuries]. *Zion* 47 (1982): 56–76.

——. "Rav Yosef Eskapa ve-Rabbanut Izmir" [Rabbi Joseph Eskapa and the Rabbinate of Izmir]. *Sefunot*, New Series 3 (18) (1985): 53–81.

——. "Zikah ve-Nittuk bein Hakhmei Turkiyah le-Hakhmei Polin u-Merkaz Eiropah ba-Me'ah ha-17" [Relation and Disengagement between the Scholars of Turkey and the Scholars of Poland and Central Europe in the 17th Century]. *Gal'ed* 9 (1986): 13–26.

——. "Le-Toledot ha-Kesharim she-bein Yehudei Izmir li-Yhudei Eretz-Yisrael ba-Me'ot ha-17 ve-ha-18" [On the History of the Relations Between the Jews of Izmir and the Jews of Palestine in the Seventeenth and Eighteenth Centuries]. *Shalem* 5 (1987): 95–114.

Baron, Salo Wittmayer. *A Social and Religious History of the Jews*. New York: Columbia University Press, 1983, Vol. 18, 2nd ed.

Bashan, Eliezer. "Hayyei ha-Kalkalah ba-Me'ot ha-16-ha-18" [Economic Life from the Sixteenth to the Eighteenth Century]. In *The Jews in Ottoman Egypt*, edited by Jacob Landau, q.v., pp. 63–112.

Beinart, Haim. *Conversos on Trial: The Inqusition in Cuidad Real*. Jerusalem: The Magnes Press, 1981.

Benardete, Mair Jose. *Hispanic Culture and Character of the Sephardic Jews*. Corrected and augmented by Marc D. Angel. New York: Sepher-Hermon Press, 1982. 2nd ed.

Ben-Arieh, Yehoshua. *Jerusalem in the Nineteenth Century*. 2 vols. New York: St. Martin's Press, 1984–1986.

Benbassa, Esther. *Un Grand Rabbin Sepharade en Politique, 1892-1923*. Paris: Presses du CNRS, 1990.

——. "Zionism in the Ottoman Empire at the End of the 19th and the Beginning of the 20th Century." *Studies in Zionism* 11 (1990): 127–40.

Benvenisti, David. *Yehudei Saloniki ba-Dorot ha-Aharonim* [The Jews of Salonica in the Last Generations]. Jerusalem: Kiryat Sefer, 1973.

Ben-Ya'akov, Abraham. *Yehudei Bavel mi-Sof Tekufat ha-Ge'onim ad Yameinu (1038–1960)* [The Jews of Iraq from the End of the Gaonic Period to Our Times (1038–1960)]. Jerusalem: The Ben-Zvi Institute, 1965.

Ben-Zvi, Itzhak [Izhak]. *The Exiled and the Redeemed*. Philadelphia: The Jewish Publication Society, New Edition, 1961.

——. *Eretz Yisrael ve-Yishuvah bi-Ymei ha-Shilton ha-Otmani* [Eretz-Israel under Ottoman Rule]. Jerusalem: Bialik Institute, 1962.

Berkes, Niyazi. *The Development of Secularism in Turkey*. Montreal: McGill University Press, 1964.

Bornstein-Makovetzky, Leah. "Pinkasim shel Batei-ha-Din be-Kushta min ha-Me'ot ha-18 ve-ha-19 ki-R'i la-Hayyim ha-Hevratiyyim ve-ha-Kalkaliyyim shel Yehudei ha-Ir [Eighteenth and Nineteenth Century Court Records from Istanbul as a Mirror of the Social and Economic Life of the City's Jews]. *Shevet Va'am*, Second Series 5 (10) (1984): 101-109.

———. "Ha-Kehillah u-Mosdoteihah" [The Community and its Institutions]. In *The Jews in Ottoman Egypt*, edited by Jacob Landau, q.v., pp. 129-216.

———. "Seridim mi-Pinkas Beit-Din Balat be-Kushta, Shenat 1839" [Remnants of the Register of the Court of Balat in Istanbul, 1839]. *Sefunot*, New Series 4 (19) (1989): 53-122.

———. "Jewish Brokers in Constantinople during the 17th Century According to Hebrew Documents." In *The Mediterranean and the Jews: Banking, Finance and International Trade (XVI–XVIII Centuries)*, edited by Ariel Toaff and Simon Schwarzfuchs, pp. 75–104. Ramat-Gan: Bar-Ilan University Press, 1989.

Bowman, Steven B., *The Jews of Byzantium, 1204-1453*. Birmingham, Alabama: The University of Alabama Press, 1985.

Braude, Benjamin and Bernard Lewis, eds. *Christians and Jews in the Ottoman Empire: The Functioning of a Plural Society*. 2 vols. New York: Holmes & Meier, 1982.

Braudel, Fernand. *The Mediterranean and the Mediterranean World in the Age of Phillip II*, translated by Siân Reynolds. 2 vols. New York: Harper and Row, 1973.

———. *Civilization and Capitalism: 15th–18th Century*, translated by Siân Reynolds. 2 vols. New York: Harper and Row, 1982.

Cahen, Claude. *Pre-Ottoman Turkey: A General Survey of the Material and Spiritual Culture, c. 1071–1330*, translated by J. Jones-Williams. London: Sidgwick and Jackson, 1968.

Çelik, Zeynep. *The Remaking of Istanbul. Portrait of an Ottoman City in the Nineteenth Century*. Seattle and London: University of Washington Press, 1986.

Chouraqui, André. *Cent ans d'histoire: L'Alliance Israélite Universelle et la renaissance juive contemporaine (1860–1960)*. Paris: Presses Universitaires de France, 1965.

Cohen, Amnon. *Palestine in the 18th Century: Patterns of Government and Administration*. Jerusalem: The Magnes Press, 1973.

———. *Jewish Life under Islam: Jerusalem in the Sixteenth Century*. Cambridge, Massachusetts: Harvard University Press, 1984.

——— and Bernard Lewis. *Population and Revenue in the Towns of Palestine in the Sixteenth Century*. Princeton: Princeton University Press, 1978.

Cohen, Hayyim J. *The Jews of the Middle East*. Jerusalem: Israel Universities Press, 1973.

Cohen, Mark R. *Jewish Self-Government in Medieval Egypt*. Princeton: Princeton University Press, 1980.

Cohen, Richard I., ed. *Vision and Conflict in the Holy Land*. Jerusalem: Yad Yitzhak Ben-Zvi, 1985.

Cook, M.A., ed. *Studies in the Economic History of the Middle East*. London: Oxford University Press, 1970.

———, ed. *A History of the Ottoman Empire to 1730*. Cambridge: Cambridge University Press, 1976.

Dankoff, Robert (translation and commentary) and Rhoads Murphey (historical introduction). *The Intimate Life of an Ottoman Statesman, Melek Ahmed Pasha (1588–1662), as Portrayed in Evliya Çelebi's Book of Travels (Seyahat-Name)*. Albany: State University of New York Press, 1991.

Davison, Roderic H. *Reform in the Ottoman Empire, 1856–1876*. Princeton: Princeton University Press, 1963.

Devereux, Robert. *The First Ottoman Constitutional Period: A Study of the Midhat Constitution and Parliament*. Baltimore: The Johns Hopkins Press, 1963.

Dumont, Paul. "Jewish Communities in Turkey during the Last Decades of the Nineteenth Century in the Light of the Archives of the Alliance Israélite Universelle." In *Christians and Jews*, edited by Benjamin Braude and Bernard Lewis, Vol. 1, pp. 209–42.

Elazar, Daniel J., et al. *The Balkan Jewish Communities*. Lanham, Maryland: University Press of America, 1984.

Emmanuel, I.-S. *Histoire de l'industrie des tissus des Israélites de Salonique*. Paris: Librairie Lipschutz, 1935.

——. *Histoire des Israélites de Salonique*. Paris: Librairie Lipschultz, 1936.

Engelhardt, Ed. *La Turquie et le Tanzimat*. 2 vols. Paris: 1882–1884.

Epstein, Mark Alan. *The Ottoman Jewish Communities and their Role in the Fifteenth and Sixteenth Centuries*. Freiburg: Klaus Schwarz Verlag, 1980.

——. "The Leadership of the Ottoman Jews in the Fifteenth and Sixteenth Centuries." In *Christians and Jews*, edited by Benjamin Braude and Bernard Lewis, Vol. 1, pp. 101–16.

Eton, William. *A Survey of the Turkish Empire*. London: 1799, 2nd ed. Reprinted by Gregg International Publishers, 1972.

Farhi, David. "Yehudei Saloniki be-Mahapekhat 'ha-Turkim ha-Tze'irim'" [The Jews of Salonica in the Young Turk Revolution]. *Sefunot* 15 (1971–1981): 135–52.

Fattal, Antoine. *Le Statut Légal des Non-Musulmans en Pays d'Islam*. Beirut: Imprimerie Catholique, 1958.

Findley, Carter V. *Bureaucratic Reform in the Ottoman Empire: The Sublime Porte 1789–1922*. Princeton: Princeton University Press, 1980.

Fischer-Galati, Stephen A. *Ottoman Imperialism and German Protestantism*. Cambridge, Massachusetts: Harvard University Press, 1959.

Fleischer, Cornell H. *Bureaucrat and Intellectual in the Ottoman Empire: The Historian Mustafa Ali (1541–1600)*. Princeton: Princeton University Press, 1986.

Franco, M. *Essai sur l'Histoire des Israélites de l'Empire Ottoman*. Paris, 1897. Reprinted, Paris: Centre d'Etudes Don Isaac Abravanel, 1981.

Frankl, Ludwig August. *The Jews in the East*. 2 vols. Westport, Connecticut: Greenwood Press, 1975. Translation of *Nach Jerusalem*. Reprint of the 1859 edition published by Hurst and Blackett, London.

Friedenwald, Harry. *The Jews and Medicine: Essays*. 2 vols. Baltimore: Johns Hopkins Press, 1944.

——. *Jewish Luminaries in Medical History*. Baltimore: Johns Hopkins Press, 1946.

Friedman, Isaiah. *Germany, Turkey and Zionism, 1897–1918*. Oxford: The Clarendon Press, 1977.

Galante, Avram [Galanté, Abraham]. *Histoire des Juifs de Turquie.* 9 vols. Istanbul: Editions Isis, [n.d.] 1985. A reprint of Galante's collected works.

Geller, Yaakov. "Ha-Yahasim ha-Bein-Adatiyyim ba-Imperyah ha-Otmanit" [Inter-Community Relations in the Ottoman Empire]. *Mi-Kedem U-mi-Yam* 2 (1986): 29–54.

Gerber, Haim. *Yehudei ha-Imperyah ha Otomanit ba Me'ot 16-17: Kalkalah ve-Hevrah* [The Jews of the Ottoman Empire in the Sixteenth and Seventeenth Centuries: Economy and Society]. Jerusalem: Historical Society of Israel, 1982.

——. *The Social Origins of the Modern Middle East.* Boulder, Colorado: Lynne Rienner Publishers, 1987.

——. "Guilds in Seventeenth-Century Anatolian Bursa." *Asian and African Studies* 11 (1976): 59–86.

——. "Yozmah u-Mishar Bein-Le'umi ba-Pe'ilut ha-Kalkalit shel Yehudei ha-Imperyah ha-Othmanit ba-Me'ot 16-17" [Entrepreneurship and International Commerce in the Economic Activity of the Jews of the Ottoman Empire in the Sixteenth–Seventeenth Centuries]. *Zion* 43 (1978): 38–67.

——. "Yehudim be-Hayyei ha-Kalkalah shel ha-Ir ha-Anatolit Bursah ba-Me'ah ha-17: He'arot u-Mismakhim" [Jews in the Economic Life of the Anatolian City Bursa in the Seventeenth Century: Notes and Documents]. *Sefunot,* New Series 1 (16) (1980): 235–72.

——. "Jews and Money-Lending in the Ottoman Empire." *Jewish Quarterly Review* 72 (1981): 100–18.

——. "Le-Toledot ha-Yehudim be-Kushta ba-Me'ot ha-17-18" [On the History of the Jews in Istanbul in the Seventeenth and Eighteenth Centuries]. *Pe'amim,* no. 12 (1982): 27–46.

——. "*Ï*ehudim be-Edirne ba-Me'ot ha-16 ve-ha-17" [Jews in Edirne in the Sixteenth and Seventeenth Centuries]. *Sefunot,* New Series 3 (18) (1985): 35–51.

—— and Jacob Barnai. *Yehudei Izmir ba-Me'ah ha-19* [The Jews in Izmir in the Nineteenth Century]. Jerusalem: Misgav Yerushalayim, 1984.

Gibb, H.A.R. and Harold Bowen. *Islamic Society and the West.* One volume in two parts. London: Oxford University Press, 1950–1957.

Göçek, Fatma Müge. *East Encounters West: France and the Ottoman Empire in the Eighteenth Century.* Oxford: Oxford University Press, 1987.

Goffman, Daniel. *Izmir and the Levantine World, 1550–1650.* Seattle: University of Washington Press, 1990.

Goldman, Israel M. *The Life and Times of Rabbi David Ibn Abi Zimra.* New York: The Jewish Theological Seminary, 1970.

Goodblatt, Morris S. *Jewish Life in Turkey in the XVIth Century.* New York: The Jewish Theological Seminary, 1952.

Grunebaum-Ballin, Paul. *Joseph Naci, duc de Naxos.* Paris: Mouton, 1968.

Hacker, Joseph. "Ottoman Policy toward the Jews and Jewish Attitudes toward the Ottomans during the Fifteenth Century." In *Christians and Jews,* edited by Benjamin Braude and Bernard Lewis, Vol. 1, pp. 117–26.

——. "'Ha-Rabbanut ha-Roshit' ba-Imperyah ha-Othmanit ba-Me'ot ha-15 ve-ha-16" [The "Chief Rabbinate" in the Ottoman Empire in the Fifteenth and Sixteenth Centuries]. *Zion* 49 (1984): 225–63.

———. "Links between Spanish Jewry and Palestine, 1391–1492." In *Vision and Conflict in the Holy Land*, edited by Richard I. Cohen, pp. 111–39. Jerusalem: Yad Itzhak Ben-Zvi, 1985.

———. "The Intellectual Activity of the Jews of the Ottoman Empire during the Sixteenth and Seventeenth Centuries." In *Jewish Thought in the Seventeenth Century*, edited by Isadore Twersky and Bernard Septimus, pp. 99–135. Cambridge, Massachusetts: Harvard University Press, 1987.

Havlin, Shlomo Zalman. "Ha-Yetzirah ha-Ruhanit" [Intellectual Creativity]. In *The Jews in Ottoman Egypt*, edited by Jacob Landau, pp. 245–310.

Hess, Andrew C. *The Forgotten Frontier: A History of the Sixteenth Century Ibero-African Frontier*. Chicago: The University of Chicago Press, 1978.

Heyd, Uriel. *Ottoman Documents on Palestine, 1552–1615*. London: Oxford University Press, 1960.

———. "The Jewish Communities of Istanbul in the Seventeenth Century." *Oriens* 6 (1953): 299–314.

———. "Alilot Dam be-Turkiyah ba-Me'ot ha-15 ve-ha-16" [Ritual Murder Accusations in Fifteenth and Sixteenth Century Turkey]. *Sefunot* 5 (1961): 135–50.

———. "Moses Hamon, Chief Jewish Physician to Sultan Süleyman the Magnificent." *Oriens* 16 (1963): 152–70.

Inalcik, Halil. *The Ottoman Empire: The Classical Age, 1300–1600*, translated by Norman Itzkowitz and Colin Imber. London: Weidenfeld and Nicolson, 1973.

———. "The Ottoman Economic Mind and Aspects of the Ottoman Economy." In *Studies in the Economic History of the Middle East*, edited by M.A. Cook, pp. 207–18. London: Oxford University Press, 1970.

———. "The Turkish Impact on the Development of Modern Europe." In *The Ottoman State and Its Place in World History*, edited by Kemal H. Karpat, pp. 51–58. Leiden: E.J. Brill, 1974.

———. "The Socio-Political Effects of the Diffusion of Fire-Arms in the Middle East." In *War, Technology and Society in the Middle East*, edited by V.J. Parry and M.E. Yapp, pp. 195–217. London: Oxford University Press, 1975.

———. "Military and Fiscal Transformation in the Ottoman Empire, 1600–1700. *Archivum Ottomanicum* 6 (1980): 283–337.

———. "Jews in the Ottoman Economy and Finances, 1450–1500." In *The Islamic World From Classical to Modern Times: Essays in Honor of Bernard Lewis*, edited by C.E. Bosworth, Charles Issawi et al., pp. 513–50. Princeton: The Darwin Press, 1989.

İslamoğlu-İnan, Huri, ed. *The Ottoman Empire and the World-Economy*. Cambridge: Cambridge University Press, 1987.

Israel, Salvator. "Solomon Avraam Rozanes — Originator of the Historiography of the Bulgarian Jews (1862–1938)." In Social, Cultural and Educational Association of the Jews in the People's Republic of Bulgaria, Central Board, *Annual* 19 (Sofia, 1984): 343–71.

Issawi, Charles. *The Economic History of Turkey, 1800–1914*. Chicago: The University of Chicago Press, 1980.

——. *Economic History of the Middle East.* New York: Columbia University Press, 1982.

Jelavich, Charles and Barbara. *The Establishment of the Balkan National States, 1804–1920.* Seattle: University of Washington Press, 1977.

Juhasz, Esther, ed. *Sephardi Jews in the Ottoman Empire: Aspects of Material Culture.* Jerusalem: The Israel Museum, 1990.

Kalderon, Albert E. *Abraham Galante: A Biography.* New York: Sepher-Hermon Press, 1983.

Kamen, Henry. "The Mediterranean and the Expulsion of Spanish Jews in 1492." *Past and Present,* no. 119 (1988): 30–55.

Karpat, Kemal H., ed. *The Ottoman State and Its Place in World History.* Leiden: E.J. Brill, 1974.

——. *Ottoman Population, 1830–1914: Demographic and Social Characteristics.* Madison: University of Wisconsin Press, 1985.

Kasaba, Reşat. *The Ottoman Empire and the World Economy: The Nineteenth Century.* Albany, New York: State University of New York Press, 1988.

Kazamias, Andreas M. *Education and the Quest for Modernity in Turkey.* Chicago: The University of Chicago Press, 1966.

Kedourie, Elie. *England and the Middle East: The Destruction of the Ottoman Empire, 1914–1921.* London: Mansell Publishing, 1987. (1st ed., London: Bowes and Bowes, 1956.)

——. "Young Turks, Freemasons and Jews." *Middle Eastern Studies* 7 (1971): 89–104.

Küçük, Abdurrahman. *Dönmeler ve Dönmelik Tarihi* [A History of the *Dönmes* and the *Dönme* Movement]. Istanbul: Ötüken Neşriyat, [n.d.] ca. 1980.

Kunt, I. Metin. *The Sultan's Servants: The Transformation of Ottoman Provincial Government, 1550–1650.* New York: Columbia University Press, 1983.

——. "Transformation of *Zimmi* into *Askeri*." In *Christians and Jews,* edited by Benjamin Braude and Bernard Lewis, Vol. 1, pp. 55–67.

Kushner, David, ed. *Palestine in the Late Ottoman Period: Political, Social and Economic Transformation.* Jerusalem: Yad Izhak Ben-Zvi, 1986.

Landau, Jacob M. *Jews in Nineteenth-Century Egypt.* New York: New York University Press, 1969.

——. *Tekinalp: Turkish Patriot, 1883–1961.* Leiden: Publications de l'Institute historique et archéologique néerlandais de Stamboul, 1984, Vol. 53.

——, ed. *Toledot Yehudei Mitzrayim ba-Tekufah ha-Othmanit (1517–1914)* [The Jews in Ottoman Egypt (1517–1914)]. Jerusalem: Misgav Yerushalayim, 1988.

Landshut, S. *Jewish Communities in the Muslim Countries of the Middle East.* London: The Jewish Chronicle, 1950.

Laskier, Michael M. *The Alliance Israélite Universelle and the Jewish Communities of Morocco, 1862–1962.* Albany: State University of New York Press, 1983.

Leven, Narcisse. *Cinquante ans d'histoire: L'Alliance Israélite Universelle (1860–1910).* 2 vols. Paris: Librairie Felix Alcan, 1911–1920.

Levi, Avner. "Ha-Itonut ha-Yehudit be-Izmir" [The Jewish Press in Izmir]. *Pe'amim,* no. 12 (1982): 87-104.

Levy, Avigdor. "The Officer Corps in Sultan Mahmud II's New Ottoman Army, 1826–1839." *International Journal of Middle East Studies* 2 (1971): 21–39.

———. "The Ottoman Ulema and the Military Reforms of Sultan Mahmud II." *Asian and African Studies* 7 (1971): 13–39.

———. "Ottoman Attitudes to the Rise of Balkan Nationalism." In *War and Society in East Central Europe*, edited by Béla K. Király and Gunther E. Rothenberg, pp. 325–45. New York: Columbia University Press, 1979. Vol. 1.

———. "Military Reform and the Problem of Centralization in the Ottoman Empire in the Eighteenth Century." *Middle Eastern Studies* 18 (1982): 227–49.

———. ed. *The Jews of the Ottoman Empire*. Princeton: The Darwin Press, 1992.

Lewis, Bernard. *Notes and Documents from the Turkish Archives*. Jerusalem: Israel Oriental Society, 1952.

———. *Istanbul and the Civilization of the Ottoman Empire*. Norman, Oklahoma: University of Oklahoma Press, 1963.

———. *The Emergence of Modern Turkey*. London: Oxford University Press, 1968, 2nd ed.

———. *The Muslim Discovery of Europe*. New York: W.W. Norton, 1982.

———. *The Jews of Islam*. Princeton: Princeton University Press, 1984.

———. "The Privilege Granted by Mehmed II to his Physician," *Bulletin of the School of Oriental and African Studies* 14 (1952): 550-63.

Loeb, Isidore. *La situation des Israélites en Turquie, en Serbie et en Roumanie*. Paris: Joseph Baer et Cie., 1877.

Lowry, Heath. "'From Lesser Wars to the Mightiest War': The Ottoman Conquest and Transformation of Byzantine Urban Centers in the Fifteenth Century." In *Continuity and Change in Late Byzantine and Early Ottoman Society*, edited by Anthony Bryer and Heath Lowry, pp. 323–38. Birmingham, England and Washington, D.C.: Dumbarton Oaks, 1986.

Löwy, A. *The Jews of Constantinople: A Study of Their Communal and Educational Status*. London: The Anglo-Jewish Association, 1890.

Mandel, Neville J. *The Arabs and Zionism before World I*. Berkeley: University of California Press, 1976.

Maoz, Moshe. *Ottoman Reform in Syria and Palestine, 1840–1861: The Impact of the Tanzimat on Politics and Society*. Oxford: The Clarendon Press, 1968.

———, ed. *Studies on Palestine during the Ottoman Period*. Jerusalem: The Magnes Press, 1975.

Mardin, Şerif. *The Genesis of Young Ottoman Thought: A Study in the Modernization of Turkish Political Ideas*. Princeton: Princeton University Press, 1962.

———. "Power, Civil Society and Culture in the Ottoman Empire." *Comparative Studies in Society and History* 11 (1969): 258–81.

Matkovski, Alexandar. *A History of the Jews in Macedonia*, translated by David Arney. Skopje: Macedonian Review Editions, 1982.

McCarthy, Justin. *Muslims and Minorities: The Population of Ottoman Anatolia and the End of the Empire*. New York: New York University Press, 1983.

McGowan, Bruce. *Economic Life in Ottoman Europe: Taxation, Trade and the Struggle for Land, 1600–1800.* Cambridge: Cambridge University Press, 1981.

Mears, Eliot Grinnell, ed. *Modern Turkey: A Politico-Economic Interpretation, 1908-1923.* New York: Macmillian, 1924.

Mehmed Pasha, Sarı. *Ottoman Statecraft: The Book of Counsel for Vezirs and Governors,* translated with an introduction and notes by Walter Livingston Wright, Jr. Princeton: Princeton University Press, 1935; reprinted, Greenwood, 1971.

Mordtmann, J.H. "Die jüdischen kira im Serai der Sultane," in *Mitteilungen des Seminars für orientalischen Sprachen* 32/2 (Berlin, 1929): 1–38.

Nahoum, Haim. "Jews." In *Modern Turkey: A Politico-Economic Interpretation, 1908-1923,* edited by Eliot Grinnell Mears, pp. 86–97. New York: Macmillan, 1924.

Nehama, Joseph. *Histoire des Israélites de Salonique.* Salonique: Librairie Molho, 1935–36 (Vols. 1–5); Thessalonique: Communauté Israélite de Thessalonique, 1978 (Vols. 6–7).

Nicolay, Nicholas de. *The Nauigations, Peregrinations and Voyages, made into Turkie by Nicholas Nicholay etc.,* translated by T. Washington. London: 1585. Reprinted, Amsterdam: Da Capo Press, 1968.

Öke, Mim Kemal. *Siyonizm ve Filistin Sorunu (1880–1914)* [Zionism and the Question of Palestine, 1880–1914]. Istanbul: Üçdal Neşriyat, 1982.

———. "The Ottoman Empire, Zionism and the Question of Palestine (1880–1908)." *International Journal of Middle East Studies* 14 (1982): 329–41.

———. "Young Turks, Freemasons, Jews and the Question of Zionism in the Ottoman Empire (1908–1913). *Studies in Zionism* 7 (1986): 199–218.

Okyar, Osman and Halil Inalcik, eds. *Social and Economic History of Turkey (1071–1920). Papers Presented to the First International Congress on the Social and Economic History of Turkey, Hacettepe University, Ankara, July 11–13, 1977.* Ankara: Meteksan, 1980.

Olson, Robert W. "Jews in the Ottoman Empire in Light of New Documents." *Jewish Social Studies* 41 (1979): 75–88.

———. "The Young Turks and the Jews: A Historiographical Revision." *Turcica* 18 (1986): 219–35.

Oscanyan, C. *The Sultan and his People.* New York: Derby and Jackson, 1857.

Parry, V.J. and M.E. Yapp, eds. *War, Technology and Society in the Middle East.* London: Oxford University Press, 1975.

Philipp, Thomas. "Beit Farhi ve-ha-Temurot be-Ma'amadam shel Yehudei Suryah ve-Eretz-Yisrael, 1750–1860" [The Farhi Family and the Changing Position of the Jews in Syria and Palestine, 1750–1860]. *Cathedra,* no. 34 (1985): 97–114.

Pitcher, Donald Edgar. *An Historical Geography of the Ottoman Empire from Earliest Times to the End of the Sixteenth Century.* Leiden: E.J. Brill, 1972.

Polk, William R. and Richard L. Chambers, eds. *Beginnings of Modernization in the Middle East: The Nineteenth Century.* Chicago: The University of Chicago Press, 1968.

Puryear, Vernon John. *International Economics and Diplomacy in the Near East: A Study of British Commerical Policy in the Levant, 1834–1853.* Berkeley: University of California Press, 1935; reprinted, Archon Books, 1969.

Quataert, Donald. *Social Disintegration and Popular Resistance in the Ottoman Empire, 1881–1908: Reactions to European Economic Penetration.* New York: New York University Press, 1983.

Ramsaur, E.E. *The Young Turks: Prelude to the Revolution of 1908.* Princeton: Princeton University Press, 1957.

Ravid, Benjamin. "Money, Love and Power Politics in Sixteenth Century Venice: The Perpetual Banishment and Subsequent Pardon of Joseph Nasi." In *Italia Judaica: Atti del I Convegno Internazionale, Bari, 1981,* edited by Vittore Colorni et al., pp. 159–81. Rome: Ministero per i Beni Culturali e Ambientali, 1983.

Renard, Raymond. *Sepharad: Le monde et la langue judéo-espagnole des Séphardim.* Mons, Belgium: Annales Universitaires de Mons, [n.d.] 1966?.

Rodrigue, Aron. *De l'instruction à l'émancipation: Les enseignants de l'Alliance Israélite Universelle et les Juifs d'Orient, 1860–1939.* Paris: Calmann-Lévy, 1989.

———. *French Jews, Turkish Jews. The Alliance Israélite Universelle and the Politics of Jewish Schooling in Turkey, 1860–1925.* Bloomington, Indiana: Indiana University Press, 1990.

Rosanes, Solomon [Rozanes, Shelomoh] A. *Divrei Yemei Yisrael be-Togarmah* [History of the Jews in the Ottoman Empire]. 6 vols. Vol. 1–3 were first published in Husijatin, 1907–1911. A second revised edition of vol. 1 was published in Tel Aviv by Devir, 1930. A second edition of volumes 2 and 3 was published in Sofia, 1937–1938. The second edition of vol. 3 and vols. 4–6 were published under the title *Korot ha-Yehudim be-Turkiyah ve-Artzot ha-Kedem* [History of the Jews in Turkey and the Lands of the East]. Volumes 4 and 5 were published in Sofia, 1934–1937; vol. 6 was published in Jerusalem by The Rabbi Kook Institute, 1945.

Roth, Cecil. *History of the Marranos,* with a new introduction by Herman P. Salomon. New York: Sefer-Hermon Press, 1974, 4th ed.

———. *The House of Nasi: Doña Gracia.* Philadelphia: The Jewish Publication Society, 1947.

———. *The House of Nasi: The Duke of Naxos.* Philadelphia: The Jewish Publication Society, 1948. Reprinted, New York: Greenwood Press, n.d.

Rozen, Minna. *Ha-Kehillah ha-Yehudit bi-Yrushalayim ba-Me'ah ha-17* [The Jewish Community of Jerusalem in the Seventeenth Century]. Tel Aviv: Tel Aviv University, 1984.

———. "Tzarefat vi-Yhudei Mitzrayim—Anatomiah shel Yahasim, 1683–1801" [France and the Jews of Egypt: An Anatomy of Relations, 1683–1801]. In *The Jews in Ottoman Egypt,* edited by Jacob Landau, pp. 421–70.

Runciman, Steven. *The Fall of Constantinople, 1453.* London: Cambridge University Press, 1965.

Ruppin, Arthur. *The Jews of To-Day,* translated by Margery Bentwich. London: G. Bell and Sons, 1913.

Scholem, Gershom. *Major Trends in Jewish Mysticism.* New York: Schocken Books, 1954, 3rd rev. ed.

———. *The Messianic Idea in Judaism.* New York: Schocken Books, 1971.

———. *Sabbatai Ṣevi: The Mystical Messiah, 1626–1676,* translated by R.J. Zwi Werblowsky. Princeton: Princeton University Press, 1977.

Sciaky, Leon. *Farewell to Salonica: Portrait of an Era.* New York: Current Books, 1946.

Shaw, Stanford J. *Between Old and New: The Ottoman Empire under Sultan Selim III, 1789–1807.* Cambridge, Massachusetts: Harvard Univesity Press, 1971.

———. *History of the Ottoman Empire and Modern Turkey. Volume I: Empire of the Gazis, 1280–1808.* Cambridge: Cambridge University Press, 1976.

———. "The Nineteenth-Century Ottoman Tax Reforms and Revenue System." *International Journal of Middle East Studies* 6 (1975): 421–59.

———. "The Ottoman Census System and Population, 1831–1914." *International Journal of Middle East Studies* 9 (1978): 325–38.

———. "The Population of Istanbul in the Nineteenth Century." *Türk Tarih Dergisi* 32 (1979): 403–14.

——— and Ezel Kural Shaw. *History of the Ottoman Empire and Modern Turkey. Volume II: Reform, Revolution and Republic, 1808–1975.* Cambridge: Cambridge University Press, 1977.

Shmuelevitz, Aryeh. *The Jews of the Ottoman Empire in the Late Fifteenth and Sixteenth Centuries.* Leiden: E.J. Brill, 1984.

Skilliter, S.A. "Three Letters from the Ottoman 'Sultana' Safiye to Queen Elizabeth I." In *Oriental Studies III. Documents from Islamic Chanceries. First Series,* edited by S.M. Stern, pp. 119–57. Cambridge, Massachusetts: Harvard University Press, 1965.

Stillman, Norman A. *The Jews of Arab Lands: A History and Sourcebook.* Philadelphia: The Jewish Publication Society, 1979.

———. *The Jews of Arab Lands in Modern Times.* Philadelphia: The Jewish Publication Society, 1991.

Sugar, Peter. *Southeastern Europe under Ottoman Rule, 1354–1804.* Seattle: University of Washington Press, 1977.

Tamir, Vicki. *Bulgaria and Her Jews: The History of a Dubious Symbiosis.* New York: Sepher-Hermon Press, 1979.

Temperley, Harold. *England and the Near East: The Crimea.* London: Longmans, Green and Co., 1936.

Toaff, Ariel and Simon Schwarzfuchs, eds. *The Mediterranean and the Jews: Banking, Finance and International Trade (XVI-XVIII Centuries).* Ramat-Gan: Bar-Ilan University Press, 1989.

Todorov, Nikolai. *The Balkan City, 1400–1900.* Seattle: University of Washington Press, 1983.

Tritton, A.S. *The Caliphs and their Non-Muslim Subjects: A Critical Study of the Covenant of 'Umar.* London: Oxford University Press, 1930.

Twersky, Isadore and Bernard Septimus, eds. *Jewish Thought in the Seventeenth Century.* Cambridge, Massachusetts: Harvard University Press, 1987.

Ubicini A. *Lettres sur la Turquie.* 2 vols. Paris, 1854. Translated as *Letters on Turkey.* London, 1856. Reprinted, Arno Press, 1973.

Udovitch, Abraham L. and Lucette Valensi. *The Last Arab Jews: The Communities of Jerba, Tunisia.* Chur: Harwood Academic Publishers, 1984.

Usque, Samuel. *Consolation for the Tribulations of Israel,* translated by Martin A. Cohen. Philadelphia: The Jewish Publication Society, 1965.

Ward, Robert E. and Dankwart A. Rustow, eds. *Political Modernization in Japan and Turkey.* Princeton: Princeton University Press, 1964.

Weiker, Walter F. *The Unseen Israelis: The Jews from Turkey in Israel.* Lanham, Maryland: University Press of America, 1988.

Ya'ari, Avraham. *Ha-Defus ha-Ivri be-Kushta* [Hebrew Printing in Istanbul]. Jerusalem: The Magnes Press, 1967.

——. "Ha-Defus ha-Ivri be-Izmir" [Hebrew Printing in Izmir]. *Areshet* 1 (1959): 97–222.

Werblowsky, R.J.Z. *Joseph Karo, Lawyer and Mystic.* London: Oxford University Press, 1962.

Winter, Michael. "Yahasei ha-Yehudim 'im ha-Shiltonot ve-ha-Hevrah ha-lo-Yehudit" [The Relations of Egyptian Jews with the Authorities and with the Non-Jewish Society]. In *The Jews in Ottoman Egypt,* edited by Jacob Landau, pp. 371–420.

Zinberg, Israel. *A History of Jewish Literature,* translated and edited by Bernard Martin. *Volume V: The Jewish Center of Culture in the Ottoman Empire.* Cincinnati: The Hebrew Union College Press, 1974.

Appendix

Authors and Their Contributions to
The Jews of the Ottoman Empire
Edited by Avigdor Levy

(Forthcoming 1992)

Angel, Marc D. "The Responsa Literature in the Ottoman Empire as a Source for the Study of Ottoman Jewry."

Barnai, Jacob. "Organization and Leadership in the Jewish Community of Izmir in the Seventeenth Century."

Başgöz, İlhan. "The *Waqwaq* Tree in the Turkish Shadowplay Theatre *Karagöz* and the Story of Esther."

Benbassa, Esther. "Associational Strategies in Ottoman Jewish Society in the Nineteenth and Twentieth Centuries."

Bornes-Varol, Marie-Christine. "The Balat Quarter and Its Image: A Study of a Jewish Neighborhood in Istanbul."

Cohen, Amnon. "Ottoman Sources for the History of Ottoman Jews: How Important?"

Dorn, Pamela J. Kamarck. "*Hakhamim*, Dervishes and Court Singers: The Relationship of Ottoman Jewish Music to Classical Turkish Music."

Dumont, Paul. "Jews, Muslims and Cholera: Intercommunal Relations in Baghdad at the End of the Nineteenth Century."

Göçek, Fatma Müge. "The Estate Register of the Chief Rabbi of Galata, 1183/1769: An Example of Ottoman Archival Information on Jews."

Gürsel, Nedim. "Some Jewish Characters in Modern Turkish Literature."

Hacker, Joseph R. "Jewish Autonomy in the Ottoman Empire: Its Scope and Limits. Jewish Courts in the Sixteenth-Eighteenth Centuries."

Hanioğlu, M. Şükrü. "Jews in the Young Turk Movement to the 1908 Revolution."

177

Juhasz, Esther. "The Material Culture of the Sephardic Jews in the Western Ottoman Empire in the Nineteenth and Twentieth Centuries."

Karpat, Kemal H. "Jewish Population Movements in the Ottoman Empire, 1862–1914."

Kayalı, Hasan. "Jewish Representation in the Ottoman Parliaments."

Kortepeter, C. Max. "Jew and Turk in Algiers in 1800."

Landau, Jacob M. "Relations Between Jews and Non-Jews in the Late Ottoman Empire: Some Characteristics."

Levy, Avigdor. "*Millet* Politics: The Appointment of a Chief Rabbi in 1835."

Lowry, Heath W. "When did the Sephardim Arrive in Salonica?—The Testimony of the Ottoman Tax-Registers, 1478–1613."

Mann, Vivian B. "Jewish-Muslim Acculturation in the Ottoman Empire: The Evidence of Ceremonial Art."

McCarthy, Justin. "Jewish Population in the Late Ottoman Period."

Ortaylı, İlber. "Ottomanism and Zionism During the Second Constitutional Period, 1908–1915."

Philipp, Thomas. "French Merchants and the Jews in the Ottoman Empire During the Eighteenth Century."

Rodrigue, Aron. "The Beginnings of Modernization and Community Reform Among Istanbul Jewry, 1854–1865."

Rozen, Minna. "Individual and Community in the Jewish Society of the Ottoman Empire: Salonica in the Sixteenth Century."

Schroeter, Daniel. "Jewish Quarters in the Arab-Islamic Cities of the Ottoman Empire."

Simon, Rachel. "Jewish Participation in the Reforms in Libya During the Second Ottoman Period, 1835–1911."

Wasserstein, David. "Jewish-Christian Relations in Eighteenth-Century Tiberias."

INDEX

Abdülhamid I (Abdul-Hamid I; ruled 1774–89), 160
Abdülhamid II (Abdul-Hamid II; ruled 1876-1909), 1, 3, 108, 116, 118, 163, 164
Abdülmecid (Abdul-Mejid; ruled 1839–61), 108, 110, 162
Accumulation of capital, 74
Adarbi, Isaac, 38
Adjiman (Acıman), Isaiah, 161
Adriatic Sea, 27
Advisors, Jewish, 18, 28–33, 76–78
Aegean Islands, 156
Aegean Sea, 27
Africa, 72, 120
African countries, 118
Agricultural property, 36
Agronomists, 99
Ahmed III (ruled 1703–30), 30, 77, 157, 158
Ahmed, Arnavud, 27
Albania, 10, 86, 102, 152, 156
Albanians, 17
Aleppo, 12, 48, 60, 64, 68, 83, 89
Alexandria, 12, 27, 36
Alexandria customhouse, 93
Algeria, 102
Ali Bey al-Kabir of Egypt (ruled 1760–73), 93, 159
Âlim, 47. *See also* ulema
Aliyah, First, 120, 163
Aliyah, Second, 120
Alliance Israélite Universelle (Abbr. Alliance, AIU), 113-115, 117, 118, 122, 149, 162, 163, 164
  alumni associations, 114
  Central Committee of, 3
  graduates, 115
  notables, 115, 117
  reading clubs, 114
  schools, 113–15, 123, 125, 149, 163
Alkabetz, Solomon, 20, 39

Almosnino, Moses, 50
Almosnino, Joseph, 142
Amara, 114
Amatus Lusitanus (Amato Lusitano) 38, 153
American University of Beirut, 100
America, 72, 118
Amsterdam, 90
Anatolia, 3, 5, 6, 8, 10, 11, 21, 36, 40, 41, 56, 60, 63, 102, 118, 151–55, 161, 164
Anatolian notables, 161
Anatomy, 38
Ancona, Jacob, 38
Ankara, 12, 39
  Battle of (1402), 151
Anti-Semitism, 123, 162
  attitudes of, 116
Antwerp, 32
Arab provinces, 16, 41, 43, 64, 102
Arabia, 147
Arabic, 101
Arabs, 17
Arba'ah Turim, 38
Ardahan, 163
Arié, Gabriel, 123
Armenian, Armenians, 17, 22, 23, 41, 43, 44, 56, 58, 78, 93, 95, 96, 101, 106, 110, 111, 115, 116, 121, 148
  Catholicos of Etchmiadzin, 44
  Catholicos of Sis, 44
  communities, 44, 105
  ecclesiastical centers, 44
  ecclesiastical leaders, 44
  millet, 106
  Patriarch of Constantinople, 44
  Patriarchate of Constantinople, 44
  Patriarchs, 43
Arms, 26
Arta (Narda), 5, 63, 95
Artillery, 30
Artisans, 79. *See also* craftsmen